# 20th-Century Britain

W. Robson

*Deputy Head*
*Harton Comprehensive School*
*South Shields*

Oxford University Press

*Oxford University Press, Walton Street, Oxford OX2 6DP*

OXFORD LONDON GLASGOW NEW YORK TORONTO MELBOURNE
WELLINGTON CAPE TOWN IBADAN NAIROBI DAR ES SALAAM LUSAKA
DELHI BOMBAY CALCUTTA MADRAS KARACHI DACCA
KUALA LUMPUR SINGAPORE HONG KONG TOKYO

© Oxford University Press 1973

Reprinted 1976, 1978

Filmset in 10/12 pt Plantin by
BAS Printers Limited, Over Wallop, Hampshire
and printed in Great Britain
at the University Press, Oxford,
by Vivian Ridler, Printer to the University

# Contents

# List of Maps

# Introduction: Britain in 1900

History is about people. A few of them are famous, but most are not. Kings, queens, statesmen, and generals usually find their way into the history books, but miners, mill-workers, shopkeepers, and their wives are seldom remembered. Yet these ordinary citizens make up the vast majority of the population, and an account of British history in the first sixty years or so of the present century must be their story. Their conditions of living and working, which were their chief concern, must also be ours. It is the historian's duty, however, not only to describe changes, but also to explain why they came about. The two main controlling influences on the fortunes of the people have always been major economic factors and the actions of politicians. It is thus that the famous find their place in history: these individuals are important because their decisions and conduct have shaped, and sometimes ended, the lives of the common folk who are the life-blood of history.

The series of economic changes which began in the late eighteenth century altered the face of Britain. The Industrial Revolution, as it is called, turned England's 'green and pleasant land' of ten million farmers and peasants into the 'workshop of the world' with over thirty million inhabitants. By 1850 Britain led the world in textiles, coalmining, iron and steel, engineering, shipbuilding, railways, and a host of other manufactures. The last thirty years of the nineteenth century saw the first challenge to Britain's pre-eminence. Germany and the United States caught up and in some fields overtook the world's workshop. Steel production, for example, increased far more rapidly in Germany and the United States than in Britain, whose industrialists showed too little interest in new developments. Cars were only in their infancy in 1900 and the first aeroplane had not yet flown, but when there was progress the Americans, Germans, and French were the pioneers, not the British.

The nineteenth century had also been a time of political change. By 1900 most men, but no women, had the right to vote and Parliament had passed laws to improve the conditions of the people who lived in the new industrial towns. But many things had not changed: King George III was on the throne in 1800 and his grand-daughter, Queen Victoria, reigned in 1900; the House of Lords had not yet admitted its inferiority to the House of Commons; the leading statesmen were still drawn from the traditional ruling classes—the

*Aspects of British life, 1900–14: a small-scale Welsh farmer, his family and their prize possessions; the shop floor of a Manchester engineering works; 'sweated labour' —girls in a hatting factory*

7

landed aristocracy and the wealthy business families. There were very few working-class men in Parliament before 1900.

In normal circumstances, the government would be formed by whichever of the major political parties, Liberals or Conservatives, had a majority of seats in the House of Commons. While the Liberals usually won more votes among the working class, the Conservatives attracted many wealthy businessmen and received solid support from the country landowners. The parties shared one fundamental principle, the assumption that Britain's wealth and power depended on trade and industry and that the government must interfere as little as possible in economic activities. This belief, normally known as *laissez-faire*, or 'leave alone', implied Free Trade, and from the middle of the nineteenth century all governments had followed a policy of reducing customs duties or abolishing them.

*Laissez-faire* also meant a minimum of government interference in the day-to-day lives of the people. In 1900 there was no health service, no national insurance scheme, and only the beginnings of an education system. The *laissez-faire* citadel had, however, been breached in some places by Acts regulating working hours, insisting on certain minimum standards of public health, and allowing local councils to improve housing conditions.

Of all the political controversies of the late nineteenth century, the bitterest was the Irish question. The north-east of Ireland (part of Ulster) was predominantly Protestant and partly industrialized, but the remainder of the country was almost entirely Catholic and agricultural. Many of the landowners in the South were English aristocrats, some of whom seldom visited Ireland. Their tenants had an abysmally low standard of living and naturally had a low opinion of the English.

Ireland returned a hundred members to the House of Commons in Westminster, but there was no separate Irish parliament, and the country was governed by a largely English administration centred on Dublin Castle. Irish resistance to the English took many different forms, but the most important group in 1900 was the Irish Nationalist Party, which regularly won over seventy Irish seats and whose main demand was a separate parliament for Ireland (Home Rule). The great Liberal statesman, W. E. Gladstone, had tried for over twenty years to solve the Irish problem and, when all else failed, had tried to persuade Parliament to grant Home Rule. In this he failed: the Conservatives and even some Liberals refused to support him. The issue was unresolved in 1900, but its importance is illustrated by the fact that the Conservatives were more commonly known as Unionists (that is, anti-Home Rule) at this time.

To the average citizen, the least interesting aspect of public affairs is foreign policy. Occasionally, however, an external issue catches the imagination of the general public. Such was the case with late nineteenth-century imperialism: Britons of all classes felt a thrill of satisfaction when they reflected that their Queen ruled a quarter of the world's population. Imperialism reached its peak with the South African War of 1899–1902, which followed a quarrel between the British government and the Boer republics of Transvaal and the Orange Free State over the republics' treatment of their British residents. After some surprising and unpalatable early defeats the British eventually prevailed, but this was the last imperial adventure.

The Boer War made exciting news and stirred up intense feelings of patriotism, but most people were not directly involved. The two world wars of the present century, on the other hand, have affected the entire population, and it is because the policies or mistakes of statesmen can lead to such disasters that diplomatic history is important. International relations in 1900 were deceptively calm. Two alliances of great powers watched each other suspiciously, France and Russia on the one side, and Germany, Austria-Hungary and a somewhat reluctant Italy on the other. Britain belonged to neither camp. She relied on her navy, by far the largest in the world, to defend herself, her Empire, and her merchant shipping. She tried to keep out of European quarrels and, at the time of the Boer War, was without friends or allies. Soon, however, what had recently been called 'splendid isolation' began to look like dangerous insecurity.

Britain's population was a mixture of rich and poor. At the top of the scale were the wealthy landowners and business and professional men earning more than £700 a year, able to live in substantial suburban houses and to employ at least two domestic servants. Lower down the ladder came the smaller shopkeepers, school-teachers, and clerks, struggling to maintain a middle-class 'image'. Nearly eighty per cent of the population belonged to the working class, but this term covered a wide range, from the printers and engine-drivers earning 50s. (£2·50) a week to the agricultural labourers who earned between 14s. (70p) and 22s. (£1·10) a week. An average working-class family had difficulty in making ends meet and it was calculated in 1900 that about a third of the population was below the poverty line. The majority had to spend every penny of the weekly wage and thus lived in fear of the future, for there were no family allowances, unemployment relief, sickness benefit, or old-age pensions.

It is against this social background that the student of history must study the actions of the 'great men'. Balfour, Lloyd George, and Sir Edward Grey are important not just because they were Cabinet Ministers. Balfour was responsible for the Act which remodelled and extended the education system; Lloyd George brought in old-age pensions and a National Insurance scheme; Grey's foreign policy led to his country's participation in a war in which three-quarters of a million British citizens lost their lives.

# Chapter 1
# Domestic Events 1900–1914

The nineteenth century ended on 31 December 1900. Although the old Queen survived it by less than a month, the attitudes, assumptions, and conventions which we think of as typically nineteenth-century faded out only gradually. Some of them were already under attack in the 1890s, but most were seriously questioned for the first time in the fourteen years which preceded the First World War. These years, sometimes called the Edwardian Era, can therefore be seen as a period of transition. Industrial workers, already organized in trade unions and soon with their own political party, waged a running battle with their employers. The Liberal party took up their cause, introduced some startling social reforms and became involved in a bitter conflict with the Unionists (Conservatives) over the powers of the House of Lords. The Empire had never been larger, but imperialism ceased to be a popular notion. Some women began to question the nineteenth-century belief that it was a man's world. Britain had to reconsider her foreign policy as the Great Powers of Europe increased their armaments. Most important of all, a few perceptive observers began to suspect that Britain's economic greatness might not be permanent. This short period was in one sense the twilight of the nineteenth century; in another it was the dawn of the twentieth.

### THE ECONOMY: ITS OBVIOUS STRENGTH AND HIDDEN WEAKNESS

Britain's power depended ultimately on the success of her industry and commerce. Both flourished before the First World War. Industrial production and exports increased, profits rose, foreign investments doubled. Britain was more prosperous on the eve of the war then ever before. But there were reasons to fear that this happy state of affairs might not last. Britain's industrial lead over her competitors was being reduced; in some industries she had lost first place; in several new lines she was making a very poor showing. Her investors were gaining large profits by helping more backward countries to establish industries which would in time present an additional challenge to her own manufacturers. To remain competitive her employers were forced to resist demands for higher wages, with the result that organized labour was becoming restive. Britain was necessarily a great trading nation and her

*'Britannia and her boys' an engraving by G. Durand—the 'boys' represent many of the nations of the Empire*

11

economy was therefore tied to world developments. Her weakness in 1914 was that too few people recognized the changes that were taking place.

Britain's most important industries before 1914 were cotton and wool textiles, coalmining, iron and steel, heavy engineering, and shipbuilding—heavy industry in other words. Each of these had expanded since the turn of the century: the number of cotton looms in Lancashire increased by a quarter and coal production went up by three-quarters between 1893 and 1913. Even these staple industries, however, were not keeping pace with their German and American rivals, partly because British manufacturers were slow to adopt new techniques. American mines, for example, made far more use of coal-cutting machinery than the British, and by 1900 the United States had become the world's leading coal producer. British cotton was still supreme, but it was significant that American operatives managed an average of twenty looms each, as against the British four. Even more alarming was the comparative failure of Britain's steel producers. Both Germany and the United States passed Britain in the 1890s and the Germans were making twice as much steel as Britain by 1908. British shipbuilders were importing large quantities of German steel.

One must take care, of course, not to exaggerate the significance of these developments. Both Germany and the United States had larger populations than Britain, and America, in particular, was vastly richer in natural resources. Both entered the industrial race late and were now inevitably catching up. By the early twentieth century Britain had lost her commanding lead but was still one of the three foremost industrial nations. This comparative decline of her heavy industry was to be anticipated; her failure in the new light industries was not. In the electrical industry and in the generation of electric power Britain was far behind Germany and the United States. Tyneside was the only part of the country where electricity was widely used as a source of power in factories. Gas, which was cheap, was preferred for street lighting and in the home. The first motor car had run in Germany in the 1880s, but British engineers were slow to turn to car manufacturing, partly because until 1896 cars were virtually prohibited in Britain: each motor vehicle had to be preceded by a man carrying a red flag. It was not until 1910 that the London General Omnibus Company began operating motor buses. Whereas all the inventions and developments of the 'first Industrial Revolution' had been British, the motor car was invented by a German, the first powered flight was made by an American, and wireless telegraphy was developed by an Italian.

Several explanations of Britain's comparative industrial failure can be offered. British firms were, on the whole, much smaller than their German and American competitors and could therefore

*Britain is left behind in the 'second Industrial Revolution': Marconi (standing) sending the first wireless message across the Atlantic*

| Steel produced (million tons) | |
|---|---|
| 1900 | 5·1 |
| 1905 | 6·0 |
| 1910 | 6·4 |
| 1915 | 8·6 |
| 1920 | 9·1 |

| Coal produced (million tons) | |
|---|---|
| 1900 | 225 |
| 1905 | 236 |
| 1910 | 264 |
| 1915 | 253 |
| 1920 | 230 |

| Raw cotton consumed (million lb.) | |
|---|---|
| 1900 | 1737 |
| 1905 | 1813 |
| 1910 | 1632 |
| 1915 | 1931 |
| 1920 | 1726 |

**Industry and Commerce**

*A German car, 1891*

Below *A French Peugeot car in England, 1896, preceded by a man carrying a red flag*

**Foreign trade and invisible exports**

often not afford new, expensive machinery. Nor could they borrow the necessary capital, for British investors found that foreign investments were more profitable. Furthermore, the new industrial processes were often extremely complex and Britain was short of scientists and advanced engineers. British universities were turning out a mere handful of engineering graduates each year, while the German annual average was 3,000. Above all, while we can now see that a relative decline was taking place, the British manufacturer at the beginning of the century was doing very well; he saw no need to change.

Britain's prosperity is demonstrated by her overseas trading record. Between the 1890s and 1913 the total value of her exports doubled, while the cost of her imports increased by half. Invisible earnings, from foreign investments, shipping, and insurance and banking services, provided her with a healthy trading surplus. The merchant navy, indeed, was far larger than any of its competitors in 1914. The exporters' success is particularly laudable in view of the growing German and American competition and the fact that, unlike Britain, most foreign countries had erected tariff barriers to protect their own industries. These obstacles had led Britain to rely slightly more on trade with the Empire and remote countries like Argentina, Japan, and China, but her exports to Europe and North America still almost doubled in value during these years, and while India was her most important export market, Germany was second.

A closer examination of the trading picture reveals some alarming features. Textiles accounted for more than half Britain's exports, but she was also exporting large quantities of textile-manufacturing machinery to India, China, and Japan. These countries would in due course become self-sufficient and even start competing in other markets. A large proportion of Germany's imports from Britain was coal, which was used as fuel for the German industry which challenged Britain in other fields. With the increased use of oil and the development of hydro-electric power, the future for Britain's coal exporters was not necessarily bright.

Britain's main imports were food and raw materials. Four-fifths of her wheat was imported in 1914, mainly from the United States, Canada, Argentina, and Australia. The maintenance of Free Trade policies, however, meant that a wide range of German manufactured goods and a vast quantity of steel were imported. In 1903 a group of Unionist politicians came to the conclusion that it was time to begin abandoning Free Trade, to raise tariffs on imports and, by protecting British industry, to safeguard the interests of manufacturers and workers alike.

The healthy state of the British economy was partly due to the large annual income from investments abroad. British investors found that shares in Canadian or South American railways and

Indian or Japanese cotton mills brought in higher dividends than did shares in domestic industry. The total amount invested abroad, which stood at £2,000 million in 1900, had risen to £4,000 million in 1914 and was yielding an annual income of £200 million. Twice as much money was invested abroad as at home in the last three years of peace. In some ways this capital investment helped British industry, for much of the money was spent on equipment, such as railway stock and textile machinery, made in Britain. On the other hand, by helping to build up the textile industry in the Far East, British speculators were damaging the long-term interests of Lancashire.

Apart from minor recessions in 1904 and 1909, business was brisk in these years and prices rose fairly steadily. Wages did not increase, however, and the purchasing power of most wage-earners was reduced. This was due partly to the popularity of overseas investment. In order to attract capital at all, British firms had to pay high dividends and were thus forced to keep wages down. The contrast of rising profits and prices on the one hand, and stationary wages on the other, led trade unionists, especially between 1910 and 1914, to press strongly for wage increases. A series of major strikes was another indication that the nineteenth century had passed and that the twentieth had begun.

**Labour troubles**

No one can dispute that Britain became a Great Power in the eighteenth century and that Britannia ruled the waves in the nineteenth primarily through the skill, resourcefulness, and energy of her industrialists, shipowners, bankers, and craftsmen. Nor can it be denied that she was still a major economic force in 1914. The City of London was still the world's financial capital, the pound sterling was widely used as an international trading currency, Britain still led the world in textiles and ships. But cracks were appearing in the edifice. It might soon begin to crumble. It would be unfair to criticize the factory-owners, investors, politicians, and trade union leaders for failing to solve the problem before it had really appeared. There is, however, a lesson to be learned: today's prosperity may contain the seeds of tomorrow's recession.

## THE UNIONIST GOVERNMENT 1900–1905

Ever since 1886, when they split over the Irish Home Rule issue, the Liberals had been in disarray. Apart from a brief spell of three years, the Conservatives or Unionists had been in power, with the Marquess of Salisbury as Prime Minister. The Unionists' record of domestic reform was unimpressive, partly because there was no minister zealous for reform and partly because Salisbury's own main interest was foreign affairs. The one member of the Cabinet who might have been expected to show enthusiasm for home policies was Joseph Chamberlain, a former Liberal. Since 1895, however, Chamberlain, as Colonial Secretary, had been preoccupied with the South African problem which had led to the Boer War in 1899.

By 1900 it seemed that the war had been won, although Boer resistance was in fact to continue for two more years. The war was popular with the people: they cheered the soldiers as they marched off to war, they sang sentimental war songs like 'Goodbye, Dolly Gray', they were delirious with excitement when they heard of the relief of Mafeking, and they made Lord Roberts, the British Commander-in-Chief, into a national hero. The only critics were a few intellectuals and about half the Liberal leaders. For these reasons it seemed to Salisbury that 1900 was a good time for an election. Often called the Khaki election, this is normally seen as an attempt by the Unionists to make political capital out of the army's success in South Africa and to take advantage of their opponents' quarrels. The gamble was successful. The Unionists won 402 seats against the Liberals' 184, while 82 Irish Nationalists and 2 members of the newly formed Labour Representation Committee were returned. The Unionists could therefore look forward to up to seven more years of power.

Apart from the death of Queen Victoria in January 1901, Salisbury's last two years of office were uneventful at home. Attention remained centred on South Africa, where the Boers, using guerrilla tactics, cast doubt on the British assumption that the war was over. Peace was finally signed at Vereeniging in May 1902 and two months later Salisbury resigned. His successor was his nephew, Arthur Balfour, a man of considerable intellect and great personal charm who had the misfortune, fatal in a political leader, of being unable to control his colleagues. He was also, by virtue of his aristocratic origins and philosophical interests, seriously out of touch with the man in the street. He was probably one of the most unfortunate of British Prime Ministers, for in his three years of office, although he was responsible for some notable reforms, including the great Education Act of 1902, everything he did earned him enemies, and he is usually held responsible for the disastrous Unionist defeat in the general election of 1906. His failure was that although his policies were well thought out and often highly beneficial, he did not realize that the voters and even the members of his own party were less disinterested than he. Every one of his policies antagonized some section of the voters and, in the end, he was left with very few supporters.

Undoubtedly, Balfour's most significant achievement was to reduce to order the chaos of English education. A brief summary of the background will show why reform was necessary and why Balfour's solution was unpopular. Before 1870 there had been no national education system, but schools had been provided by

*Election Result 1900*

| | |
|---|---|
| Unionist | 402 |
| Liberal | 184 |
| Irish Nationalist | 82 |
| Labour Representative Committee | 2 |

**Balfour, Prime Minister**

15

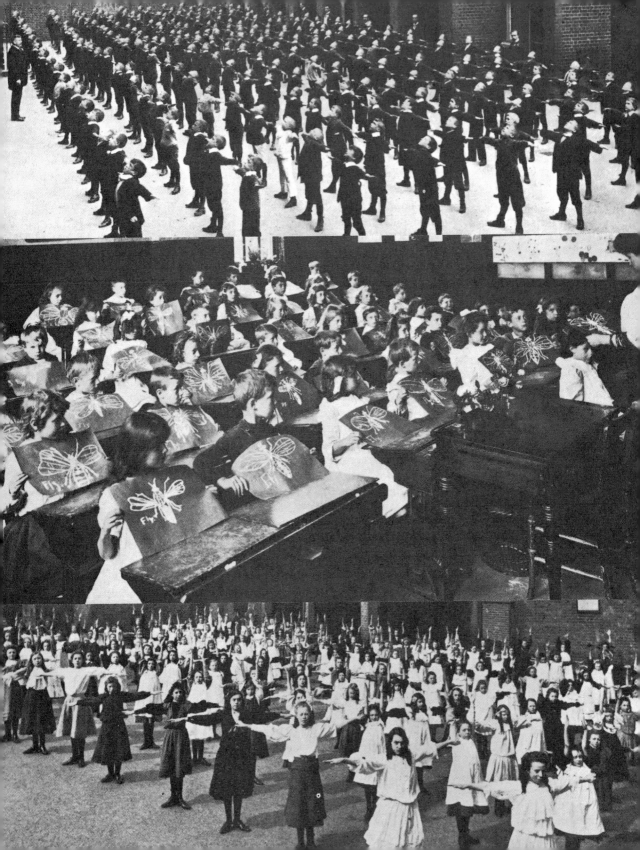

voluntary societies, closely linked to the churches, and supported by government grants. The majority of these voluntary schools had belonged to the Church of England. The Education Act of 1870 stated that the voluntary schools should continue, but that where there were insufficient schools, locally elected 'school boards' should be empowered to levy a rate to pay for new 'board schools'. This had immediately aroused religious controversy, for Nonconformists objected to the continued government subsidies for Church of England (and Catholic) schools, while Anglicans denounced the board schools as pagan. By 1902 elementary education was free and attendance at school was compulsory up to the age of twelve everywhere; and in most parts of the country the school boards had raised the leaving age to fourteen.

A further problem was that the board schools and the voluntary schools were supposed to provide elementary education only. They were expected to teach the three Rs and scripture, but not to meddle in higher mathematics, science, history, geography, or languages. Secondary education was available only in the grammar schools, which charged fees. When some school boards began to run higher classes in their schools and to present their pupils for external examinations they were accused of exceeding their proper powers.

Balfour's Education Act of 1902, which was drafted by a senior civil servant, R.L. Morant, abolished the school boards and made the county and county borough councils responsible for elementary, secondary, and technical education. The voluntary schools were to be brought partly under local council control and to be supported out of the rates. This was clearly a sensible measure, for it replaced a complicated and often contradictory pattern with a single system. Secondary schools (similar to modern grammar schools) were not to become free, but local authorities were permitted to provide scholarships enabling a proportion of their elementary-school pupils to transfer to secondary schools.

The Act was bitterly opposed, for reasons which had little or

nothing to do with education. The Nonconformists, who had hoped that the church schools would be abolished altogether, were furious when they discovered not only that they would survive, but that they would be supported out of the local rates. Opposition was especially strong in Nonconformist Wales, where several people were imprisoned for refusing to pay their rates. The Liberals, and in particular Lloyd George, who came from a Welsh Nonconformist background, successfully exploited the issue. They did not stop the Act, but they won back large numbers of Nonconformist votes. It is significant that the Unionists did not win a single Welsh seat in the 1906 general election.

The government's Irish policies lost it few votes, but added to the disharmony with which the party was plagued by 1905. The Irish Land Purchase Act of 1903, sponsored by George Wyndham, the Irish Secretary, went a long way towards meeting the grievances of the Irish tenant farmers who so bitterly resented the ownership of Irish land by English landlords. The Act provided for the purchase of the land by the government and its transfer to the peasants, who would then repay their debt to the government over a period of sixty-eight years. This satisfied most tenants and was not opposed by the landlords. When the more extreme Unionists learned, however, that Wyndham was planning to go further by reforming Irish local government, although not to grant Home Rule, they objected and forced both the abandonment of the scheme and the resignation of Wyndham himself. Balfour's reputation within the Unionist party slumped, first because he had contemplated a slight surrender to the Home Rulers, and secondly because he had sacrificed one of his ministers.

The third sensible policy to harm Balfour was the Licensing Act of 1904. Excessive drinking among the working class was one of the scandals of Victorian society; far too many children went hungry because their fathers, and sometimes mothers, were persistent drinkers. The Temperance Movement, which was closely linked to the Nonconformist churches and to the Radical wing of the Liberal party, waged a relentless campaign against 'the demon drink'. The aim of Balfour's Licensing Act was to close some public houses in areas where there were too many, but to compensate the breweries which owned them out of a fund provided by the brewing trade itself. Temperance crusaders immediately denounced Balfour for 'endowing the trade'. The government had tried to pass a useful social reform, while at the same time treating the brewers fairly. The Liberals seized and exploited the opportunity to win back votes, especially Nonconformist ones, to their side.

The harm done to the Unionist cause by these policies was slight, however, in comparison to the disastrous effects of the tariff reform controversy of 1903–5. Ever since the mid-nineteenth

**Irish Land Purchase Act
1903
Licensing Act
1904**

*We are determined on unceasing War against 'The Drink' that would relentlessly destroy Our Country and her Sons. (Temperance postcard)*

"Mr. Balfour, therefore, went down un-honoured, unwept, un——" (A Voice: "Un-'ung!")

**Tariff reform controversy**

**Joseph Chamberlain**

century Britain had pursued a Free Trade policy. Politicians of both parties agreed that low tariffs, by encouraging international trade, helped British industry. Furthermore, Free Trade meant cheap food, which both helped the British working class and allowed employers to pay relatively low wages and thereby to keep their prices down. The result of Free Trade policies, however, was that when Britain's industrial supremacy was challenged in the late nineteenth century foreign, especially German, manufactured goods flooded onto the British market. At the same time, Britain's ability to sell her products abroad was reduced by foreign tariffs.

The change came in 1903, when Joseph Chamberlain, the Colonial Secretary, announced his conversion to higher tariffs. Of all the British statesmen who have failed to become Prime Minister, Joseph Chamberlain was probably the greatest. Born of a wealthy Birmingham family, he made his fortune as a screw manufacturer in that city. He entered politics as a radical Liberal and, as Lord Mayor of Birmingham, made an enormous contribution to the solution of the city's housing problem. On his election to Parliament, Gladstone was forced to consider him for Cabinet office and he played a prominent part in the Liberal government of 1880–5. There can be little doubt that he would ultimately have succeeded Gladstone as Liberal leader. Then, in 1886, came the first of his turning-points. Although sympathetic towards the Irish National-ists, he could not agree with Gladstone's Home Rule plans and, together with a group of other 'Liberal Unionists', he deserted his leader. Gradually, he moved closer to the Unionist party and was made Colonial Secretary by Lord Salisbury in 1895. Thenceforth his chief interest was the Empire and above all, of course, South Africa. Like most politicians and the mass of the public at the turn of the century, Chamberlain believed in imperialism, but he was too intelligent to be captivated merely by the thought of acquiring additional overseas territories. He described the Empire as an 'undeveloped estate'; he saw that German and American competi-tion was beginning to damage the interests of British industry and proposed closer trading links between Britain and the Empire as a solution.

Following the Colonial Conference of 1902 Chamberlain began to consider the idea of 'imperial preference'. In May 1903 he announced his conversion: he wanted tariffs to be levied on foreign imports, but not on imports of goods from the Empire. This would have the double advantage of binding the territories of the Empire more closely together and protecting British industry from the competition of imported manufactured goods.

Chamberlain's announcement caused uproar. The Cabinet was immediately split and in September five of its members—four Free Traders and Chamberlain himself—resigned. Unable to win over the Cabinet, Chamberlain took the issue to the country. He formed the Tariff Reform League and expounded his proposals to packed public meetings all over the country. If the Unionist party was shocked and divided, the Liberals were delighted and united. Rallying to the Free Trade banner, they sent Asquith off in pursuit of Chamberlain. Following him round the country, Asquith answered all his arguments and stressed again and again that tariffs meant higher bread prices. Both sides simplified the issue: Asquith claimed that it was 'the big loaf against the little loaf'; Chamberlain replied, 'Tariff reform means work for all.'

The political significance of the controversy is not that the people preferred Free Trade to tariff reform, although it does appear that Asquith was generally better received than Chamberlain. It was important, rather, because the Unionist leaders, and Balfour in particular, were unable to make up their minds. For two years Balfour tried to reach a compromise between the Free Traders and the tariff reformers in his party, but no one was ever convinced that he had succeeded, or, indeed, that he knew his own mind. The Unionist party was in disarray; Balfour could not rely on the support of his back-benchers in the House of Commons; in 1904–5 the Unionists lost one by-election after another. It was widely felt that if the Unionists were divided on a major issue of public policy and if their leader was unable to control his rank and file, they were no longer fit to rule.

Throughout Balfour's period of office his policies lost his party votes, sometimes deservedly, often not. But not all of these lost votes went to the Liberals. A meeting of trade union representatives and socialist societies in London in 1900 had passed this historic resolution:

> That this conference is in favour of establishing a distinct Labour Group in Parliament, who shall have their own Whips, and agree upon their policy, which must embrace a readiness to co-operate with any party which for the time being may be engaged in promoting legislation in the direct interests of labour, and be equally ready to associate themselves with any party in opposing measures having an opposite tendency.

This was the origin of the Labour Representation Committee, the direct ancestor of the Labour party. The resolution was proposed by Keir Hardie, often regarded as the father of the British Labour movement. The L.R.C.'s first secretary was James Ramsay MacDonald, who was to become, in 1924, the country's first Labour Prime Minister. The character of the L.R.C. must be appreciated: it owed its origin mainly to the trade unions; it was financed almost entirely by the trade unions; its aim was to bring pressure on Parliament to pass Acts which helped labour in general and the trade unions in particular. It was not a socialist party. In many

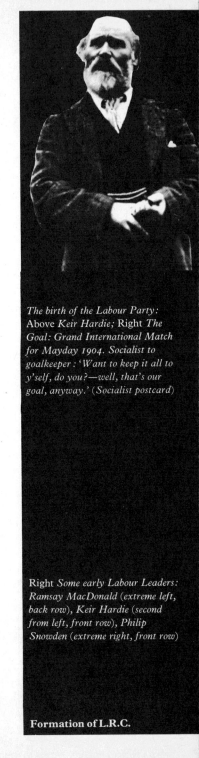

*The birth of the Labour Party:* Above *Keir Hardie;* Right *The Goal: Grand International Match for Mayday 1904. Socialist to goalkeeper: 'Want to keep it all to y'self, do you?—well, that's our goal, anyway.' (Socialist postcard)*

Right *Some early Labour Leaders: Ramsay MacDonald (extreme left, back row), Keir Hardie (second from left, front row), Philip Snowden (extreme right, front row)*

**Formation of L.R.C.**

# The Socialist Resolution

## Submitted to the House of Commons by Keir Hardie, April 23rd, 1901

"THAT considering the increasing burden which the private ownership of land and capital is imposing upon the industrious and useful classes of the community, the poverty and destitution and general moral and physical deterioration resulting from a competitive system of wealth production which aims primarily at profit-making, the alarming growth of trusts and syndicates, able by reason of their great wealth to influence governments and plunge peaceful nations into war to serve their own interests, this House is of opinion that such a state of matters is a menace to the well-being of the Realm and calls for legislation designed to remedy the same by inaugurating a Socialist Commonwealth founded upon the common ownership of land and capital, production for use and not for profit, and equality of opportunity for every citizen."

ways, it was not yet a party at all. Fifteen L.R.C. candidates stood at the 1900 election and two, of whom Hardie was one, were returned.

By no means all the trade unions took part in the meeting which produced the L.R.C. and only a minority contributed to its upkeep. An event in the following year transformed the trade unionists' attitude to political action. Following a railwaymen's strike in South Wales, the Taff Vale Railway Company sued the men's union for damages, claiming that the union should make good its losses during the period of the strike. The House of Lords, as the final court of appeal, decided in favour of the company, awarding it £23,000 in damages. This was a grave blow to the Amalgamated Society of Railway Servants. It was even more serious for the trade union movement as a whole, for it meant that in future any union calling a strike could be sued for damages: strikes, in other words, were as good as illegal.

**Taff Vale case**

Trade unionists demanded a reform of the law relating to strikes. Balfour did nothing but appoint a Royal Commission to investigate the subject. Exasperated, many union leaders turned to the L.R.C., whose number of affiliated members doubled in 1902. Nor were the union leaders alone in drawing this conclusion. Many working-class voters clearly agreed with them, for L.R.C. candidates were returned at three by-elections in 1902–3.

The L.R.C. was still, of course, only a minute political force. But Taff Vale and Balfour's failure to bring in a Bill to amend the law meant that the L.R.C. would resolutely oppose the Unionists. The challenge was made more serious by the agreement in 1903 between MacDonald and the Liberal Chief Whip to the effect that L.R.C. and Liberal candidates would not oppose each other in the next election. There were now over two million trade union members in Britain, and it seemed certain that the vast majority of them would be against Balfour.

A final nail in the coffin of Balfour's hopes of remaining Prime Minister was the outcry which was raised in 1905 over the importation of Chinese coolies to work in the Rand goldmines in South Africa. After the defeat of the Boers the British government was directly responsible for the administration of the Transvaal, where the mine-owners found that they were short of cheap labour. The government allowed them to bring in indentured Chinese labourers, coolies who bound themselves to a number of years' work in South Africa. The main criticism of the scheme was that the coolies were accommodated in squalid compounds, or labour camps, which they might not leave except to go to work. The Liberals denounced the government's inhumanity in allowing this 'Chinese slavery', while trade unionists argued that it was 'an affront to labour'. As so often happens, the affair was exaggerated out of all proportion: the

*Lunatic to Labour: 'When are you coming inside?' (Conservative postcard)*

**'Chinese slavery' and resignation of Balfour**

Unionists were represented as hard-hearted men of property to whom labour was merely a commodity to be bought and sold.

Mainly because of the continuing disputes over tariff reform and the abysmal by-election record of the government, Balfour decided to resign in December 1905. His only hope of an early return to office was that disagreements among the leading personalities of the Liberal party would prevent the formation of a government. He was disappointed. The Liberals agreed to serve under Sir Henry Campbell-Bannerman, who, on becoming Prime Minister, asked King Edward VII to dissolve Parliament and order a general election.

### THE LIBERAL GOVERNMENTS 1905–1914

**Campbell-Bannerman**

Although the Liberals had been out of office for ten years, the Cabinet formed in December 1905 was rich in experience and well endowed with talent. Campbell-Bannerman himself was from an extremely wealthy Scottish business family, but generally thought to belong to the radical wing of the party. He was a plain, down-to-earth speaker, not to be underestimated in debate. He once crushed Balfour's high-flown phrases with 'Enough of this foolery!' His weakness was his age (he was in his seventieth year) and his uncertain health. He disappeared from the political scene for two months every year in order to visit the Austrian spa town of Marienbad, where another frequent visitor was King Edward VII.

The undisputed second man in the Liberal team, and Chancellor of the Exchequer, was Herbert Asquith. Nearly twenty years younger than his chief, Asquith did not enjoy the same advantages of inherited wealth. He came from a solid middle-class Yorkshire family and had made his own reputation by his brilliant performance as a barrister and M.P. Asquith was one of Britain's great middle-of-the-road statesmen: he believed in social and political progress and was prepared to fight hard to achieve them, but he loved and respected the traditions and institutions of his country. He was no revolutionary. Above all, he delighted in surrounding himself with men and women whose wit and intellectual brilliance matched his own. The members of his own family were all outstandingly talented and Asquith revelled in the company of clever young people. His opponents, and some colleagues, thought him too casual, even lazy. They probably misunderstood him. He realized that most problems are far more complex than politicians like to pretend; he always waited for the right opportunity before acting.

Also in the Cabinet were Asquith's close friends, R.B. Haldane (Secretary for War) and Sir Edward Grey (Foreign Secretary). The young Welsh radical fire-brand, David Lloyd George, became President of the Board of Trade and Winston Churchill, who had

left the Unionists over the tariff reform controversy, was appointed to a junior office outside the Cabinet.

The new government's first task was to fight a general election and to secure for itself an adequate House of Commons majority. Here, everything was in its favour: the Unionists had antagonized two important sections of the electorate, the Nonconformists and organized labour, with their Education and Licensing Acts, their failure to reform trade union law after the Taff Vale case, and the 'Chinese slavery' blunder. Most important of all, the party had torn itself apart over tariff reform. The outcome was an unprecedented Unionist defeat. The Liberals won 377 seats against the Unionists' 157, while the Irish Nationalists secured 83 seats and the L.R.C. 29. A further 24 trade union backed members, not attached to the L.R.C., were returned. The Liberals had a majority of 84 over all other parties, but since the Irish and Labour members normally supported them their position was overwhelmingly strong. Such was the tide against the Unionists that Balfour himself lost his seat, although he was able to return later at a by-election.

Surprisingly perhaps, the first two years of the new government's life saw few significant reforms. The most important achievement was the Trade Disputes Act of 1906, which reversed the Taff Vale decision by stating that employers could not sue unions for damages. Two small Acts in 1907 had far-reaching effects on the education service. A Bill proposed by the Labour party (as the L.R.C. now called itself) enabled local authorities to provide school meals for children from poor homes, and another Bill in the same year provided for the medical inspection of all schoolchildren.

The remainder of the Liberal government's plans were frustrated by the Unionist-dominated House of Lords. It is necessary here to define the function and powers of the House of Lords, for a first-class political and constitutional battle now arose over the use made of the Lords by the Unionist Party. The process of legislation, or law-making, in Britain is lengthy and complicated. A Bill (or draft law) has to pass through several stages in each House of Parliament. When both Commons and Lords have passed the Bill, it goes to the Crown for the Royal Assent, whereupon it becomes an Act and part of the law of the land. Theoretically, a Bill may be rejected by either House or by the Crown, but no monarch since Queen Anne has used the royal veto, and by the early twentieth century it was fairly well accepted that most important Bills, and all money Bills, if passed by the Commons, would also be passed by the Lords. The constitutional position, however, was complicated by a party political factor. Party majorities in the Commons fluctuated according to the whims of the electorate, but the Lords was always overwhelmingly Unionist. A Unionist government would therefore have no difficulty in passing Bills, for it could rely on the Lords to

| Election Result 1906 | |
|---|---|
| Liberal | 377 |
| Unionist | 157 |
| Irish Nationalist | 83 |
| L.R.C. | 29 |
| Trade Union | 24 |

**Trade Disputes Act 1906**

**The House of Lords**

*Edward VII and Queen Alexandra*

approve whatever it had managed to steer through the Commons. A Liberal government, on the other hand, might anticipate trouble. In 1893 Gladstone had induced the Commons to pass an Irish Home Rule Bill, only to see it thrown out by the Lords by 419 votes to 41.

Shortly after the 1906 election, Balfour and Lord Lansdowne, the Unionist leader in the Lords, agreed to use the House of Lords to embarrass the government. The Unionists could no longer pass Bills, for they had lost control of the Commons, but they could use their majority in the Lords to defeat Liberal Bills to which they objected. This dangerous policy was soon applied: an Education Bill was rejected in 1906, a Bill to abolish the right of some people to two or more votes was defeated in the same year, two Scottish Land Bills were thrown out in 1907, and a Licensing Bill met a similar fate in 1908. Campbell-Bannerman objected to what he considered were unfair tactics, but Balfour and Lansdowne continued their campaign. The Unionists had found a way of retaining power despite their rejection by the mass of the electorate.

The crisis over the role of the House of Lords reached its climax in the years 1909–11, by which time Asquith had succeeded Campbell-Bannerman. The elderly Prime Minister had resigned on 6 April 1908 and died a fortnight later. An interesting sidelight is that the pleasure-loving King Edward VII was on holiday at Biarritz in south-west France at the time and, rather than break his holiday, he summoned Asquith to Biarritz. This is the only time in history that a British Prime Minister has been officially installed in office in a foreign hotel. Some reconstruction of the Cabinet was necessary. Asquith appointed Lloyd George to the Exchequer and made Churchill President of the Board of Trade.

Lloyd George's first budget, in 1909, was the immediate cause of the constitutional battle. Faced with the need to provide money for extra social services (see pages 29–30) and naval building (see pages 42–43), he had to increase taxes. The necessary revenue was raised by increased death-duties, higher duties on tobacco and spirits, an extra 2d. (1p) on income tax and a new supertax on incomes over £3,000 a year. He also introduced special taxes on motor vehicles and petrol to provide money for road improvement. The most controversial item in the budget, and financially the least important, was the proposal to impose a twenty per cent tax on profits made from the sale of land. The effect of these land value duties was that a man who bought a piece of land for £10,000 and sold it for £15,000 would have to pay £1,000 in tax to the Treasury. In all, Lloyd George was proposing to raise an extra £15 million a year, a huge sum by Victorian and Edwardian standards. In his budget speech he appealed to the public spirit of his listeners:

The money thus raised is to be expended, first of all, in insuring the inviolability of our shores. It has also been raised in order not merely to relieve but to prevent unmerited distress within those shores. It is essential that we should make every necessary provision for the defence of our country. But surely it is equally imperative that we should make it a country even better worth defending for all and by all.

The Unionists howled in protest, claiming that the budget confiscated property and introduced socialist principles. They set up a Budget Protest League and held public meetings to denounce Lloyd George. This suited the little Welshman, perhaps the last truly great performer on a public platform seen in Britain. He in turn made a series of public speeches in defence of the budget. Some of them were violent attacks on the Unionist landowners:

There are many in the country blessed by Providence with great wealth, and if there are amongst them men who grudge out of their riches a fair contribution towards the less fortunate of their fellowcountrymen they are very shabby rich men.                    (Limehouse, 30 July 1909)
Who made ten thousand people owners of the soil, and the rest of us trespassers in the land of our birth?          (Newcastle, 9 October 1909)

In utterances such as these Lloyd George appeared to be a revolutionary, or at least to be threatening revolution. But he had his more sober moods:

Here are you a nation of nearly forty-five millions, one of the greatest nations the world has ever seen, a nation whose proficiency in the art of government is unrivalled, a nation which has no superior in commerce or in industry . . . It has founded the greatest and most extensive empire the world has ever witnessed.          (London, 3 December 1909)

It is difficult to attach a label to David Lloyd George. Born in 1863, brought up by his shoemaker uncle in Criccieth in North Wales, articled to a solicitor at fifteen, he owed his success to his sharp brain and, above all, to his wonderful power of oratory. He entered Parliament in 1890 as a Liberal, but nowadays we should probably call him a Welsh Nationalist. He was in politics to fight for Welsh tenant farmers and labourers and against English landlords. Since then, especially since achieving Cabinet office in 1905, he had matured. Proud of Britain's industrial and commercial achievements, proud of her political traditions, he wanted to progress in the direction of social justice and democracy. He was not against inequalities of wealth, but he thought that the rich had a responsibility to the rest of the community. He resolutely resisted the idea that political power should be concentrated in the hands of a minority.

It is unlikely, then, that Lloyd George deliberately set out to infuriate the rich or to provoke the Unionist peers to open opposition. Asquith and Churchill, who gave him solid support throughout, were not the men to be party to such a plot. Lloyd George himself might sometimes sound like a socialist revolutionary, but the budget was the responsibility of the Cabinet as a whole and the ministers were all representatives of the middle-of-the-road Liberal tradition.

Such was the anger of the Unionists over the budget that they decided to use their House of Lords majority to reject it. The budget was passed by the Commons on 4 November 1909 by 379 votes to 149 and rejected by the Lords on 30 November by 350 votes to 75. This was foolish. No law said that the Lords might not reject a budget, but there was a long constitutional tradition that the Commons' decision on questions of taxation was final. Two days after the Lords' vote Asquith carried the following resolution in the Commons:

That the action of the House of Lords in refusing to pass into law the financial provisions made by this House for the service of the year is a breach of the Constitution and a usurpation of the rights of the Commons.

**Constitutional Crisis 1909–11**

The Lords' rejection of the budget brought the whole question of the Unionists' use of their House of Lords majority into the open. Unless the law were changed, no Liberal government could exercise power. Was Britain really a democracy or was the Unionist party permanently in control? The trouble was that an Act of Parliament was needed to reduce the powers of the Lords and that such a Bill would have to be passed by the Lords themselves. There was only one way round this difficulty: if necessary, the King would have to be asked to create sufficient Liberal peers to swamp the Unionist majority in the Lords. Both Edward VII and Asquith were extremely reluctant to take this step and the King, shortly after the Lords' vote on the budget, told Asquith that he would do so only after two general elections, one to show that the electorate approved of the budget and one to test its opinion on Asquith's proposed reform of the Lords' powers..

*Election Result January 1910*

| | |
|---|---|
| Liberal | 275 |
| Unionist | 273 |
| Irish Nationalist | 82 |
| Labour | 40 |

Parliament was dissolved in December 1909 and the first election held in January 1910. The Unionists made substantial gains, increasing their representation to 273, while the Liberal total fell to 275. The balance was held by the Irish Nationalists with 82 and the Labour Party with 40. Since both the Irish and Labour supported the Liberal government on the budget and the reform of the House of Lords, Asquith remained Prime Minister, but henceforth he had to pay much more attention to the wishes of his allies. Whatever his other plans, he would now have to do something about Irish Home Rule.

Shortly after the reassembly of Parliament, both Houses passed the controversial budget. Asquith then drafted a Bill to reduce the powers of the House of Lords. In the middle of the crisis, on 6 May 1910, King Edward died. His successor, George V, tried hard to reach a solution and at all times acted fairly and correctly. On the new King's advice, a conference between the leaders of the two main parties met at Downing Street between June and November but, although it made considerable progress, it broke down over the Unionists' insistence that the House of Commons alone should not be able to change the law on fundamental matters like Irish Home Rule.

Asquith then asked King George V to repeat his father's promise to create Liberal peers if necessary and had Parliament dissolved again. The results of the December election of 1910 were virtually identical to those of January: Liberals 272, Unionists 272, Irish 84, Labour 42. The majority in favour of reform of the House of Lords and Home Rule was 126. Asquith introduced his Parliament Bill, which deprived the Lords of the power to reject money Bills, gave them the right to delay other Bills for two years only, and reduced the maximum time between general elections from seven years to five. The Parliament Bill was passed by the Commons in May by a large majority, then sent to the Lords. Some Unionists, the die-hards, wanted to reject it outright, but when Asquith informed Lansdowne of the King's promise to create peers, sufficient Unionists gave way to allow the Bill's passage by 131 votes to 114

| *Election Result December 1910* | |
|---|---|
| Liberal | 272 |
| Unionist | 272 |
| Irish Nationalist | 84 |
| Labour | 42 |

*'New Year Bargains in Coronets':
a cartoon mocks the Liberal plan
to create between four and five
hundred new peers*

**Parliament Act**

on 10 August. Lansdowne and his colleagues realized that it was better to have a delaying power than to be swamped by Liberal peers and thus to lose control altogether.

The Parliament Act of 1911 is usually thought to be as important a landmark in British constitutional history as the great Reform Act of 1832. It meant that Britain was now undeniably a democracy, that the party which won a majority in the House of Commons would not only form the government, but be able to carry out its policies. Also, by providing for more frequent elections, it gave the voters more control over their representatives and the government.

To the politicians, the struggle over the House of Lords was the great issue of the years 1909–11 and Irish Home Rule the central problem of 1912–14. The mass of the people were probably more impressed by the series of social reforms which Asquith's government implemented. Many historians have since observed that in these years the Liberals laid the foundations of the Welfare State. Although this may be an exaggeration, the government did try to relieve the hardships of old people, the sick, the unemployed, and underpaid workers. By modern standards their achievements were insignificant. They did, however, represent another major attack on the principle of *laissez-faire*.

**Social Reforms**

*Social Security 1908*
Old age pension (per week)   25p (single)
   37½p (couple)

The first of these measures was the provision in the 1908 budget, introduced by Asquith, for the payment of old-age pensions to people over seventy. In the interests of economy and so as not to discourage thrift, the amount of the pension was kept down to 5s. (25p) a week for single people and 7s. 6d. (37½p) for married couples. Anyone with an income exceeding £31.10s. (£31.50) a year would receive no pension at all. Trifling though the sum was, it was a godsend to thousands of old people and their hard-pressed families who tried to care for them. Ironically, Asquith did not get the credit. This went to Lloyd George, who succeeded Asquith as Chancellor immediately after the budget. By 1909 half a million old people were regularly collecting their 'Lloyd George' from the Post Office.

*Social Security Expenditure*
(million pounds)

|  | 1900 | 1910 |
|---|---|---|
| Poor relief | 8·4 | 12·4 |
| Old age pensions | | 8·5 |
| Housing | | 0·6 |

No entirely satisfactory solution to the problem of unemployment was devised, partly because most economists still believed that the threat of unemployment and hardship was necessary to make people work hard. The Labour Exchanges, however, set up in 1909, which were an extension of a scheme begun by the Unionists in 1905, were an attempt to assist the casual labourer to find new work quickly. Also in 1909 a Trade Boards Act provided for special committees to deal with the sweated trades—those where hours of work were long and wages low, and where there were no trade unions to protect the workers' interests. The trades most concerned were tailoring, millinery, and the manufacture of chains, lace, and paper boxes. The trade boards, comprising representatives of the employers and the employees and some outsiders, were to fix minimum wages.

The most far-reaching of the social reforms was the National Insurance Act of 1911, which was also one of Lloyd George's special concerns. The Act covered the entire manual labour force. Every worker earning less than £160 a year had to have a stamped insurance card. The stamps represented weekly contributions of 4d. (1½p) from the worker, 3d. (1¼p) from the employer, and 2d. (1p) from the government. In return, workers would receive free medical treatment from 'panel' doctors, and sick pay of 10s. (50p) a week and disablement and maternity benefits. The free medical treatment, however, applied only to insured workers, not to their families. In addition, men employed in the seven trades most liable to seasonal unemployment would qualify for unemployment benefit of 7s. (35p) a week for up to fifteen weeks in any one year. This section of the Act covered rather more than two million workers, while the sickness benefit provisions applied, by 1914, to nearly fourteen million people.

This was a tremendous step away from traditional nineteenth-century attitudes. It appeared to be an admission that the state had some responsibility for the material well-being of its less fortunate members. But it fell far short of the Welfare State: the amounts paid in sickness and unemployment benefit were inadequate to maintain a family, only a minority of workers were covered against unemployment, and the government passed over the administration of the scheme to friendly societies and trade unions, which could register as approved societies. It has even been suggested that healthy and employed workers were being forced to subsidize the sick and unemployed. This, of course, is the essence of any form of insurance and the only alternative would have been for the government to pay the whole cost out of general taxation. No one would have stood for that in 1911.

These, together with the school meals and medical inspection provisions of 1907, were the main social achievements of the Liberals. How important were they? All the benefits they provided were meagre. They did little to help pupils from poor homes to advance to higher education. They hardly touched the housing problem. It is easy to denounce the 'great Liberal reforms' as illusions. But no government can advance too far ahead of public opinion, and many members of the public had great difficulty in swallowing these modest changes. The achievement of Asquith and Lloyd George was to make men think differently about what governments might and should do.

The Liberal government had already, with the Trade Disputes Act of 1906, helped its Labour allies over one hurdle. Another loomed up in 1908–9 when W.V. Osborne, the secretary of the

*Social Security 1911*
All workers earning less than £160 a year (about 14 million)
Benefits: sick pay 50p a week
free medical treatment
disablement payment
maternity payment
Additional payment to seasonal workers (about 2 million) unemployment benefit: 35p a week for a third of the year.

*Elderly Londoners collect their 'Lloyd George', 1909*

**Osborne Judgement 1909**

Walthamstow branch of the Amalgamated Society of Railway Servants, claimed that the payment of a proportion of the union funds to the Labour party was illegal. The House of Lords decided in favour of Osborne in December 1909. This was a catastrophic blow to the new party, whose election funds came almost entirely from the trade unions. Also, since M.P.s did not yet receive an official salary, most Labour Members were supported out of union funds. The Labour party's problem was partly solved by the government's decision in 1911 to pay M.P.s a salary of £400 a year.

**Trade Union Act 1913**

The Osborne Judgement was not reversed, however, until 1913, when the Trade Union Act allowed unions to pay a 'political levy', provided that the members expressed their agreement in a ballot, and provided that members had the right to 'contract out'. In other words, trade union members who did not wish to support the Labour party could refuse to pay that part of their union dues which it would have received.

The Osborne Judgement and the rather undistinguished performance of the Parliamentary Labour Party led some of the more extreme trade union leaders to contemplate direct action. Between 1910 and 1912 strikes by dockers, railwaymen, miners, and others threatened to cripple industry. Some of the organizers were known

*Government propaganda: Lloyd George points out the advantages of his National Insurance scheme*

# THE DAWN OF HOPE.

NATIONAL INSURANCE AGAINST SICKNESS AND DISABLEMENT

**MR. LLOYD GEORGE'S** National Health Insurance Bill provides for the insurance of the Worker in case of Sickness.

to sympathize with French Syndicalist ideas, according to which trade unions should use the strike weapon to disrupt industry and bring down the government. The rank and file were not Syndicalists. They went on strike because prices were rising while wages remained stationary.

The strikes were remarkable for the number of men involved and for the violence which often accompanied them. During the South Wales miners' strike in November 1910, troops had to be used to break up riots at Ton-y-Pandy. In 1911 the dockers of London, Liverpool, and Manchester all struck at once, and two men were killed when soldiers tried to restore order in Liverpool. Potentially the most dangerous stoppage was the national railway strike of August 1911. It lasted only four days, but it affected the whole of the north and the Midlands. Serious disorder seemed likely until Lloyd George helped the two sides to reach a settlement. The largest number of men to come out at one time were the 850,000 miners who struck in March 1912. Other industries depended on coal to such an extent that more than a million other workers were made idle. Here again, the government had to intervene. The miners went back to work when a miners' Minimum Wage Act was promised.

Perhaps as significant as these outbreaks of industrial violence was the trade union reorganization which took place. A huge new union, the National Transport Workers' Federation, looking after the interests of dockers, tram crews, and general labourers, was formed by Tom Mann and Ben Tillett in 1910. Three of the railway unions joined together in the National Union of Railwaymen in 1912. These new unions covered the whole country. Strikes in the future would not be confined to single factories or regions; whole industries would be paralyzed. This growth in the power of organized labour struck alarm into middle-class employers and shareholders. To them the most sinister development of all was the Triple Alliance of 1914, an undertaking by the Railwaymen, the Transport Workers' Federation, and the Miners' Federation to co-operate in future if necessary. Acting together, the members of the Triple Alliance could bring the economy to a standstill. Here was another instance of transition: the nineteenth-century unions struggled to survive and to protect their members' interests; the twentieth-century unions might be able to hold the country to ransom.

Violence came also from another, entirely unexpected, quarter—the women. A few educated ladies and a handful of male sympathizers had been arguing in favour of votes for women since the 1860s, but no one paid much attention to them until 1903, when Mrs. Emmeline Pankhurst founded the Women's Social and Political Union. The suffragettes, as they were called, were never

**Strikes 1910–12**

**Trade Union reorganization**

*Labour troubles, 1910–12: striking Welsh miners forage for coal on a pit heap; troops guard coal carts during the 1911 railway strike; a strike meeting at Tower Hill in London, 1912*

## The Suffragettes

Left *Sylvia Pankhurst (Christabel's sister) addresses an impromptu meeting in the East End in 1912.* Right *Emily Davidson's sacrifice*

Below *Some suffragettes tried to win support from working class women. This banner was made for use in all industrial disputes where women were involved.* Below right *Mrs. Pankhurst arrested again*

# The Daily Mirror

#### THE MORNING JOURNAL WITH THE SECOND LARGEST NET SALE.

o. 2,782. MONDAY, SEPTEMBER 23, 1912 One Halfpenny

JFFRAGETTES MOBBED AND BEATEN IN WALES: HAIR TORN FROM THE HEADS OF MR. LLOYD GEORGE'S INTERRUPTERS.

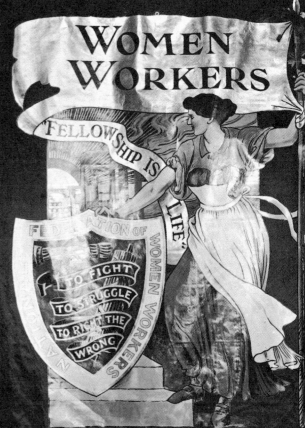

more than a small minority of middle-class women, but they soon won massive publicity for their cause. They began by interrupting political meetings, especially those addressed by Liberal ministers. They argued that since only the government could pass the legislation necessary to give women the vote, there was no point in attacking Unionist politicians. Asquith, who was never sympathetic to the women's cause, was their special target, but Grey and Lloyd George, who were not opposed in principle to votes for women, also had to contend with female hecklers.

Although an Act of 1907 allowed women to sit on county and borough councils, the suffragettes did not relax their campaign. Numerous militants, of whom Mrs. Pankhurst's daughter, Christabel, and Annie Kenney were the first, were sent to prison for failing to pay fines after being convicted of disrupting public meetings. From 1909 imprisoned suffragettes adopted the hunger-strike tactic, which led to the extremely unpleasant forcible feeding of women prisoners. Mrs. Pankhurst's claim that 'The argument of the broken pane is the most valuable argument in modern politics' heralded a new stage in the campaign. After a lull in 1910 and 1911, the suffragettes began an all-out programme of violence in 1912. Rejoicing in their self-sacrifice for the cause, young women broke windows, including those of 10 Downing Street, chained themselves to the railings outside Buckingham Palace and the Houses of Parliament, set fire to letters in pillar boxes, burned down churches and empty houses, and slashed pictures in public galleries. The most tragic and futile gesture was Emily Davidson's. She threw herself in front of the King's horse as the field rounded Tattenham Corner in the 1913 Derby. She died the next day.

The suffragettes' violence won them few friends. Public opinion was probably better disposed towards them before the militancy of 1912–13 than after. The government was concerned to maintain public order, but also tried to make reasonable concessions to just demands. To deal with the hunger-strikers, it had the 'Cat and Mouse Act' passed in 1913. This allowed prisoners who went on hunger-strike to be temporarily released, but provided for their re-arrest when they had recovered their health. The government also introduced a Parliamentary Reform Bill in 1913 and let it be known that an amendment in favour of women's suffrage would be accepted. To everyone's surprise, the Speaker refused to accept the amendment when it was moved; the Bill was accordingly dropped. The 'Cat and Mouse Act' and the unsuccessful Reform Bill did nothing to improve relations between the suffragettes and Asquith, who was on one occasion personally assaulted. The campaign continued until the outbreak of war, when it was abruptly suspended.

After the 1910 elections the survival of the Liberal government depended upon the goodwill of the Irish Nationalist Members of

Parliament. Their support was conditional upon another attempt to grant Home Rule to Ireland. From one point of view, the opportunity to solve the Irish problem was ideal, for the Nationalists were now led by John Redmond, a responsible and statesmanlike Irishman who was fully prepared to co-operate with the British government so long as Ireland was given her own parliament. The Unionists, however, were more determined than ever to resist. They now took full advantage of the Ulster Protestants' opposition to Home Rule and brought the United Kingdom to the brink of civil war.

Asquith introduced the third Irish Home Rule Bill in April 1912 (the first two had been defeated in 1886 and 1893). It stated that Ireland was to have her own parliament in Dublin, but that it was to deal only with local Irish matters and that the United Kingdom Parliament was to remain supreme. Ireland was to send forty-two members to Westminster.

The Ulster Protestants reacted strongly even before the Bill was brought in. Their objection was partly economic—they were afraid that Ulster's wealth would be siphoned off to support the backward South—but mainly religious: 'Home Rule means Rome Rule!'. Sir Edward Carson, a Dublin-born Protestant barrister and Unionist M.P., organized the Ulster Volunteers, a private army of Protestants pledged to resist Home Rule by force if necessary. On 9 April 1912 Carson and Andrew Bonar Law, the new Unionist leader, took the salute at a parade of the Ulster Volunteers.

Bonar Law, who was of Scots-Canadian origin, had become leader of the Unionists in 1911 when Balfour was forced to resign. He was a compromise candidate, appointed because the party could not agree between two better-known contestants, Austen Chamberlain (Joseph's son) and Walter Long. Weak, unsure of his own position, inclined to act irresponsibly, Bonar Law was carried away by the enthusiasm of his more extreme colleagues, men like Lansdowne and Carson, on the Irish question. Obviously trying to justify his leadership of the party, he delivered a dangerous and provocative speech at a party rally at Blenheim Palace in July 1912:

I can imagine no length of resistance to which Ulster will go, which I shall not be ready to support, and in which they will not be supported by the overwhelming majority of the British people.

It was only to be expected that the Catholic Nationalists in the South would retaliate. Redmond's political position was challenged by Arthur Griffith, who founded Sinn Fein ('We Ourselves'), a party pledged to the total separation of Ireland from Britain. At the same time, a second private army, the Irish Volunteers, appeared in the South.

It is often said that in this tense situation Asquith did nothing,

*Sir Edward Carson addresses an anti-Home Rule rally, 1913*

**Irish Home Rule problem**

**Buckingham Palace
conference 1914**

but pursued a policy of 'wait and see', hoping, like Mr. Micawber, that something 'would turn up'. He should have carved Ireland up into Catholic and Protestant areas; he should have put Carson and Bonar Law in prison; he should have done something. Criminal charges could quite possibly have been brought against Carson and Bonar Law. They had encouraged the formation of a private army whose function could only be to wage civil war; they had made public speeches containing passages which were probably seditious. Asquith must have been tempted, but he knew that one solves nothing by locking up one's political opponents, that, even with Carson behind bars, Ulster would have continued to resist Home Rule. Similarly partition, even though it would almost certainly have to be adopted in the end, was at present unacceptable to Unionists like Lansdowne, who owned land in Southern Ireland, and to Redmond, who would be overthrown by the Nationalists and derided by Sinn Fein if he gave way over Ulster. But Asquith was not inactive between 1912 and 1914. An almost continuous round of meetings and a mountain of letters and memoranda on the subject over a period of two years hardly justifies the normal condemnation of the 'wait and see' policy.

Bonar Law continued to make trouble. Hopefully, but not very realistically, he asked the King in September 1913 to dismiss Asquith. Two months later he took the foolhardy step of appealing to the army officers in Dublin to disobey orders to enforce Home Rule. In the previous year several trade union leaders had been imprisoned for circulating a pamphlet urging soldiers not to shoot strikers. An indirect result of Bonar Law's appeal was the declaration in March 1914 by a group of cavalry officers at The Curragh, the military headquarters near Dublin, that they would resign rather than obey orders to crush an Ulster rebellion. After some confusion, Asquith himself took over the War Office and the Curragh Mutiny was crushed. That the loyalty of the armed forces was in question was an indication of the strength of feeling on the Irish issue.

In April 1914 the Ulster Volunteers successfully landed a shipload of rifles and ammunition at Larne. The Irish Volunteers replied by enrolling more men, but when they tried to import arms at Howth in July the police and troops attempted, unsuccessfully, to stop them. Sinn Fein claimed that the British government had allowed the Larne gun-running and that it was prejudiced in favour of the Ulster Protestants.

Asquith continued to seek a compromise solution. At the King's suggestion, a conference of the interested parties met at Buckingham Palace in July 1914. The participants were Asquith and Lloyd George for the government, Bonar Law and Lansdowne for the Unionists, Redmond and Dillon for the Nationalists, and

37

Carson and Craig for the Ulstermen. Temporary partition at least now seemed inevitable, but the delegates could not agree as to which areas might be excluded from Home Rule. The Buckingham Palace conference, according to Winston Churchill, 'lost itself in the muddy by-ways of Fermanagh and Tyrone'. The conference lasted for three days and failed.

The outbreak of the First World War on 4 August 1914 put the Irish question into temporary cold storage. It was Asquith's intention to pass the Home Rule Bill, making use of the Parliament Act to overcome the Lords' opposition, but to exclude six of the Ulster counties for six years. Whether this would have been acceptable to all sides is doubtful; a similar solution provoked civil war in 1920. The Bill was passed in September 1914, but its operation was suspended for the duration of the war.

Asquith's government faced a larger number of severe crises than any other peacetime administration. Two of them—the House of Lords controversy and Ireland—threatened the very structure of political and social life. Two others—the strikes and the suffragette campaign—were only slightly less serious. The government had hardly surmounted its obstacles triumphantly, but it had survived, had prevented a breakdown of law and order, and had also carried through a number of hotly contested social reforms. So much for the placid mill-pond of Edwardian England. In some ways it was a relief to go to war.

# Chapter 2
## Foreign and Defence Policies
## 1900–1914

Unionists and Liberals differed sharply on most domestic issues, but their foreign and defence policies were broadly similar and consistent. The aim of every Foreign Secretary is to serve his country's interests and it is the duty of the ministers in charge of the armed forces to see that the country is able to protect those interests in war if necessary. Both Lord Lansdowne, the Unionist Foreign Secretary, and Sir Edward Grey, the Liberal, endeavoured to protect, but not to extend, the British Empire and to improve relations with foreign governments as far as possible. They did not wish to attach Britain to either of the European alliances (see page 9). So long as no one Power dominated the Continent of Europe, Britain was happy to stand apart. It followed from this that Britain did not need a large army, although it was desirable that her small professional force should be highly efficient. The Empire could not be defended, however, unless the Royal Navy maintained its superiority, not only over any other navy, but over any two others.

If neither Lansdowne nor Grey wished to become entangled in European alliances, then why did Britain go to war in 1914? Unfortunately, perhaps, their attempts to resolve Britain's differences with France and Russia were much more successful than their overtures to Germany, with the result that Britain was drawn gradually towards the Franco-Russian *Entente*, although she never joined it. When, for reasons which did not concern Britain and over which she had no control, the two European alliances went to war, Britain was under strong pressure to help France. Even so, she might have remained neutral had it not been for the German invasion of Belgium, a country which Britain was bound by treaty to defend.

The Foreign Office's main concern at the turn of the century was the Far East (see map). The decadent Chinese empire, with its massive population, was an attractive market for western industrialists, and British, German, and French traders, supported by their respective governments, had secured concessions from the Chinese. Japan, throwing off some of its Oriental traditions and copying western techniques, had recently seized Korea from China and was interested in the adjacent province of Manchuria. Both the British and the Japanese governments, however, were alarmed at the progress of the Russians, whose influence was extending

*Map 1 The Far East in 1900*

southwards from eastern Siberia into Manchuria. In 1898 Russia seized the Chinese city of Port Arthur.

The revolt in Peking by the fanatical anti-foreign Chinese Boxers in 1900 provoked swift retaliation by the Powers and an almost unprecedented instance of united action. An international relief force consisting of contingents from Japan, Russia, Britain, France, and Germany relieved the besieged foreign legations in Peking and compelled the Chinese to recognize the principle of the 'open door'. Foreigners, in other words, were to be free to trade with China.

The Russians' apparent intention to add Manchuria to their empire led Joseph Chamberlain to approach the German government with an outline plan for an Anglo-German alliance. Part of Chamberlain's aim was to persuade the Germans to co-operate in resisting further Russian expansion in the Far East. When the German government showed little interest in the idea, the Foreign Office turned to the Japanese, who readily agreed to a treaty with Britain. The Anglo-Japanese alliance of 1902, often seen as marking the end of 'splendid isolation', stated that if one of the partners were involved in war with one other Great Power, the other partner would remain neutral, but that war with two or more Powers would compel the other signatory's intervention. The alliance was clearly directed against Russia, but also indirectly against Russia's ally, France. When war between Russia and Japan broke out in 1904, France remained neutral and the Japanese were able to win a convincing victory. In 1905 Russia gave up southern Manchuria to Japan. From the British point of view, the results of the Japanese alliance had been highly satisfactory. These events do, however, show that in 1900–2 Britain did not think herself naturally committed to the Franco-Russian side in the European struggle, and was even looking for a chance to reach an agreement with Germany.

The main obstacle to friendship between Britain and Germany was Kaiser William II's ambition to build a great German fleet. This direct challenge to Britain's mastery of the seas caused alarm in the Admiralty. Chiefly through the efforts of Sir John Fisher, the First Sea Lord, whose plans won the approval and support of King Edward VII, Britain began in 1904–5 to modernize the Royal Navy and to build new ships. The Navy was reorganized into three main fleets, one in the Mediterranean (based on Malta), an Atlantic fleet (based on Gibraltar) and a Channel fleet (based on the home ports). Instead of trying to patrol the seven seas, the Admiralty was concentrating on meeting the German menace. Most significant of all, a new battleship, the *Dreadnought*, was built secretly, launched in 1906, and completed in 1907. The *Dreadnought*, the first of a new class, could out-gun any ship afloat and rendered all other battleships obsolete. Instead of admitting their inability to compete,

**Anglo-Japanese alliance 1902**

Above *The launching of the first submarine for the Royal Navy, 1901*

**Anglo-German naval race**

40

Map 2 *Morocco in 1905*

*H.M.S. Dreadnought*

the Germans copied the *Dreadnought*. Thus began the Anglo-German naval race, which cost both countries millions of pounds and which prevented the British government from reaching with Germany the kind of *entente* or understanding which she was to make with France and Russia.

Relations between Britain and France had been strained for some years, partly because France was allied to Britain's rival in the Far East, Russia, partly because of quarrels over African colonies. In 1903–4 Lansdowne set out not to secure an Anglo-French alliance, but to remove the causes of discord. Some of the spade-work was done by King Edward VII, who won over French public opinion on a state visit to Paris in 1903. In 1904, with the outbreak of the war between Russia and Japan, the French were alarmed that they might be drawn in on the opposite side to Britain. They were very willing to enter into discussions, therefore, and the Anglo-French *Entente* was signed in April 1904. It was concerned solely with colonial matters and said, in effect, that while Britain was to have a free hand in Egypt, she would not object to France taking over Morocco. It said nothing at all about co-operation against Germany. On the other hand, it was significant that just as Britain's relations with Germany were deteriorating she was moving closer to France.

The *Entente* was soon put to the test. Morocco was still officially independent, although the French hoped to bring it under their influence. In March 1905, however, the Kaiser visited the Moroccan port of Tangier and announced that Germany had great and growing interests in Morocco. This direct challenge to France precipitated a major international crisis, but when a conference of the Great Powers met at Algeciras in Spain in January 1906 to discuss the matter, Britain gave solid support to her new partner. The Germans, finding themselves isolated apart from their Austrian allies, gave way.

At the time of this first Moroccan crisis a series of very secret talks between British and French generals began. Although authorized by Haldane, the War Minister, they were so secret that they were not revealed even to the whole Cabinet. These conversations were continued intermittently thereafter and were another indication that Britain was drifting into a close association with France.

Simultaneously, Haldane carried out a number of army reforms, designed not to increase the size of the British army, but to make it more efficient and economical. A general staff was created to replace the antiquated over-all command and bring Britain into line with Continental practice. Haldane also organized an Expeditionary Force of six infantry divisions and one cavalry division, ready for rapid mobilization and capable of being sent to the Continent at short notice. Minute by European standards, this force was highly efficient and was to play a vital part in the fighting

*Map 3 Europe before 1914*

of August and September 1914. As a second line, the yeomanry and
volunteers were made into a Territorial Force, whose function was
to be home defence. Finally, public schools and secondary schools
were encouraged to form Officers' Training Corps, so that if war
did come the army would have sufficient young men capable of
becoming officers.

Taken together, the Anglo-French military conversations and
Haldane's army reforms show that the British government was
beginning to contemplate the prospect of taking part in a Continental war against Germany. This represented an extraordinary
change in British policies between 1900 and 1906, a change which
was due to France's readiness to respond to friendly British
overtures and to the German Kaiser's obsession with his naval
programme.

The die was not yet cast, however. On taking office, Campbell-
Bannerman's Liberal government reduced the naval building
programme and suggested to Germany that the international
Disarmament Conference at The Hague in 1907 should discuss the
reduction in the size of navies. The Germans were unwilling to call
a halt while their rivals were still ahead and the race continued.
Thanks to Campbell-Bannerman's pause, Germany was even begin-

**Haldane's army reforms**

**Failure of Liberals to reach
agreement with Germany**

ning to catch up. Reluctantly, and in response to public demand, Asquith's Cabinet decided to lay down eight Dreadnoughts in 1909 and a further five in each of the next two years. The slogan 'We want eight, and we won't wait' had swept the country.

Meanwhile, the Foreign Office, now under the guidance of Sir Edward Grey, had taken another decisive step away from isolation. Following the *Entente* with France, it was perhaps natural that Britain should seek a similar agreement with France's ally, Russia. An Anglo-Russian Convention was duly signed in August 1907. Like the French *Entente* of 1904, it was concerned only with colonial matters and merely sought to remove causes of possible disagreement. Russia's defeat by Japan meant that there was no longer any risk of confrontation in China, but the nearness of the southern border of Russia to India had alarmed British statesmen for more than half a century. Accordingly, Russia promised to keep out of Afghanistan and Tibet and the two countries divided Persia into spheres of influence and promised to respect each other's rights there. As with the French *Entente*, there was no mention of European issues. Britain was not committed to supporting Russia in her quarrels with Austria-Hungary or Germany. There was, in fact, no reason why Grey should not make a similar agreement with the Germans, and it seems clear that for some time he continued to hope that he might be able to do so.

The most likely cause of a European war was the Eastern Question, which no longer directly concerned Britain. As the Turkish, or Ottoman, Empire contracted, the Balkan nations (Greeks, Serbs, Rumanians, and Bulgarians) asserted their independence. The Great Powers to the north, Russia and Austria-Hungary, jealously competed for influence over the Balkan states, although neither necessarily wanted to seize extra territories. The Russians, who had religious and cultural links with the Balkan peoples, were generally more successful. The Austrians, on the other hand, with an empire containing numerous different national groups, were alarmed at the growth of nationalism in south-east Europe. They thought that an arrogant and expanding Serbia, for example, would soon want to absorb the Serb territories of the Austrian empire. Austria's policy of frustrating the ambitions of Serbia received full support from the Germans, who had their own plans to increase their trade and influence in Turkey.

In 1908 the Austrian Foreign Minister, Aehrenthal, carried out a bold stroke by formally annexing Bosnia-Hercegovina, a Turkish territory which the Austrians had occupied since 1878 (see Map 4). The Turks were in no position to object, but the move was bitterly resented by Serbia, for Bosnia-Hercegovina was inhabited by Serbs and the Serbian government had hoped to annex the provinces at a favourable moment in the future. The Serbs appealed to their

**Anglo-Russian Convention 1907**

**The Eastern Question**

**Austrian annexation of Bosnia-Hercegovina 1908**

patrons, the Russians, but when the latter learned both that Germany was solidly behind Austria-Hungary and that neither the French nor the British governments were prepared to take any positive action, they backed down. Apart from suggesting that the Bosnian question be discussed by a European conference, a proposal which Aehrenthal turned down, Grey played no part in the affair. The incident is, however, interesting in that it was a dress rehearsal for the outbreak of the First World War: it began with a dispute between Austria-Hungary and Serbia and expanded to involve Germany and Russia. The difference was that in 1914 France and Britain became entangled also.

Grey took a neutral line in 1908: the Anglo-Russian Convention of 1907 said nothing about Bosnia-Hercegovina or any other European territory. The Anglo-French *Entente* did, however, refer to Morocco, and when the Germans sent a gunboat, the *Panther*, to the Moroccan port of Agadir in June 1911 the British and French governments stood firmly together. Grey was alarmed lest the German gesture might be a prelude to an attempt to establish a naval base on Morocco's Atlantic coast, a base from which German raiders could attack British merchant ships in the North Atlantic. The crisis lasted throughout the summer and autumn of 1911, but Germany eventually gave way, partly because the British government clearly stated its support for France. In July, speaking at a dinner in the Mansion House in London, Lloyd George said:

**Moroccan crisis 1911**

> I would make great sacrifices to preserve peace. I conceive that nothing would justify a disturbance of international goodwill except questions of the gravest national moment. But if a situation were to be forced upon us, in which peace could only be preserved by the surrender of the great and beneficent position Britain has won by centuries of heroism and achievement, by allowing Britain to be treated, where her interests were vitally affected, as if she were of no account in the Cabinet of Nations, then I say emphatically that peace at that price would be a humiliation intolerable for a country like ours to endure.

Germany received a small central African territory as compensation and gave up her claims to Morocco.

Their co-operation over Morocco drew Britain and France closer together, but Grey and his colleagues still did not abandon hope of an agreement with Germany. Regular discussions took place, and in 1912 Haldane was sent on a mission to Germany. The price demanded by the Kaiser's government for a suspension of the naval race and an *entente*, however, was a promise by Britain that she would remain neutral in the event of a European war. Britain could have German friendship only if she deserted France. Grey could not accept this.

**Haldane's mission to Germany 1912**

Later in 1912 Britain and France reached a naval agreement whereby some British ships were moved out of the Mediterranean

**Anglo-French naval agreement 1912**

Map 4 *The Balkans in 1900*
Right Map 5 *The Balkans in 1914*

**Balkan wars 1912–13**

**Military preparations**

so as to increase the Royal Navy's superiority in the Atlantic and the Channel. France, meanwhile, assumed responsibility for patrolling the Mediterranean. This naval co-operation, together with the military conversations, had the effect of converting the *Entente* into something close to a military alliance. Even so, Britain and Germany were not yet enemies: the two governments reached agreements in 1913 and 1914 on colonial questions and the German railway-building activities in Turkey—the 'Berlin-Baghdad railway'.

If naval rivalry prevented Anglo-German friendship, it was the Eastern Question which provoked European war. The prelude came in 1912–13 when, as a result of two wars in the Balkans, Turkey's hold on Europe was virtually eliminated and Serbia was doubled in size (see Map 5). The expansion of Serbia alarmed the Austrians, some of whose Serb subjects were beginning to demand inclusion in Serbia. Grey, by organizing an international conference in London, played an important part in reducing the risk of European war, and it is important to note that he still pursued a neutral policy on the Eastern Question. His increased commitment to France did not lead him to back France's ally, Russia, or her protégé, Serbia.

The increasing tension in the Balkans, the two Moroccan crises, and the naval race led the Great Powers to believe that a European war was possible, and even likely. They all increased their military preparedness: Germany increased the strength of her army, raised a huge sum in extra taxation, and completed the widening of the Kiel Canal, to allow Dreadnoughts to pass from the Baltic to the

45

North Sea; France increased her period of compulsory military service from two years to three; Russia added half a million men to her peacetime strength. The British army was not increased, but expenditure on the Royal Navy was raised from £33 million in 1905 to over £50 million in 1914.

Thus armed, the Great Powers were ready for war. But war was not inevitable. The fantastic armaments of the United States and the Soviet Union have not driven them into war. Only if political leaders are willing to risk war, even to invite it, do hostilities break out. In the summer of 1914 too many leaders calmly accepted the prospect.

Not unexpectedly, the Eastern Question provided the spark. Archduke Franz Ferdinand, the heir to the Austrian throne, was assassinated by a Serb patriot in Sarajevo, the capital of Bosnia, on 28 June 1914. The Austrian chancellor, Berchtold, seized this opportunity to humiliate Serbia. A war to punish the Serbian government would destroy for a generation the Serb challenge to Austrian security. Remembering the events of 1908, Berchtold did not expect Russia to intervene on the Serbian side.

Berchtold received firm support from the German Kaiser and his chancellor, Bethmann-Hollweg, both of whom wanted Austria-Hungary to crush its troublesome little neighbour. The Germans could see that if Russia decided to support Serbia there was a risk of a European war, but the Kaiser was prepared to face this risk and his generals even welcomed it. The latter wanted war in 1914, for they thought that Germany could then defeat both Russia and France, and that her task would grow progressively more difficult as her prospective enemies rearmed.

Encouraged by the backing of his senior partner, Berchtold issued a crushing ultimatum to Serbia on 23 July. The Serbs gave way on most points, but not all, and on 28 July Austria-Hungary declared war. In Britain, Asquith and Grey were sure that a European war was now inevitable, but Britain's role was still unclear. If Russia went to war with Austria-Hungary and Germany, France would be drawn in on the Russian side. Would Britain side with France? The two countries had been drawn closer together ever since 1904, but there was still no treaty obliging Britain to help France in a war. Opinion among Cabinet ministers and Liberal M.P.s was divided: some, like Grey, would have liked to have given a clear statement of Britain's intention to assist France against Germany; others, like Lloyd George and the more radical ministers, wanted to stay out of a continental war. These divisions of opinion prevented Grey from pledging Britain to any particular course of action. In any case, the German generals were so contemptuous of Britain's little army that a British warning would probably have had no influence on the course of events. Grey

*Newspaper posters (and sellers) in August 1914*

**British Cabinet divided**

suggested a London conference of the ambassadors of the Great Powers, but this was rejected by the Germans.

**Russian mobilization**

Events now unfolded logically and remorselessly. On 31 July Tsar Nicholas II signed the order for general Russian mobilization. This put the control of German policy into the hands of the generals, who insisted on immediate German mobilization, which meant war. The Germans had only one war plan, the Schlieffen Plan. Drawn up to deal with the danger of simultaneous wars with France and Russia, the Schlieffen Plan envisaged a holding operation against Russia, while France was knocked out in a lightning six-week campaign which depended on an invasion of north-eastern France through Belgium. Once the Russians had begun to mobilize, there could be no delay: speed was the essence of the Schlieffen Plan. Accordingly, Germany declared war on Russia on 2 August and on France a day later. German troops began to cross the Belgian frontier almost immediately. The Tsar's decision to mobilize and the rigidity of the German plan had pushed Europe over the brink.

**The Schlieffen Plan**

The invasion of Belgium gave Grey an opportunity to bring an almost united Britain into the war. By a treaty of 1839, Britain was bound to protect Belgium's independence. In answer to Grey's inquiry, France had readily undertaken not to invade Belgium in 1914, while Germany had failed to give satisfaction. On 3 August Grey told the Commons that the Cabinet intended to declare war if the Germans invaded Belgium. He received a promise of full Unionist support from Bonar Law and, to everyone's surprise, Redmond made a similar gesture on behalf of the Irish. Two radical ministers resigned and the Labour party withheld its approval, but the Commons reflected the almost unanimous public opinion.

On 4 August, as the German divisions marched into Belgium, a British ultimatum was delivered in Berlin. No satisfactory reply was received by midnight, and the Great War had begun. Next day, crowds rejoiced in the streets of London. Ecstatic patriotism gripped every European capital—Berlin, St. Petersburg, and Paris saw identical scenes. Everyone felt sure that the war would be short and would end in glorious victory.

War broke out in 1914 because the continental Great Powers had conflicting interests and because their leaders were prepared to contemplate the use of force. Britain was not directly responsible for the coming of war. Lansdowne's policy, continued by Grey, was to settle differences between Britain and foreign governments, to remove possible causes of discord. The Japanese Alliance, the French *Entente*, and the Russian Convention were part of this policy. Its logical extension would have been similar agreements with Germany and Austria-Hungary. The naval race prevented an

*Britain goes joyfully to war, August 1914: patriotic parade down Whitehall, London*

Anglo-German settlement. It is pointless to blame either Germany for wishing to build a navy or Britain for seeking to preserve her naval supremacy, but it is necessary to realize that this naval rivalry drove Britain steadily into the arms of France. Two verdicts on Sir Edward Grey are possible: either he was an honest and talented statesman who did his best to keep Europe at peace, or he made the fatal mistake of allowing British policy to drift from neutrality to undeclared alliance. Lloyd George said that the governments of Europe 'stumbled and staggered into war'. Perhaps this is also true of the British government.

Socially, there were many similarities between Edwardian and Victorian Britain. Class distinctions were well defined and carefully preserved, although talented individuals could move upwards. The wealthy could lead a life of leisured luxury while many of the poor waged a continuous struggle against adversity. There were glaring inequalities of wealth, yet few signs of revolt. Each class treated its superiors with genuine respect. The pace of life was slower than it has been since the First World War: the motor car was a rich man's luxury, the aeroplane was an amazing new invention, films were an interesting novelty, but in general the Edwardians' lives were similar to their parents'. Most road transport was still horse-drawn, fashion showed subtle variations but no major changes, married women were expected to work only in the home. The astute observer might have anticipated that a transformation was on the way, but there was none of the restless bustle of subsequent decades.

**Population**

The population of the United Kingdom increased from forty-two million to forty-five million between 1901 and 1911, thus almost maintaining the rapid expansion of the Victorian period. Although the birth-rate was declining, the death-rate was also falling, mainly because fewer children were dying in infancy and the first years of childhood. This was partly due to medical improvements and to the setting up of Infant Welfare Centres, which gave advice to mothers and distributed free milk to those in need. There were only twelve such centres in 1906, but their efforts and those of family doctors had brought the infant mortality rate down to below ten per cent for the first time by 1916. The only part of the United Kingdom whose population did not increase was Ireland. Her surplus population continued to emigrate to Great Britain, the United States, and the Dominions. For the United Kingdom as a whole the emigration figures reached a record level between 1911 and 1913.

*Population* (millions)

|  | 1901 | 1911 |
|---|---|---|
| U.K. | 37·0 | 40·8 |
| S. Ireland | 4·5 | 4·4 |

About three per cent of the forty-five million belonged to the upper and upper middle classes (people with incomes exceeding £700 per year). They included the landowners and wealthy industrialists and bankers, as well as the more successful professional men. The very rich landowners had been hit by the agricultural depression of the late nineteenth century, but low taxation permitted them still to live in large houses, dress elegantly, and employ

**Social classes**

49

*Class distinctions: Painting of an upper-class wedding; a middle-class family; a working-class family — the father has a handful of pawn tickets*

numerous domestic servants. A large proportion of the aristocracy now derived at least part of its income from business and industry, thus blurring the distinction between upper and middle classes. Comparatively few of the English rich were idle. Many devoted themselves to public affairs, business, or the armed forces. Politicians like Salisbury, Balfour, and Lansdowne belonged to this 'patrician' class; they were moved not by financial need but by the desire to serve.

A further four million people, with incomes between £160 and £700 per year, belonged to the lower middle class. These were the less successful businessmen, shopkeepers, and most of the professional men. Clerks considered themselves to be middle-class, but most of them earned less than £3 a week in 1910.

A family qualified for middle-class status if it kept domestic servants. Mrs. Beeton suggested in 1888 that households with incomes over £150 a year should have a maid, that those with over £500 a year should have a cook and a maid, and that anyone with more than £1000 a year should employ a cook, two housemaids, and a manservant. Servants' wages were low, but they received free board, lodging, and clothes. A maid might earn 5s. (25p) a week, a cook 8s. (40p), and a valet 14s. (70p) or 15s. (75p). In the 1890s, apparently, footmen's wages in London depended on their height:

*A shopping expedition: Oxford Street in 1907*

*Cheap bread attracts young customers to an East End shop in 1912*

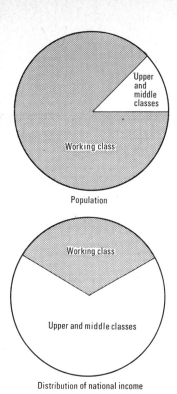

Population

Distribution of national income

*Food Prices 1913–14*

| | |
|---|---|
| Meat | 4p per lb |
| Bacon | 3p per lb |
| Cheese | 3½p per lb |
| Eggs | ½p each |
| Bread | 2½p large loaf |
| Milk | 1p pint |
| Tea | 8p a lb |
| Sugar | 1p a lb |
| Flour | ½p a lb |
| Potatoes | ¼p a lb |
| Butter | 13p a lb |

**Working-class standard of living**

a six-foot-tall first footman might receive 16*s.* (80p) a week, while a second footman of five foot six would be paid only 8*s.* (40p).

It was calculated in 1911 that the upper and middle classes, numbering between five and six million people, took two-thirds of the national income, while the working class of thirty-nine million existed on the remaining third. The lowest-paid of all workers were the women in the sweated trades, while the worst-paid men were the agricultural labourers, of whom there were 650,000 in 1911 and whose earnings were often less than £1 a week. Semi-skilled workers in the building industry, machine operators, and miners earned between 25*s.* (£1.25) and 30*s.* (£1.50) a week, while the aristocracy of the working class were the men in highly skilled trades—printers, engineers, and engine-drivers, some of whom received between 50*s.* (£2.50) and 60*s.* (£3) a week. The average adult man was paid 30*s.* (£1.50) for a fifty-four hour week in 1913–14.

The years between 1900 and 1914 saw the reverse of the late nineteenth-century trend in wages and prices. Between 1875 and 1900 prices had fallen while wages remained stationary, with the result that the working-class standard of living rose. After 1900 there was a slow rise in prices, which was not accompanied by increases in wages. Wage-earners, therefore, were worse off in 1914 than in 1900.

Pre-First World War prices may appear low, but it should be remembered that wages averaged 30*s.* (£1.50) a week and that families were large. Most of a family's earnings would go on rent, food, and clothes; there was seldom anything left for luxuries; weekly budgets had to be reckoned in pennies and halfpennies. Rent might account for 5*s.* (25p) of the weekly wage. Food had to be filling rather than appetizing or nutritious, and most working-class families would be able to afford each week only one joint of 'butcher's meat', at about 9*d.* (4p) per pound. Bacon, which could be thinly sliced, offal, trotters, and cow-heels were more economical and more popular. Tea was the standard beverage, but it was comparatively expensive: even the multiple grocers like Liptons charged 1*s.* 7*d.* (8p) per pound. The basic item in any diet was bread, the price of which had fallen to 5*d.* (2p) or 6*d.* (2½p) for the quartern loaf (4lb. 5¼oz.).

Prudent working-class housewives took advantage of every opportunity to economize. This meant buying the cheaper kinds of food and buying at the right time. Walter Greenwood's *There was a Time*, a partial autobiography in which he describes his early life in Salford, provides an illustration of this:

Where the weekly roast was concerned the shrewd and thrifty housewives were aware that they had the butchers at a disadvantage. Refrigerators had yet to supplant iceboxes, and the customers knew that the butchers knew that if the stock were not cleared by closing time it would be rotten or have to be given away by Monday, when the dawn crush at the pawnshop told its tale of empty purses. An hour or so before midnight (Saturday), while the pubs resounded with the uncertain harmony of tipsy vocalists, wives congregated outside the shops under the spluttering naphtha flares. It only needed one butcher to start for all to follow suit. Standing on the pavement, sometimes on a chair in front of a circle of upturned faces, he brandished aloft the unsold stock: 'Here y'are, ladies. Shoulder o' lamb—eighteen pence.'

Taking advantage of the butchers' growing alarm, the customers forced them into a Dutch auction and came away with far more meat than they could otherwise have afforded.

Even though the price of clothes had fallen in the late nineteenth century, the purchase of a new suit, dress, or pair of shoes was a major step. There was a flourishing trade in second-hand clothes. Coal, however, at about a pound per ton, was comparatively cheap. The only other items on which poorer families would spend money were household utensils, furniture (very rarely), doctor's bills, drink, and gambling. The latter two items would vary according to the man's sobriety and prudence. Holidays were beyond the means of most families, while bicycles, costing four or five pounds, were a symbol of middle-class status. Only the wealthier business and professional men could afford motor cars, the cheapest of which cost between a hundred and two hundred pounds.

Serious poverty, the inability to provide themselves and their families with adequate food, clothing, and shelter, afflicted a distressingly large proportion of the population. Researches carried out at the turn of the century by Charles Booth in London and Seebohm Rowntree in York revealed that almost a third of the nation lived in poverty. Rowntree calculated that a married couple and three children needed a weekly income of £1. 1s. 8d. (£1.08½) and found that forty per cent of the working-class population of York fell below this minimum. His weekly budget is detailed opposite.

Only about fourteen per cent of the working class actually earned less than Rowntree's minimum. Rowntree referred to this group as the sufferers from 'primary poverty'. Nearly twice as many people were affected by 'secondary poverty'; their wages could have kept them above the poverty level had not a proportion gone on such items as medical expenses, travel, drink, and gambling.

The Temperance Movement's claim that 'Drink is the curse of the working classes' was still substantially true. Rowntree saw heavy drinking as the most important cause of 'secondary poverty' and calculated that the average working-class family spent 6s. 11d. (34½p) a week on drink. The Temperance Movement, closely linked to the Nonconformist churches, and, to some extent, to the trade unions and the new Labour movement, had made some headway among the

| | |
|---|---|
| Food for husband and wife | |
| Food for three children | |
| Rent | |
| Clothing for adults | |
| Clothing for children | |
| Fuel | |
| Sundries (light, household equipment, soap, etc.) | |

*Crisp Street market, East End of London, 1904*

| | | |
|---:|---:|---:|
| 6s. | 0d. | |
| 6s. | 9d. | |
| 4s. | 0d. | |
| 1s. | 0d. | |
| 1s. | 3d. | |
| 1s. | 10d. | |
| | | |
| | 10d. | |
| £1 | 1s. | 8d. |

upper working class, the more skilled, better-educated workers. Tragically, it was those who could least afford money for drink who indulged the most. Their folly brought misery to themselves and their dependants; yet it is easy to understand their longing for some escape from drudgery and squalor.

Some insight into the conditions of the 'primary poor' is provided by one of Rowntree's detailed case-studies. A typical lorry-driver, with a wife and two children, had total earnings, over an eight-week period, of £8. 14s. 6d. (£8.72½). His expenditure, including food, rent, fuel, clothing, and medical expenses, amounted to £8. 14s. 9d. (£8.74). Mr. Micawber would have concluded, 'Result: misery'; Rowntree amplified this: an eighteen per cent protein deficiency and a nine per cent calorie deficiency. The family lived in a three-roomed house, for which they paid 3s. (15p) a week. There was a tap, but no sink, in the living-room; there were no carpets; the principal items of furniture were a table, two wooden easy chairs, a sofa, and an occasional table. Their menu of meals for a week in February 1901 has survived:

55

|          | *Breakfast* | *Dinner* | *Tea* | *Supper* |
|----------|-------------|----------|-------|----------|
| *Friday* | bread | bread | bread | none |
|          | butter | butter | butter | |
|          | tea | toast | tea | |
|          | | tea | | |
| *Saturday* | bread | bacon | bread | tea |
|          | bacon | potatoes | butter | bread |
|          | coffee | pudding | shortcake | kippers |
|          | | tea | tea | |
| *Sunday* | bread | pork | bread | bread |
|          | butter | onions | butter | meat |
|          | shortcake | potatoes | shortcake | |
|          | coffee | Yorkshire | tea | |
|          | | pudding | | |
| *Monday* | bread | pork | bread | one cup |
|          | bacon | potatoes | butter | of tea |
|          | butter | pudding | tea | |
|          | tea | tea | | |
| *Tuesday* | bread | pork | bread | bread |
|          | bacon | bread | butter | bacon |
|          | butter | tea | boiled eggs | butter |
|          | coffee | | tea | tea |
| *Wednesday* | bread | bacon and | bread | none |
|          | bacon | eggs | butter | |
|          | butter | potatoes | tea | |
|          | tea | bread | | |
|          | | tea | | |
| *Thursday* | bread | bread | bread | none |
|          | butter | bacon | butter | |
|          | coffee | tea | tea | |

Debt was a normal feature of most working-class people's lives. Housewives who were not good managers often found themselves in debt to the grocer or general dealer, whose corner shop was the source of most of their provisions. It was because of this that pawn-broking was among the most flourishing of businesses in working-class areas. Not only valuable articles like clocks and watches, but suits of clothes, basic items of furniture, and even blankets were regularly 'popped' by housewives desperately trying to raise a few extra shillings. In some families it was routine that the best clothes were pawned on Monday morning and redeemed on Friday evening when the wages were paid. Walter Greenwood, who worked for a time as an assistant in a pawnbroker's shop, describes the Monday morning rush:

**Poverty**

*The poor: Top the cheapest available overnight accommodation, the Salvation Army's 'penny sit-up'; Right St. Pancras workhouse 1900; 'down-and-outs' in St. James's Park*

As I shot back the top bolt I saw the latch rise. The noise without now resembled that at a football match. Even this was exceeded when I kicked the bottom bolt back, the door was flung wide and I had to fly out of the way of a stampede of shawled and clogged women, aprons bulging with things to be pawned. Mrs. Boarder was in the van and, by the time I had reached the safety of the counter's other side, she and those at the front had piled their stuff on the counter like revolutionaries throwing up a barricade. Mrs. Boarder's contribution extended the counter's width and it was heaped so high that it quite concealed her daughter Hetty who had helped carry some of the burden. The shop was packed, spilling into the backyard. Without a glance at his customers the pawnbroker came from the safe carrying three canvas bags. He was followed by Reggie, acolyte-fashion, bearing the leather-bound book of account. Everybody watched the silver and copper being poured into the till's compartments and the paper money at the back.

The main cause of poverty after 1918 was unemployment. This was not such a serious problem in the Edwardian era. The statistics are unreliable, but it seems that the level of unemployment up to 1910 averaged six per cent and was much lower in the last three years of peace.

The unemployed, the aged, and widows had no Welfare State to help them before the beginning of the Liberal reforms (see Chapter 1). People reduced to poverty had to rely on their savings, friendly societies, trade unions, the generosity of friends and relatives, pawnbrokers or, as a last resort, the Poor Law, the only form of state relief for the poor. The structure of the Poor Law system was essentially unchanged from that set up by the Act of 1834: parishes were grouped in Poor Law unions, each controlled by an elected

57

board of guardians, and each providing a workhouse. The basic principle was 'less eligibility': apart from some old people, invalids, and mothers with young children, relief was available only to those who entered the workhouse, where conditions were deliberately made unpleasant so that idlers would be discouraged.

By the turn of the century workhouses were less horrific than in the days of Oliver Twist, for elderly married couples were now allowed to live together and workhouse infirmaries were becoming less drab and unhygienic. Nevertheless, one third of the children in workhouses died each year. The payment of 'out-relief' to paupers who were not required to enter the workhouse was also becoming more common, although the donations were granted grudgingly by the wary guardians. Walter Greenwood's widowed mother was on one occasion forced to apply to the Salford guardians for 'out-relief':

We went, Mother, Sister and I, to the Board. A row of wooden forms faced a table at which the three Guardians sat. There could not be any doubt as to what they were guarding. This was in a canvas bag on the table in front of them. There was an account book at its side.

The applicants were old men and women for the most part. They sat there dejected, motionless and silent except for wheezes and coughs. When the old men were called to the table for interrogation each took off his cap respectfully and stood holding it in front of him with both hands.

Our turn came. My sister and I stood either side of Mother facing the Guardians. The canvas bag was open in front of the paymaster, coins spilling from its mouth. Mother answered the questions; the Guardians put their heads together and mumbled, then the paymaster, looking at the applicant said: 'Very well. Half a crown.' He took a coin from the store and tossed it across the table. It bounced, revolved on its rim and stopped. The man reached for his pen to enter the item in the accounts.

Thus was charity blended with prudence. To her credit, Mrs. Greenwood preferred hunger to humiliation and proudly rejected the paltry offer. The old Liberal idea that ratepayers' money must not be squandered and that idleness must be discouraged still prevailed. But the tide was beginning to turn. Most of the members of the Royal Commission on the Poor Law, which sat from 1905 to 1909, rejected the principle of 'less eligibility'. They had learned, for example, that unemployment was not a symptom of laziness but a product of trade fluctuations over which workers had no control. They reported in favour of old-age pensions, labour exchanges, and national insurance. The Liberal government put some of these recommendations into practice (see pages 29–30), but the last vestiges of the Poor Law were to survive for a further twenty years.

Nearly all working-class families lived in houses rented from private landlords. None could afford to buy their own houses and very few houses were built by local authorities: the council house was a thing of the future. Standards varied, but most people lived in streets of terraced houses without gardens, with the front door

**Housing**

often opening directly into the living-room. The élite of the working class might have two rooms, a 'parlour' and a kitchen downstairs and two bedrooms upstairs. The family would live on week-days in the large, square kitchen, with its open hearth where all the cooking was done. The Sunday roast was cooked in an oven adjoining and heated by the coal fire. The single tap and sink would either be in the separate scullery or in a corner of the kitchen. Bathrooms, indoor lavatories, and hot water systems were virtually unknown. Less fortunate families lived in cheaper, more compressed accommodation. In many areas houses were often constructed as pairs of flats, with one family downstairs and another upstairs; back-to-back houses were still common in west Yorkshire; tall tenement blocks were normal in parts of London and central Scotland. Flats and tenements had fewer rooms than self-contained houses; some had no independent water supply; in many cases several families had to share a single outside lavatory.

Middle-class housing standards varied even more, ranging from the successful businessman's huge suburban mansion standing in its own grounds to slightly larger versions of the working-class terraced houses. Just as there was a clear distinction between middle and working-class in employment and dress, so there was in housing. Even the clerks and elementary schoolteachers had small gardens protected by iron railings at the front, indoor lavatories and bathrooms and, a clear indication of status, either basements or attics as servants' bedrooms. The grander, detached villas, with their arched doorways, marble floors, and little turrets, represented that mixture of medieval castle and cathedral so beloved by Victorians and Edwardians. That 'an Englishman's home is his castle' was often almost literally true.

The British people were probably better clothed at the end of the nineteenth century than ever before, largely because the invention of new machines made it possible to produce cheaper clothes and footwear. New clothes, however, were still a luxury for the poor. Second-hand clothes shops and market stalls flourished, and garments were usually passed on from one member of a family to another, and from employers to servants. The new clothes and shoes which working-class people bought were usually obtained through clothing clubs, whose agents collected weekly contributions from the customers. Men in irregular employment could not, of course, keep up weekly payments and, in any case, often preferred the immediate advantage of a pint of beer to the distant prospect of new shoes for the family. Many children went barefoot to school and, in some towns, the police force ran charitable funds to provide boots and shoes for poor children. One reason why few very poor people attended church was that they had no respectable 'Sunday clothes'.

Fashion, of course, is a meaningless term for those who can afford

*Working-class housing in Liverpool*

*The three classes: topper, bowler, and cloth cap.* Below *Ladies' fashion, 1907*

no more than the bare essentials, but for the wealthy few the Edwardian Age was gay and flamboyant. That ugly Victorian appendage, the bustle, had been abandoned by about 1890 and ladies of fashion preferred blouses and skirts after the turn of the century. The skirts, naturally, still reached to the ground. Hair-styles and hats were the most striking features of the Edwardian lady's appearance. The hair was brushed forward from the back and piled in a mass on the top. Above this splendour floated a wide-brimmed, ornate hat, fixed to the hair by a long hat pin. The only major change in women's clothing was that the materials were much lighter in weight than before 1900. This was due in part to the vogue of new sports like lawn tennis and cycling.

Only slight changes were apparent in men's styles. City business-men were less likely to wear top hats and tails than before, and had taken to lounge suits, with bowler hats in winter and straw boaters in summer. Everyone wore a hat. Indeed, the nature of a man's headgear was an excellent guide to his social status: the three main classes might be renamed topper, bowler, and cloth cap.

The general standard of the nation's health was unsatisfactory before 1914. The Public Health reforms of the Victorians had largely eliminated the epidemics of diseases like cholera, but a low standard of living and squalid housing lessened the people's resis-tance, while the absence of a free health service prevented them from obtaining adequate medical treatment. Tuberculosis was rampant; rickets (a bone disease caused by malnutrition) was common among working-class children. In 1917 army medical examinations revealed that ten per cent of the conscripts were totally unfit for service, that

*Edwardian schools: over-crowding, poor facilities and harsh discipline led to widespread dissatisfaction. In many parts of the country in 1911 schoolchildren, supported by their parents, staged 'strikes'*

**Health**

another forty-two per cent had marked disabilities, and that a further twenty-two per cent had partial disabilities. The Edwardians had begun to tackle some of the problems. Infant Welfare Centres and Health Visitors helped to reduce the infant mortality rate, but school meals and medical examinations brought only a slight improvement in children's health, while the National Insurance Act of 1911 made free medical treatment available only to the insured workers, not their families. Resistance to the Welfare State idea was still strong: the sick poor could be treated free of charge by the Poor Law District Medical Officers, but only after they had proved to the guardians that they were destitute. By this time, of course, they were often incurable. Another generation of rising living standards, better housing, and improved medical services was needed to produce a significant change.

Although the politicians of the major parties appear to have agreed that a free health service would merely encourage idleness and discourage thrift, they had all come to accept a universal and free education system. Even here, however, the influence of *laissez-faire* was not dead; elementary education was free, but the parents of most secondary-school pupils had to pay fees. The Liberal governments after 1905 made some attempts to persuade local authorities to increase the number of secondary-school scholarships available to poorer children, and the total number of secondary-school pupils rose from 94,000 in 1905 to 200,000 in 1914. Even so, no more than one in forty elementary-school children passed on to secondary education. Not even the Liberals believed in equality of opportunity.

**Education**

They did not seek to break down class barriers; they merely assisted exceptionally talented and industrious children, blessed with parents who were prepared to make sacrifices on their behalf, to climb from one class to another.

University expansion was further evidence that Englishmen had at last realized the importance of education. Once again, however, the Edwardians' achievement was significant mainly as a promise for the future. New universities were founded at Manchester, Liverpool, Leeds, Sheffield, and Bristol between 1903 and 1909 and university colleges were set up in five other towns before 1914, but the number of students in each of these institutions was small. Indeed, Britain's total student population in 1913 was only 9,000, which compared unfavourably with Germany's 60,000. It was no coincidence that German industry had overtaken and was drawing away from Britain's by 1914.

The small number of university students and the fact that far too few of them studied science and engineering were dangerous omens for the nation's economic prospects. Even worse was the failure to tap the great reservoir of working-class talent. Clever boys and girls from poor homes had little chance of going to secondary schools and virtually no chance of reaching university, for there was still no national system of scholarships and student grants. That there was a craving for education is proved by the success of the Workers' Educational Association, which was founded in 1904–5. The W.E.A., which ran courses of lectures and classes in a wide range of subjects, but with an emphasis on economics and history, had nearly two hundred branches and over 11,000 members by 1914. Many eminent university lecturers and schoolmasters gladly took classes (some of them even refusing fees), believing that they were meeting a major social need. Some of the W.E.A. students were minor trade union

**Workers' Educational Association**

*WEA summer school at Oxford, 1912*

officials, but most were ordinary, intelligent working-class men and women who would, two generations later, have progressed naturally from grammar schools to state-aided universities.

**Newspapers**

One of the most striking social changes of the Edwardian period was the appearance of popular newspapers. The Harmsworth brothers, Alfred and Harold, realized that universal education had created a reading public which could not afford to buy papers like *The Times* and the *Daily Telegraph,* and which did not have sufficient knowledge of or interest in politics to wade through the lengthy reports of public speeches and Parliamentary debates which were the staple diet of those traditional newspapers. Alfred Harmsworth, who later became Lord Northcliffe, realized that an enormous market awaited anyone who could produce a cheap and simple daily paper. After a few experiments, he launched the *Daily Mail* in 1896.

The *Daily Mail* differed from all other dailies in that it cost only a halfpenny, as against the penny of its cheapest competitors, and in its novel style of journalism. The articles were short, the vocabulary was simple, and the lay-out was attractive. The *Daily Mail* did not ignore politics, but it simplified issues and often presented its readers with ready-made opinions. Harmsworth's aim was to entertain as well as to inform. He therefore gave his readers what they wanted: crime, sensation, feature articles, and sport, as well as political news. Wars were good for newspaper sales, and by taking a strongly anti-Boer line Harmsworth both profoundly influenced public opinion and boosted the sales of the *Daily Mail.* One of his more foolhardy strokes was to invent, during the Boxer risings in Peking in 1900, the story that the occupants of the British legation had been massacred. Several weeks later the *Daily Mail* had to admit that the story was a complete fabrication.

Several competitors quickly appeared. The *Daily Express* was founded by C.A. Pearson in 1900; the *Daily News* and *Daily Chronicle* both reduced their price to a halfpenny in 1904, and in 1911 appeared the *Daily Herald,* the first popular daily to support the trade union movement. None of them presented a successful challenge to the *Daily Mail.* Harmsworth not only dominated the new market which he had created; he was determined to extend his empire. He started the *Daily Mirror* as a women's paper in 1904. When it failed, he converted it into a cheap daily picture paper, aimed at a slightly less-educated readership than the *Daily Mail*'s. Soon it too was making big profits. The stroke of business which brought him most prestige, however, was his purchase of *The Times* in 1908. Not even Harmsworth, who was now Lord Northcliffe, dared radically to change this sacred British institution, but he did try to increase its sales by reducing the price.

The influence of the newspaper revolution was nationwide. Special trains carried the early editions of the popular dailies from London to the provinces, and in 1900 the *Daily Mail* began printing a northern edition in Manchester. Provincial dailies were the chief sufferers. Some, like the *Manchester Guardian* and the *Birmingham Post*, survived, but others went out of business.

The emancipation of women, another result of the growth of popular education, had hardly begun by 1914. Despite the efforts of Mrs. Pankhurst and her followers, women were still without the vote. In many other senses, too, the role of women was still the same as in Victorian times. The working-class woman was a drudge, her middle-class counterpart was a household manager, and the upper-class lady was an ornament. Large families kept most married women fully occupied, and there were still only a few occupations open to single girls. Although the census figures reveal an increase in the number of female clerks and book-keepers, a large army of girls was still employed in the sweated trades, such as millinery and laundry work. The great majority of working women, however, were domestic servants, of whom there were one and a half million in 1911, the highest figure ever recorded in a census. This is evidence of middle and upper-class prosperity and of the lack of opportunities for women in factories, shops, and offices. Apart from the sweated trades, virtually the only women employed in industry were the mill-girls of Lancashire. There were some indications that a change in women's status was on the way, such as slight modifications of fashion and an increased participation by women in sport, but it was the First World War which caused the great transformation.

**The role of women**

Among the many social changes of the twentieth century, the increased volume and acceleration of transport has been outstanding. In this respect, as in so many others, the Edwardian era was one of promise rather than fulfilment. Most British people rarely travelled more than a few miles from their birth-place in the course of their lives. Holidays were for the fortunate few. Nowadays thousands of families go off in the car for picnics by the seaside or in the country on Sunday afternoons; their grandparents walked to the public park to listen to a band concert. Cars were often unreliable and always expensive.

**Transport**

The standard method of travel over long distances was the railway. The national network was in the hands of about twenty private companies, such as the Great Eastern, the London and South Western, and the North British. Each maintained its rolling stock in distinctive colours, prided itself on a high standard of service, and expected loyalty from its employees. This was the golden age of the steam locomotive, and it is noteworthy that the speeds achieved by main-line expresses in 1914 were seldom bettered between the wars. The railways' function was not only to carry passengers and freight quickly between the main centres of population, however. They

In 1902 the Great Western engine 'City of Truro' reached 100 m.p.h.

*Day trips to the seaside or into the country were the only holidays possible for the working class*

Right *Blackpool beach in 1903*

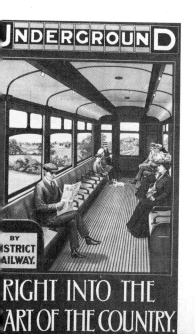

provided the only link between the remote villages and the outside world. Every part of the country had its pattern of single-track branch lines, along which slow, ancient engines would puff wheezily once or twice a day.

A new invention had recently speeded up transport within towns. The electric tram had begun to supersede its horse-drawn predecessor in the 1890s, and by 1905 most towns and cities had a system of municipally owned tramways. Although noisy, electric tram-cars were quite fast and cheap. In London, the trams were supplemented by the underground railway, which was electrified and considerably extended after 1905. One result of these changes was that working-class people were able to live in new estates on the edges of towns and be transported cheaply to work in the town centres. This revolution in living patterns had to wait, of course, until the new houses were available.

65

Until the repeal of the 'Red Flag Act' in 1896, motor cars had been almost illegal in Britain. This was one of the reasons why the British car industry was so slow to develop. Even after the turn of the century motorists did not receive much official encouragement. A twenty miles per hour speed limit was imposed on all roads in 1903 and it was not until 1909 that the government began to spend money on the improvement of roads. Before this, motor vehicles threw up clouds of dust as they passed and were rightly regarded as a public menace.

Cars, of course, were expensive. Even doctors sometimes did their rounds on bicycles. Nevertheless, there were 120,000 cars and 110,000 motor cycles on Britain's roads by 1913. Motor lorries and buses were still in their infancy, but there was sufficient traffic (more than half of it horse-drawn) to cause serious congestion in the streets of London and other major cities in the years immediately before the First World War.

Any intelligent observer could see that motor vehicles had a great future. 'Flying machines' were a different matter; the miracle was that they flew at all. A few daredevil eccentrics might risk their lives in competing for prizes, or entertain astonished crowds with their 'flying circuses'. A Frenchman called Blériot even managed to skim his machine across the Channel in 1909, although it is significant that he was unable to clear the cliffs of Dover. The Wright brothers had, after all, made the first powered flight as recently as 1903. It was hardly surprising that few people took flying seriously in 1914. Once again, the decisive breakthrough was to come during the war.

*London traffic in 1910 and 1912. Motor buses began to replace horse buses in 1910*

*Motor vehicles produced in Britain—cars, motor cycles, buses, lorries (thousands)*

| | |
|---|---|
| 1905 | 32 |
| 1910 | 144 |
| 1915 | 407 |
| 1920 | 651 |

66

The Edwardians stood in time between the Victorians and ourselves. In most respects their society was nearer the nineteenth century than the twentieth. The First World War, not the death of Queen Victoria, was the great watershed. Rigid class distinction, low working-class living standards, inadequate housing and health services were all typical of the late nineteenth century. Yet just as a study of the economic and political history of Britain immediately before 1914 reveals the first signs of new problems and forces which were profoundly to influence later developments, so an examination of the social history of the same period reveals a changing attitude towards poor relief and health services, a slow expansion of education, the eruption of the popular press, and the beginnings of a transport revolution.

**Church attendance**

That the Edwardian Age was a half-way house may be finally demonstrated by reference to people's church-going habits. There is a myth that the Victorians were devoutly religious. In fact, probably no more than half the population of Victorian England went to church regularly and it seems clear that many working-class people never attended at all. The middle-class families were the ardent church-goers. A religious census of 1886 revealed that thirty per cent of London's population attended church on a particular Sunday. Seventeen years later the figure had fallen to twenty per cent. Yet daily family prayers were still normal in many Edwardian households. On the surface, the Victorian tradition was intact; underneath, the foundations were beginning to subside.

# Chapter 4
# The First World War
# —Military Events

Left *They went to war in cattle trucks and they died like cattle*

**Kitchener**

The Great War, known to a generation of Europeans simply as The War, was a momentous disaster. Its origins lay in the grand designs and out-dated thinking of small men exercising too much power, men like Kaiser William II and Tsar Nicholas II; in an exaggerated concern for national prestige; above all, in an ignorance of the implications of modern warfare. The war was a monster which, once unleashed, was beyond the control of statesmen or generals. It claimed the lives of ten million men and maimed or disfigured twice as many again. It brought crashing down in ruins four great empires, made possible a Communist revolution in Russia, and prepared the way for the rise of upstart dictators like Hitler and Mussolini. Britain, which escaped devastation and political breakdown, never recovered from its economic effects. But the war involved a social revolution: total war brought everyone into action, and those who rubbed shoulders with their betters in the trenches, in the munitions factories, or in the hospitals, never quite accepted the Edwardian class distinctions again.

## THE WESTERN FRONT

The Germans expected a short war. In fact, if they did not win quickly their chances of winning at all were slight. Most people on the Allied side also thought that it would be over by Christmas 1914. Asquith and his Cabinet were confident that the French army, supported by the small but highly trained British Expeditionary Force, would beat the Germans. They did not anticipate four years of war, the raising of mass armies, vast casualty lists, or the need to mobilize the nation's resources. In August 1914 Sir Edward Grey said: 'If we are engaged in war, we shall suffer but little more than we shall suffer if we stand aside.'

As soon as war was declared, Asquith appointed Lord Kitchener Secretary of State for War. This was a popular move, for Kitchener had had a brilliant military career in the Sudan, the Boer War, and India. Unfortunately, he had little knowledge of Europe, was unused to working with politicians, and was unequal to the task of providing supplies for the huge armies which he found it necessary to call into being. In one respect he was more far-sighted than his Cabinet colleagues: he predicted that the war would last at least three years.

69

In accordance with pledges already given, the British Expeditionary Force was promptly sent to France. About 100,000 men, rather less than had been promised, crossed the Channel in August to take up a position on the French left. Individually, they were excellent soldiers and unrivalled as riflemen. Their weaknesses were their lack of numbers, the absence of trenching tools, field telephones, and wireless, and the fact that the War Office had not seen fit to equip them adequately with machine-guns. They also had an indifferent commander. Sir John French was a somewhat unimaginative general, and his reluctant attempts to communicate with his French allies were impeded by his total ignorance of their language.

The B.E.F. saw action for the first time on 23 August 1914 at Mons in Belgium. As the French army tried, unsuccessfully, to carry out its Plan 17, according to which it was to invade Lorraine and Luxembourg, the German right wing swept through Belgium. Having brushed aside the Belgian army, the German armies encountered only the weakened French left wing and the B.E.F. The British made a gallant stand at Mons, but were heavily outnumbered and had to retreat.

In the last week of August and the first week of September the Schlieffen Plan nearly succeeded. The Allies retreated two hundred miles to the line of the River Marne (see Map 6). Here the French counter-attacked. Such was the urgency that half a French division was rushed to the battlefield in Paris taxi-cabs. The British played little part in the Battle of the Marne, which was a French success. It ended German hopes of a quick victory and committed both sides to a long war. It was followed by a German retreat and a race to the sea as the Germans tried to grab the Channel ports and the Allies fought to stop them. After a bitter struggle in Flanders in October and November (the First Battle of Ypres) the Allies saved the ports and kept a tiny foothold in Belgium. The trench line was now established. It extended from the Belgian coast southwards through Artois and Picardy to Compiègne, then along the River Aisne to Verdun, then along the frontier to Switzerland. All of Luxembourg, most of Belgium, and a tenth of France were in German hands.

The war of movement was over. The two intricate systems of trenches and dug-outs were separated by a few hundred yards of no-man's-land, pitted with shell holes and strewn with barbed wire. Trenches were an adequate protection against rifle and machine-gun fire and, except in the case of a direct hit, against artillery shells. Life in the trenches was usually terrifying for even the bravest of men, and always unpleasant. To the almost constant roar of gun-fire and the likelihood of being (at best) buried alive as a shell exploded, were added the discomfort of water which was sometimes knee-deep, the stench of decomposing bodies, and the ever present problem of lice. Time spent in the front line was a combination of look-out duty

**British Expeditionary Force in France**

**Mons**

**Battle of the Marne**

**Trench warfare**

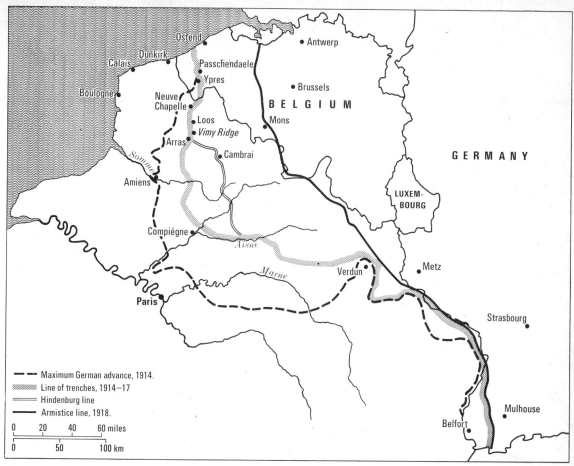

Map 6 *The Western Front in the First World War*

on the firing-step, rest in the dug-out, and occasional patrols into no-man's-land. Patrols were hazardous by night and almost suicidal by day.

The commanders believed that intensive artillery barrages would obliterate the enemy trenches and that the infantry would then be able to break through. Such was the idea behind every offensive. Shelling never had the desired effect: thirty-seven million shells were fired in the Battle of Verdun, but neither side was eliminated. After several hours of heavy bombardment the front-line troops were ordered 'over the top'. Weighed down with equipment, the infantry-men could move only slowly and were easy targets for the defenders. Wave after wave advanced to a death made all the more certain by the defenders' machine-guns. The British lost 60,000 men on the first day of the Battle of the Somme. The generals apparently never realized that the enemy trenches could not be blasted out of existence and that advancing infantry would be massacred by machine-guns.

These facts explain the lack of movement and the enormous

casualties. The soldiers and junior officers who had to endure life in the trenches soon lost that early idealistic enthusiasm, best expressed in Rupert Brooke's famous poem, 'The Soldier':

> If I should die, think only this of me:
> That there's some corner of a foreign field
> That is for ever England. There shall be
> In that rich earth a richer dust conceal'd;
> A dust whom England bore, shaped, made aware,
> Gave, once, her flowers to love, her ways to roam,
> A body of England's, breathing English air.

Survivors speak of the incessant noise and the ever growing fear, which in many cases became intolerable. Sufferers from acute shell-shock were invalided out of the forces and some never recovered. Disillusionment with the generals and the war itself soon set in. The private soldier's sense of futility is seen in the song 'We're 'ere because we're 'ere . . .', while Wilfred Owen's 'Anthem for Doomed Youth' puts into memorable words the despair of a sensitive young officer:

*Troops moving up to the Front*

*The trenches*

> What passing-bells for these who die as cattle?
> Only the monstrous anger of the guns.
> Only the stuttering rifles' rapid rattle
> Can patter out their hasty orisons.
> No mockeries for them from prayers or bells,
> Nor any voice of mourning save the choirs,—
> The shrill, demented choirs of wailing shells;
> And bugles calling for them from sad shires.

They all hated the war and cursed the men who directed it; yet they enjoyed strong bonds of comradeship. Many a wounded junior officer disobeyed orders to stay in England and returned to his battalion in France.

By the end of 1914 there were 270,000 British troops in France. The B.E.F. had already suffered 100,000 casualties. 'Kitchener's Army' steadily grew in size in 1915 as the eager volunteers were quickly trained and sent to the front. The year saw two British offensives and one major German attack, but no territorial changes. A minor British victory of Neuve Chapelle in March was not followed up, while a German attack in April and May (the Second Battle of Ypres) caused heavy losses of men, but yielded the Germans no advantage. In this battle the Germans used poison-gas for the first time, thus adding further to the horrors of trench warfare without finding a way out of the deadlock. Sir John French's complaint of a shortage of shells may have been a valid excuse for his failure; it certainly caused a political storm at home (see page 88).

**Fighting in 1915**

A British offensive at Loos in September and October cost 50,000

casualties but did not break the German lines. Its main result was a shake-up in the high command. Sir Douglas Haig replaced Sir John French as commander of the B.E.F., while Sir William Robertson was appointed Chief of the Imperial General Staff. Robertson thus took over control of strategy from Kitchener, who was still popular with the public but whose Cabinet colleagues had begun to see his short-comings.

In the first half of 1916, the Germans attempted to capture the key French fortress of Verdun. After murderous shelling and savage fighting Verdun remained in French hands, but the cost was half a million casualties. Joffre, the French Commander-in-Chief, called for a combined Allied attack in the summer and Haig gladly agreed. Unfortunately, they chose the River Somme for their offensive, the strongest point in the German line. Haig, nevertheless, was confident of victory and stuck to the routine formula of artillery barrage followed by infantry assault. According to the theory, when these two stages had been successfully completed, the cavalry would break through. With this aim in mind, Haig kept 700,000 horses in France throughout the war.

**Battle of the Somme 1916**

The Somme was a ruinous failure. Between July and November the British lost 420,000 men, while the French lost nearly 200,000. German casualties were probably not quite equal to the combined Allied losses. The Allied advance varied between three and seven miles. Those of the early volunteers who survived the Somme forfeited there their youthful enthusiasm. Henceforth poets like Wilfred Owen were the true representatives of the soldiers' feelings.

Undeterred by these failures, the Allied commanders persisted in the belief that the war could be won by a direct assault on the German positions. Early in 1917 Nivelle, the new French commander, persuaded Lloyd George, who had become British Prime Minister, that a combined offensive would succeed. The military situation had not changed; Nivelle's self-confidence and persuasive tongue were the main reasons for Lloyd George's consent. As one

*One of the 420,000 British casualties at the Somme*

**Allied Nivelle Offensive 1917**

**French mutinies**

**Battle of Passchendaele 1917**

historian has remarked: 'Nivelle talked well in fluent English, which is more than one could say of Haig.'

The British generals had no enthusiasm for the Nivelle Offensive, but agreed to attack in April. Any hopes of a breakthrough should have vanished when the Germans withdrew to the heavily fortified Hindenburg Line. The attack was nevertheless launched and yielded the usual heavy crop of casualties and little or no gains. Neither the British at Arras nor the French on the Aisne made any important advance. The only real success was the capture of Vimy Ridge by the Canadians. Worse than the failure to break through was the effect of the offensive on the morale of the French army. Widespread mutinies threatened to destroy its effectiveness as a fighting force. Even the replacement of Nivelle by Pétain, the hero of Verdun, failed to restore enthusiasm. For the rest of the year the British would have to bear the main brunt of the fighting.

Haig duly attacked again between August and November 1917 in Flanders. His aim was to capture the Belgian ports, which the Germans were using as U-boat bases. Another theory is that he wanted to win a great victory before the Americans could arrive to steal the glory. The United States had entered the war in April 1917, but significant numbers of American troops did not reach the front until mid-1918. Haig's Flanders offensive is usually known as the Battle of Passchendaele and must rank with the Somme as one of the most futile battles in British history. The usual preliminary bombardment completely destroyed the drainage system, without eliminating German resistance. When the infantry advanced they marched into a sea of mud, in which hundreds of men drowned. At the cost of 324,000 casualties, Haig's army advanced four miles.

Ironically, just as the well-tried tactics were again being proved wrong at Passchendaele, a novel device was succeeding further south. Massed tanks were used for the first time at Cambrai in November 1917. Nearly four hundred of them broke right through the German lines and into the open country beyond. So unexpected was this success that reserves of infantry and cavalry were not available to exploit the advantage and the Germans recaptured the lost ground within ten days.

With the exception of the attack on Verdun in 1916, the Germans had remained on the defensive on the Western Front since 1914. They were, after all, in possession of enemy territory and if they could hold it they were bound to get favourable peace terms. The events of 1917 changed the picture. Russia's collapse gave the Germans the chance to transfer men from the Eastern Front to the west. More important still, it was obvious that by late 1918 and 1919 there would be a huge American army in France. Ludendorff, the German commander, had two alternatives: either an immediate attack to destroy the French and British armies and so win the war, or eventual defeat as his enemies' numbers grew. If the offensive failed, Germany would lose the war, but she would also lose if it were not attempted.

The Germans attacked in March 1918, striking first at the weakest point in the British line on the Somme. They were immediately successful. The British reeled back forty miles in a few days. Ludendorff then struck south against the French and in May his troops reached the Marne for the first time since September 1914. As the French withdrew towards Paris and the British retreated on the Channel ports an alarming gap appeared between the Allied armies. Haig issued his famous order: 'With our backs to the wall and believing in the justice of our cause each of us must fight to the end.'

Fresh troops were sent over from England, Americans were rushed to the front, and the Allies at last agreed to appoint a single commander-in-chief, the French general, Foch. By July the German attack had lost its momentum. The Allied armies had been defeated, but not destroyed. The German troops were battle-weary and dispirited when they found that their great effort had not brought final victory. The French made the first Allied counter-attack on the Marne on 18 July and were able to push the Germans back four miles. British tanks broke through the German lines at Amiens on 8 August, a day which Ludendorff described as 'the black day of the German army'. Throughout August and September Foch and Haig attacked, steadily driving the Germans back until all the ground lost in the spring and summer had been regained. Ludendorff saw that his gamble had failed. He informed the German government that the war was lost and that an immediate armistice was necessary. There is no doubt that German resistance could have continued into 1919, but Ludendorff was right: ultimate defeat was now inevitable. The armistice came into effect at 11 a.m. on 11 November 1918.

The Allied victory on the western Front was due above all to the entry of the United States into the war, not because the American

**Tanks at Cambrai 1917**

**German Ludendorff Offensive 1918**

*A French sentry prepared for a gas attack*

troops made an especially important contribution, but because the prospect that they would give massive reinforcement to the Allied armies forced Ludendorff into a desperate and unsuccessful gamble. The Allied commanders showed no sign of finding a solution to the problem of trench warfare. They had too little faith in new weapons and techniques. Aircraft were used for reconnaissance purposes and, towards the end, for bombing raids, but played only a small part in the Allied victory. The tank, however, was a weapon with which imaginative generals might have won the war much earlier. Tanks proved their worth at Cambrai in 1917, but it was not until August 1918 that this near-perfect answer to barbed wire, trenches, and machine-guns was allowed to play the decisive role which it should have done.

> Generals are chosen, so I'm told,
> For being very, very old.

### THE OTHER FRONTS

**Problem of helping Russia**

The French and British commanders believed throughout that the war had to be won on the Western Front. Not everyone agreed. The Russians, although they won some impressive victories against the Austrians, were manifestly inferior in equipment and organization to the Germans. They needed the help of the western Allies, but this presented problems. German control of the Baltic closed the most obvious route, while the northerly sea route to Archangel and Murmansk was extremely hazardous, especially in winter. There remained the passage through the Straits and the Black Sea, but this was closed also when Turkey entered the war on Germany's side in October 1914.

The need to supply the Russians with military equipment and the hope that Turkey might be knocked out of the war prompted Lloyd George, the Chancellor of the Exchequer, and Winston Churchill, the First Lord of the Admiralty, to support in 1915 the idea that the Royal Navy might force its way through the Dardanelles and capture Constantinople. A fleet of old battleships was sent into the Straits in March 1915, but when several were sunk by mines the fleet withdrew. The plan was now changed: Allied troops would land on the Gallipoli peninsula and take Constantinople from the land.

**The Gallipoli campaign and its results**

The Gallipoli campaign (see Maps 7 and 8) was disastrously mismanaged. The commander, Sir Ian Hamilton, was to begin with, short of men because Sir John French and Joffre resisted every attempt to divert troops from the Western Front. But Hamilton's own incompetence was the main cause of the failure. By delaying his attack he gave the Turks time to prepare their defences. He made

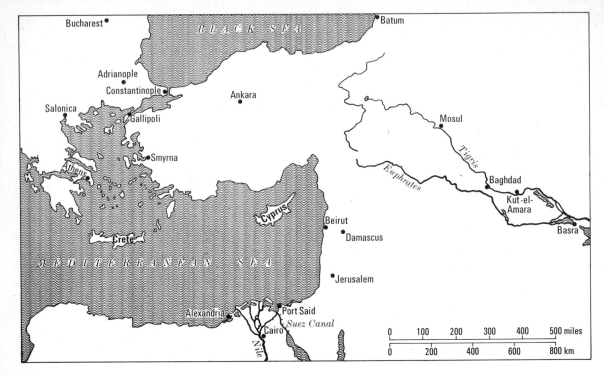

Map 7 *The Middle East and the First World War*

no adequate preparations for an amphibious operation. When his men were ashore he gave no clear orders and himself remained aboard a battleship.

The British, Australian, and New Zealand troops who landed in April 1915 got no further than a line of trenches along the shore, where they were subject to continuous, accurate Turkish fire. A further landing at Suvla Bay in June was more successful, but was not followed up. Throughout the campaign the Turks retained control of the heights of the rocky peninsula and prevented the British and Dominion troops from advancing beyond the coast.

The expedition was a costly failure. Winston Churchill was blamed and removed from the Admiralty. When the military high command was changed in late 1915 no one was in favour of continuing the attempt to seize the Dardanelles. A highly successful withdrawal (the only well-managed part of the campaign) was carried out in December 1915 and January 1916. Debate has raged ever since as to whether Constantinople could have been taken and whether its capture would have helped the war effort more than marginally. The decision to withdraw from the Dardanelles certainly harmed British prestige in the area and was among the reasons for Bulgaria's declaration of war on the side of Germany and Austria-Hungary in November 1915. This in turn contributed to the defeat of Serbia and the virtual extinction of the Allied cause in south-east

Map 8 *The Dardanelles*

Europe. To keep the flame alive, the French insisted on maintaining an Allied force of 600,000 men (200,000 of them British) at Salonika in northern Greece. This army remained immobile for two years, suffering terrible privations and being decimated by malaria.

The Allies continued to supply the Russians via the northerly route. German U-boats and mines sank a large proportion of this traffic, including the ship carrying Kitchener to Russia in 1916. Kitchener's death was a disaster to most British people, but Lord Northcliffe remarked cynically (and perhaps astutely): 'Providence is on the side of the British Empire after all.' Allied aid was not sufficient to sustain the Tsar against the dual challenge of the German army and internal discontent. His regime was toppled in

**Russian Revolution 1917**

March 1917 and although his successors at first tried to keep Russia in the war they were overthrown by Lenin and the Bolsheviks in November. The Eastern Front had already disintegrated and Lenin quickly made peace at Brest-Litovsk in March 1918. The end of the war in the east allowed German troops to be transferred to the Western Front, but not so many as might have been anticipated, for the vast territories ceded by the Russians at Brest-Litovsk had to be garrisoned by Germans.

**Italian Front**

The Italian Front almost collapsed also. Two years of static trench warfare between the Italians and Austrians in north-east Italy ended in October 1917 when, with German assistance, the Austrians won a great victory at Caporetto. Much of the Italian army disappeared in headlong flight, but enough stood firm to resist on the line of the River Piave. Here, with Allied support, they won revenge in the Battle of Vittorio Veneto in October 1918.

**Palestine and Mesopotamia**

British forces were also involved in two important 'side-shows' in the Middle East. The Palestine campaign began as an attempt to prevent the Turks from invading Egypt and seizing the Suez Canal, while the advance into Mesopotamia from the Persian Gulf was intended to protect Britain's oil supplies. Neither side made much progress in Palestine until the British, under General Allenby, began to advance in late 1917. Allenby took Jerusalem in December 1917, then, by winning a major victory at Megiddo in September 1918, was able to make a triumphal entry into Damascus. Allenby's success was in part due to a revolt of Arab tribesmen against the Turks, stimulated by Colonel T.E. Lawrence. In Mesopotamia a premature advance in 1916 ended with the surrender of General Townshend's force at Kut-el-Amara, but reinforcements were sent and by the end of 1917 Baghdad and the precious oil supplies were in British hands.

It is sometimes wrongly claimed that the Allied victory in 1918 was due to the collapse of Germany's allies. It is true that in the second half of 1918 Turkey, Bulgaria, and Austria-Hungary were forced to sue for peace, but their defeat was not the cause of the

German surrender. The successful Allied offensive on the Western Front brought the war to an end.

## THE WAR AT SEA

The German naval challenge was the main reason why Britain drifted into an undeclared alliance with France before 1914. The Royal Navy retained its numerical superiority and would have had no difficulty in preventing the Germans from invading Britain. What were its other roles? It could, and did, blockade German ports, thus weakening the German war effort by limiting the supply of raw materials and causing food shortages. By destroying German surface vessels it could safeguard Allied merchant shipping. When the Germans began to use submarines, or U-boats, to attack merchant ships, however, the Navy was faced with a new problem, one which it almost failed to solve.

Unlike any other country, Britain's very existence depended on her overseas trade and a regular supply of food and raw materials which had to be transported in merchant ships. At the beginning of the war several German cruisers in the Far East, the Indian Ocean, and the Atlantic began sinking British merchantmen, but their success was bound to be temporary. The cruiser *Emden* was sunk by ships of the Australian navy in the Indian Ocean in November 1914 and a German squadron was destroyed by the British in the Battle of the Falkland Islands in December. Contrary to expectations, the German High Seas Fleet stayed in harbour, while the British Grand Fleet remained in readiness at Scapa Flow in the Orkneys. The blockade was established and British control of the seas seemed secure.

**German surface raiders**

Then, in 1915, German submarines began to torpedo Allied merchant ships. U-boats could attack unexpectedly and were able to escape detection by the Royal Navy; they were an immediate success. The Germans had to be careful not to alienate neutral opinion, however. In May 1915 the British liner *Lusitania*, some of whose passengers were American, was sunk off the Irish coast with a heavy loss of life. The Allied press represented the sinking of the *Lusitania* as a dastardly war crime, and did not mention that the vessel was carrying munitions. Most Americans sympathized with the Allied cause in any case, and the *Lusitania* incident showed that if the U-boats began sinking American vessels the United States would probably go to war. The German navy consequently restricted its submarine attacks to Allied ships during 1915 and 1916, while the Royal Navy developed such devices as the hydrophone and the depth-charge in attempting to deal with the menace.

**U-boats**

For almost two years the great fleets stayed in harbour at opposite sides of the North Sea. The Admiralty and the British people longed

**Naval strategy**

for a major sea battle, another Trafalgar. A great victory would, of course, have given a wonderful boost to Allied morale, but it would have had little practical effect. So long as the German High Seas Fleet kept out of the way it was not damaging the Allied war effort. On the other hand, a German naval victory would have been a total disaster for the Allies. If a substantial part of the British fleet had been destroyed, the Germans could have sunk merchantmen at will and brought Britain to her knees. As Winston Churchill said, the British Commander-in-Chief was the one man who could lose the war in an afternoon.

Hoping to achieve such a victory, Scheer, the German commander, tried to lure part of the British Grand Fleet into the North Sea in May 1916. After complex manoeuvres the two fleets came into brief contact on 1 June. The Battle of Jutland was not a second Trafalgar. The British sustained more damage, but the Germans again withdrew into port, never to emerge until the end of the war. In a sense, of course, Jutland was a British victory. Jellicoe had not lost his fleet and he had forced the Germans to abandon their attempt to challenge British supremacy.

**Battle of Jutland, 1916**

**Unrestricted submarine warfare**

The Germans now reverted to submarine tactics and in February 1917 announced that they were about to begin unrestricted submarine warfare: U-boats would sink any Allied or neutral vessel encountered in the seas around Britain, off the French Atlantic coast, or in the Mediterranean. The German high command knew that the extension of submarine attacks to neutral vessels would probably provoke the United States into a declaration of war, but calculated that Britain would be starved into submission before the Americans were ready.

The plan nearly worked. Although the United States entered the war in April 1917, a million tons of Allied shipping, two-thirds of it British, was sunk in the same month. British and American shipyards could not keep pace with such losses and Britain was soon down to six weeks' supply of wheat. Senior British naval officers confessed that they were powerless to stop the sinkings, and when Lloyd George suggested that warships might be used to escort convoys of merchant vessels the Admiralty replied that merchant navy captains were not sufficiently skilled navigators to be able to keep station in convoy. Lloyd George rode roughshod over the admirals' objections and forced them to accept the convoy system, which was an immediate success. During 1917 and 1918 only one per cent of ships sailing in convoy was sunk, while a quarter of those sailing singly was destroyed.

**Convoy system**

The adoption of the convoy system was one of the decisive steps of the war; Britain would otherwise have been obliged to sue for peace before the end of 1917. As it was, she survived, encouraged now by the prospect of American assistance and eventual victory.

THE END OF THE WAR

A small minority of British people, including Ramsay MacDonald and some other members of the Labour party, had continuously opposed the war as unnecessary and immoral. A further group thought that it should not be fought to a bitter end, and that the Allied governments should try to reach a peace settlement with the Germans. Lloyd George realized that the minimum terms acceptable to Britain and France must include Germany's evacuation of Belgium and the return of Alsace-Lorraine to France, and that the German government would submit on these points only when its armies had been defeated.

Lloyd George's position was made more difficult by the American President Wilson's assertion that the United States, as an 'Associated Power', was fighting neither for conquests nor for the destruction of Germany, but to uphold international justice. In January 1918 Wilson published his peace formula, the Fourteen Points, which included the following proposals:

> II. Absolute freedom of navigation upon the seas . . . alike in peace and in war . . .
>
> VII. Belgium . . . must be evacuated and restored, without any attempt to limit the sovereignty which she enjoys in common with all other free nations.
>
> VIII. All French territory should be freed and the invaded portions restored, and the wrong done to France by Prussia in 1871 in the matter of Alsace-Lorraine . . . should be righted.
>
> X. The peoples of Austria-Hungary . . . should be accorded the freest opportunity of autonomous development.
>
> XIII. An independent Polish state should be erected which should include the territories inhabited by indisputably Polish populations . . .

**Lloyd George's peace terms**

Lloyd George was reluctant to agree to the freedom of the seas, but the remainder of the Fourteen Points were highly satisfactory. In a speech to an audience of trade unionists in January 1918 he outlined a similar peace plan:

> We are not fighting a war of aggression against the German people . . . Nor are we fighting to destroy Austria-Hungary or to deprive Turkey of its capital . . .

But what was high-minded idealism from Woodrow Wilson was little short of hypocrisy from David Lloyd George. He knew that in the military situation of early 1918 the German government would

**Armistice terms**

*An air duel between German and Russian fighters*

not accept what amounted to an Allied demand for surrender.

The successful Allied offensive in August and September changed the situation. Ludendorff demanded an armistice and the German government approached Wilson in October. He left the signing of the armistice to the commanders in the field, who, acting on instructions from London and Paris, offered very harsh terms. The German army was to withdraw beyond the Rhine, the German fleet was to be surrendered to the British, and Germany was to evacuate all territories conquered from Russia. Faced with defeat in the west, a naval mutiny at Kiel, and revolution at home, the Kaiser abdicated and fled to neutral Holland, leaving his generals to sign the armistice in a railway carriage at Compiègne on 11 November.

The news was received at first with stunned surprise. Then London erupted in wild celebrations, which lasted for three days. All work stopped; crowds thronged the streets; a bonfire was lit in Trafalgar Square. Every town saw similar scenes. At the front it was different. When the guns stopped the soldiers were disturbed by the strange quietness. After the initial relief that they had achieved the impossible and survived, they grew disgruntled and irritable. Morale dropped and discipline disintegrated. They all wanted to go home. Edmund Blunden writes:

Leaving company headquarters in the first evenings, I could feel much the same difficulty in the abrupt change from a long war to silence. I scanned the eastern darkness as though, if I looked hard enough, the familiar line of lights would be playing there. The silent darkness was in some way worse than those assistants of vengeance. I wanted them. Youth had been subdued to what it worked in.

# LORD KITCHENER SAYS:-

'MEN, MATERIALS & MONEY ARE THE IMMEDIATE NECESSITIES. ......

DOES THE CALL OF DUTY FIND NO RESPONSE IN YOU UNTIL REINFORCED — LET US RATHER SAY SUPERSEDED — BY THE CALL OF COMPULSION?'

Lord Kitchener Speaking at Guildhall. July 9th 1915

## ENLIST TO-DAY.

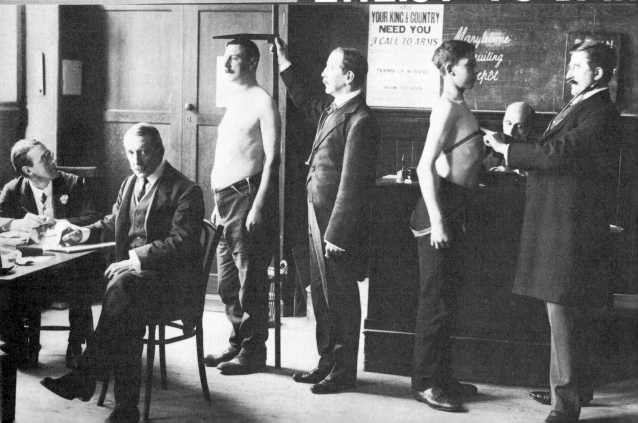

# Chapter 5
# The First World War
# —Domestic Events

Contrary to most expectations, the war had a profound effect on the life of the nation. It caused a massive extension of government interference in people's lives and a change in the structure of government itself. As the early hopes of a quick victory receded, it became necessary to raise mass armies, to equip them with munitions, to take control of the railways and the coal mines and, eventually, to impose food rationing. It was originally hoped that the war could be left to the Navy and the small professional army, but by 1918 every man, woman, and child in Britain had become involved. This huge national effort explains the almost hysterical rejoicing in November 1918. It also explains why Britain was never the same again.

ASQUITH'S LIBERAL GOVERNMENT 1914–1915

*Recruiting propaganda and its results*

Despite many threats of resignation, only two members of Asquith's Cabinet, the radicals Morley and Burns, resigned when war was declared. The government which had led Britain into war was charged with the task of winning it. Asquith and most of his colleagues thought that their job would be to exercise over-all supervision and to leave the fighting to the generals and admirals.

**Kitchener**

In accordance with this policy Asquith appointed Lord Kitchener to the post of Secretary of State for War. Kitchener was popular in the country and his appointment undoubtedly brought public opinion over to the government's side. His appeals for recruits were also dramatically successful. His management of the War Office, however, was undistinguished, and his contributions to Cabinet meetings were few and unimpressive.

**Political truce**

With the exception of Kitchener, who belonged to no political party, the Cabinet was still entirely Liberal. The Unionists remained out of office. But party conflict in the House of Commons was largely suspended. The Unionists supported the war and saw their task as making sure that ministers kept up to the mark. The parties later decided that there should be no general election until the war was over.

**Defence of the Realm Act 1914**

The main emergency measure the government took in 1914 was to get Parliament to pass a Defence of the Realm Act, which gave the government wide and ill-defined powers. It could issue regulations 'as to the power and duties of the Admiralty and the Army

85

Council for securing the public safety and the defence of the Realm'. This was later used to justify the curtailment of licensing hours and the dilution of beer, but its immediate effect was to restrict the issue of war news to the press and to impose censorship on cables and foreign correspondence.

Kitchener soon dispelled his colleagues' optimism about a short war. He predicted that it would last three years and insisted that an army of seventy divisions must be raised as quickly as possible. The entire Cabinet was opposed to conscription, so an enormous recruiting campaign was launched. Posters bearing a picture of Kitchener screamed 'Your country needs YOU!', mob orators like Horatio Bottomley harangued enthusiastic recruiting meetings, music-hall artists sang the popular recruiting songs. The film *Oh What a Lovely War!* gives an excellent impression of the mood of hysterical patriotism which swept the country. Recruiting stations were swamped by eager young men whose chief concern was to get to the front before it was all over. There were 750,000 recruits by the end of September 1914 and an average of a further 125,000 a month until June 1915. By March 1916 two and a half million men had volunteered for the army. The response was far better than Kitchener had expected. It was also more than the army could cope with: there were not enough barracks or rifles or uniforms for all the volunteers.

In such a highly-charged atmosphere rumour and prejudice ran riot. Patriotic elderly ladies surreptitiously handed white feathers to young men not in uniform. Soldiers home on leave from the front, when thus approached, were sometimes amused, but often deeply hurt. Anti-German feeling was whipped up by rumours of German atrocities in Belgium, stories which usually bore no relation to the truth. Concert-goers took a sudden dislike to the music of Beethoven and Bach. Shopkeepers with German names frequently had their windows broken and their premises wrecked by mindless Saturday night revellers. Children patriotically kicked and stoned dachshunds. Even the Royal Family succumbed to the clamour: the King changed the family name from Saxe-Coburg-Gotha to Windsor. Some of the rumours have been embellished in the retelling, but many people believed that a band of angels had been seen above the battlefield at Mons, although the believers do not appear to have included any members of the B.E.F. The most fantastic story was that thousands of Russian troops had landed at Aberdeen, *en route* for the Western Front. A later version of the myth added that you could tell they were Russians by the snow on their boots.

As Chancellor of the Exchequer, Lloyd George had the task of raising enough money to pay for the huge armies and their supplies. He did this partly by raising income-tax and partly by borrowing. During Lloyd George's time at the Treasury income-tax rose from

*Actresses helped the recruiting campaign*

*Men were happy to enlist and their wives urged them to serve. The London women on the right use the 'White Feather Flag' as encouragement*

**Recruiting**

1s. 3d. (6p) in the pound in 1914 to 3s. (15p) in the pound in 1915. By 1918 the standard rate had reached 6s. (30p) in the pound. The National Debt increased from £625 million in 1914 to £7,809 million in 1918.

**Finance**

Before 1914 Lloyd George had also dealt with labour problems, and he continued to work for harmony between government and trade unions in the first two years of war. He was helped by the co-operative attitude of the trade union leaders who agreed in August 1914 to keep strikes to a minimum. The Chancellor's main achievement in this direction was the Treasury Agreement of March 1915, by which union leaders pledged themselves to accept the 'dilution' of the labour force: union rules were waived so that unskilled men and women could be employed in munitions factories.

**Labour relations**

. In the early months of the war Asquith's government had the confidence and support of the House of Commons and the public at large. By mid-1915 some voices were raised in criticism. Unionist back-benchers, the Labour party, and the Irish Nationalists, backed by Northcliffe's newspapers, began a campaign against the government in general and Churchill in particular. Using Sir John French's complaint that his failure on the Western Front was due to a shortage of shells, they denounced the government's inefficiency. Furthermore, the Dardanelles expedition had been a conspicuous failure and led to the resignation of the First Sea Lord, Sir John Fisher. The government's critics castigated the First Lord of the Admiralty, Churchill, for launching the campaign and demanded his removal from office.

Asquith bowed before the storm. After consultations with Lloyd George and Bonar Law, he agreed in May 1915 to the formation of a coalition government. Asquith remained Prime Minister, but five prominent Unionists and the leader of the Labour party, Arthur Henderson, joined the Cabinet. Churchill yielded the Admiralty to Arthur Balfour and moved to relative obscurity as Chancellor of the Duchy of Lancaster. His opponents still did not give up, and he was dismissed from office altogether in November 1915. The most significant feature of the new government was the creation of a Ministry of Munitions in response to the complaints about a shortage of shells. Apparently sacrificing the prestige of high office, Lloyd George took over the new ministry, where he devoted his talents and energy to the stimulation of war industry.

**Formation of coalition 1915**

88

## ASQUITH'S COALITION GOVERNMENT 1915–1916

**Ministry of Munitions**

Created in response to anger over the Dardanelles débâcle and the shell shortage, the new government took appropriate action. The political and military leaders soon decided to cut their losses and abandon the Dardanelles. The shell shortage was Lloyd George's problem. He created a new ministry from nothing, partly by recruiting onto his staff businessmen with a knowledge of industry but no experience of the Civil Service. Abandoning the War Office practice of dealing only with a few specialized firms, he offered contracts to a large number of private firms, some of which made enormous profits out of the manufacture and sale of arms. He tackled labour problems in co-operation with Arthur Henderson, who was actually President of the Board of Education but, in effect, Minister of Labour. Between them they persuaded the unions to accept even more dilution and to refrain from striking. At the same time, Lloyd George sought to resist the recruitment of munitions workers into the forces. The Ministry of Munitions was successful: the generals soon had no complaints about a shortage of shells. The value of so many extra shells was questionable; the significance of an enormous increase in the production of machine-guns was not. Another wise and far-sighted move on Lloyd George's part was to take over from the Admiralty, and develop, the idea of the tank. Kitchener naturally disapproved of tanks.

**McKenna's financial policies**

McKenna, who became Chancellor of the Exchequer in 1915, continued Lloyd George's policy of borrowing and raising taxes. His one revolutionary step was to impose import duties of thirty-three and a third per cent on luxuries such as cars, clocks, and watches. This was a sensible idea, for he both raised extra revenue and limited foreign trade at a time when merchant ships were liable to submarine attack. Nevertheless, it was a denial of the cardinal Liberal principle of Free Trade, and was tolerable only as a wartime emergency measure. As well as raising the National Debt by borrowing from private investors, the government also borrowed £1,000 million from the United States during the war. This sum was considerably exceeded by the amount loaned by Britain to her allies and the question of the repayment of inter-Allied debts was to be a thorny problem after the war.

For the ordinary citizen, the main financial result of the war was inflation. Prices rose threefold, and although wages lagged behind until 1917 they caught up in 1918. Most people were better off, however, for nearly everyone was in regular employment and many were in more highly paid jobs than before 1914.

Until early 1916 service in the armed forces was entirely voluntary. But the end of the war was still not in sight, and Britain was committed to maintaining a huge army in France. Heavy casualties

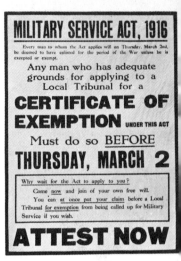

# MILITARY SERVICE ACT, 1916

Every man to whom the Act applies will on Thursday, March 2nd, be deemed to have enlisted for the period of the War unless he is excepted or exempt.

Any man who has adequate grounds for applying to a Local Tribunal for a

## CERTIFICATE OF EXEMPTION UNDER THIS ACT

Must do so BEFORE

# THURSDAY, MARCH 2

Why wait for the Act to apply to you?
Come now and join of your own free will.
You can at once put your claim before a Local Tribunal for exemption from being called up for Military Service if you wish.

# ATTEST NOW

*Left Call-up of married men, 1916*

meant that the recruitment rate must be kept up. Many politicians, especially those on the Unionist side, began to demand compulsory conscription, and they were supported by newspapers like the *Daily Mail*. The problem was twofold: although there was still a steady flow of volunteers, too many engineers and craftsmen, whose skills were needed in the munitions factories, were leaving for the army; secondly, the fact that able-bodied young men were able to evade military service was widely resented.

In January 1916 Parliament passed a Military Service Act, which made enlistment compulsory for all unmarried men between the ages of eighteen and forty-one, but exempted from service those men in 'reserved occupations', of which munitions work and coal-mining were the most important. The government thus sought to maintain the forces at the strength of two and a half million which they had reached by early 1916, and at the same time to prevent a run-down of vital war industries. The Act also contained a provision that conscientious objectors were to be interviewed by local tribunals, which might exempt them from combatant duties if satisfied that they were not merely trying to 'dodge the column'. Public opinion was strongly against the conscientious objectors, but many of them served heroically in ambulance units at the front. Others worked on the land or in industry.

In May 1916 the Military Service Act was extended to cover married men also. Conscription had the desired effect of maintaining the level of enlistment and satisfying the demands of industry. The exemption of munitions workers and miners, however, did mean that the number of recruits was less after the Military Service Acts than before.

*Women's Ambulance Corps*

Men who joined the army were to a large extent replaced in their civilian jobs by women. The massive contribution of women was one of the most significant and lasting social effects of the war. Women did work which had previously been the exclusive preserve of men. This proof of their competence and reliability opened up a new range of occupations for them and had far more effect than the suffragettes' campaigns in bringing about women's suffrage. The suffragettes abandoned their violent activities as soon as war was declared and all women immediately began to try to contribute to the war effort, if only by handing out white feathers. In July 1915 Christabel Pankhurst, militant as ever, led a march of 30,000 women down Whitehall, chanting, 'We demand the right to serve!' The right was soon granted: nearly three-quarters of a million women took clerical jobs, either in the Civil Service or with private firms; a quarter of a million worked on the land; 800,000 joined engineering firms, mainly in the munitions industry. Others worked as conductresses, and even drivers, on buses and trams, while large numbers trained as nurses. Many of the volunteers were married women who had not worked at all before the war, but some 400,000 were recruited from domestic service. Even so, the total number of domestic servants fell by only a third during the war.

Suffragette violence was one of Asquith's pre-war problems. Ireland was another. This too at first appeared to have subsided. The Home Rule Act was at last passed in September 1914, but its operation was postponed until six months after the end of the war. There the problem seemed to rest: Redmond pledged the support of the Irish Nationalists to Asquith's government; thousands of loyal Irishmen volunteered for the army, although the government

*Dublin damaged during Easter Rising, 1916*

wisely did not attempt to extend conscription to Ireland.

But the Irish calm was deceptive. A small minority of fanatical Irish Nationalists, calling themselves the Irish Republican Brotherhood, saw Britain's involvement in war as an ideal opportunity to strike a blow for Irish freedom. Sir Roger Casement, a former Colonial Office official, went secretly to Germany as an agent of the Brotherhood. There he asked the German government for arms to use in an Irish rebellion and tried unsuccessfully to recruit volunteers among the Irish prisoners of war in German prison camps.

The rising was planned for Easter 1916. Shortly before the appointed day a German submarine landed Casement on the Kerry coast, where he was immediately arrested. A German ship carrying arms and explosives had already been intercepted by the Royal Navy. All prospects of success appeared to have vanished, and most of the would-be rebels decided to abandon the attempt, but on Easter Monday, while most of the officers of the British garrison were at the Fairyhouse races, a group of extremists seized several key points in Dublin and Padric Pearse read the Declaration of the Irish Republic from the steps of the Dublin General Post Office. Only 1,500 Irishmen took part in the Easter Rising, which was crushed by the British troops after four days of fighting, but not before some of the finest buildings in Dublin had been destroyed. About 450 Irishmen and 100 British soldiers were killed.

The Irish people showed little sympathy with the rebels: Dublin women whose husbands were at the front treated them with contempt. The rising might almost have been forgotten had not the British commander ordered the execution of Pearse and fourteen other rebel leaders. (The future Irish President, Eamonn de Valera,

## The Easter Rising 1916

*Sinn Fein members interned after the Easter Rising*

**Asquith replaced by Lloyd George 1916**

escaped only on the grounds that he was an American citizen.) In the eyes of the Irish public, the executions turned foolish fanatics into martyrs in the national cause. Whatever chance there was of reconciliation between Britain and Ireland perished in front of the firing-squads in Kilmainham Gaol.

The continuing military failures led, in late 1916, to new criticism of Asquith's leadership. Although a wise and skilful statesman in peacetime, Asquith lacked the energy and dynamism necessary in the leader of a nation involved in total war. His original decision to leave the war to the military experts had clearly proved unsatisfactory, yet he had no new ideas. The principal demands for change came, naturally, from Unionist leaders like Bonar Law and Carson, but they had an ally in Lloyd George, who had taken over as Secretary for War on Kitchener's death in June 1916. Another prominent member of the anti-Asquith group was Max Aitken, the Canadian owner of the *Daily Express*, later to become Lord Beaverbrook.

Lloyd George, inspired partly by personal ambition and partly by the certainty that he could win the war for Britain, tried to persuade Asquith to hand over the direction of the war to a committee presided over by himself: Asquith was merely to be the government figure-head. Although most of the Liberal ministers backed Asquith, Lloyd George had the support of the Unionists. Seeing that national unity could not be preserved if he remained Prime Minister, Asquith resigned in December 1916. Lloyd George became Prime Minister at the head of another all-party coalition government. He had the support of the whole Unionist party and most of the Labour party, but about half of the Liberal M.P.s remained loyal to Asquith, who

93

refused to serve under Lloyd George.

The fall of Asquith was a milestone. The transfer of over-all command to Lloyd George was as important a contribution to the Allied victory in the First World War as was Churchill's assumption of power in the Second. Lloyd George sometimes acted rashly and often made mistakes, but no one could doubt his determination, energy, and courage. No other statesman could have led Britain through the third and fourth years of war. In another sense, the change was critical. It marked the break-up of the Liberal party. Apart from a brief reconciliation in the 1920s, the Liberals never recovered from the split of 1916 and soon after the end of the war they ceased to be a major political force.

## LLOYD GEORGE'S COALITION GOVERNMENT 1916–1918

Lloyd George began his task by streamlining the machinery of government. Instead of the traditional Cabinet, he set up a War Cabinet of five members, Bonar Law, Henderson, Curzon, and Milner in addition to himself. Apart from Bonar Law, who was Chancellor of the Exchequer, the members of the War Cabinet were not in charge of major government departments. They therefore had time to meet daily and to devote their attention to whatever problems, military or civil, were most urgent. Generals, admirals, and other ministers were called in to meetings of the War Cabinet whenever their advice was required.

**State control of industry**

The transfer of power from Asquith to Lloyd George meant the death of Old Liberalism; it also saw the end of *laissez-faire*, at least for the duration of the war. Lloyd George was committed to total war, which meant the mobilization of all the nation's resources. He set up a string of new ministries, dealing with shipping, labour, food, national service, and food production. Unimpressed by the abilities of many of his colleagues in the House of Commons, he brought in businessmen to run some of the new ministries. State control was ruthlessly extended: all British merchant ships were requisitioned, the coalmines were nationalized for the duration of the war, and the government took action to control prices.

**The Dominions and Smuts**

Lloyd George also showed some appreciation of the part which the Dominions were playing in the war. Although a conference of Dominion Prime Ministers in London in March 1917 achieved little, the British Prime Minister accepted their demand to be treated as equals. His consultations with Dominion governments brought him into contact with General Smuts of South Africa, a former Boer leader and now South African Minister of Defence. Lloyd George was so impressed by Smuts that he asked him to stay in London and appointed him to the War Cabinet in 1917.

German unrestricted submarine warfare in 1917 seriously threat-

**Food rationing**

ened Britain's supplies of food, but it was not until January 1918 that rationing was introduced, more in response to an irrational panic on the part of housewives than because food stocks were running low. The first ration cards applied only to meat, but in July rationing was extended to cover sugar, butter, margarine, and cooking-fat. Strangely, the main effect of rationing was slightly to increase food consumption, as most people made a point of buying their full ration.

**Propaganda**

Lloyd George thought not only of practical problems like manpower, munitions, and food. He set up a Ministry of Information under Lord Beaverbrook in February 1918, attempting to bolster Allied morale, win over doubting neutrals, and undermine the German war effort by skilful propaganda. The Ministry of Information exploited the skills not only of journalists like Lords Northcliffe and Rothermere, but also of men of letters like Rudyard Kipling.

During the last two years of the war the government acted with vigour and confidence. Lloyd George's bullying of the Admiralty into acceptance of the convoy system is a good example of his methods. Asquith and his band of dissident Liberals remained in opposition, but voted against the government only once.

**The Labour Party**

While the Liberal party was falling apart, the Labour party was preparing to take its place. Although Arthur Henderson resigned from the War Cabinet in 1917, several Labour ministers continued in office. Also, in 1918 the party's constitution was revised and a clear programme was drawn up. This contained the vital Clause IV, pledging a future Labour government to the nationalization of all the main industries.

**Representation of the People Act 1918**

The final year of the war saw two highly significant pieces of legislation, neither related to the war effort. The Representation of the People Act of 1918 finally granted the right to vote to all men over the age of twenty-one. It broke new ground by giving votes to women for the first time, but only women over the age of thirty were enfranchised. Parliament decided that men voters should not be outnumbered by women. A clause in the Act which had only temporary effect was that which gave voting rights to men between the ages of nineteen and twenty-one who had served in the war.

**Education Act 1918**

The other great measure was the Education Act of 1918, which established a general leaving age of fourteen for elementary schools. Somewhat optimistically, the Act also laid down that all young people between the ages of fourteen and eighteen should attend day continuation classes while at work. This attempt to bridge the gap between school and work failed when shortage of money in the 1920s prevented local authorities from building the necessary day continuation colleges. Finally, the Act established a system of state scholarships to allow secondary-school pupils to attend universities.

YESTERDAY - THE TRENCHES

# Chapter 6
# Unfulfilled Expectations 1918–1929

THE ECONOMIC PROBLEMS OF THE 1920s

Amid general rejoicing, which was an expression of relief rather than triumph, the armistice bringing the First World War to an end came into effect at eleven a.m. on 11 November 1918. This had been the most destructive war the world had ever known and until 1939 it was referred to simply as The War.

Now that the carnage was ended, what would follow? David Lloyd George, who remained Prime Minister until 1922, promised that Britain would become 'a fit land for heroes to live in' and most people expected that with peace would come prosperity. The governments of the 1920s, however, were unable to deal with, or even to understand, the economic difficulties which faced the nation. The tragedy of the 1920s and 1930s was that the 'heroes' of the Great War were often worse off than their fathers had been before 1914.

Britain had ceased to be the 'workshop of the world' long before 1914, but she had remained one of the three leading manufacturing and trading nations. Her main sources of wealth were her coalmining, cotton, and heavy engineering industries, her merchant navy and the banking and insurance services of the City of London. The hardships of the inter-war years were in part due to the failure of British politicians, industrialists, and economists to realize that, if prosperity was to be restored, it would not necessarily be based on the same activities as before 1914. In 1920 the new American President, Warren Harding, looked forward to a return to 'normalcy'; so did Lloyd George and his colleagues. They were all disappointed: what was normal in 1914 could not be normal after the war.

**Post-war boom**

In the first months of peace it seemed that prosperity was no idle dream. Britain experienced an economic boom: prices rose, but so did wages, and despite the rapid demobilization of the armed forces there was full employment. Britain's former customers in Europe, North and South America and Asia were eager to buy the goods, especially cotton cloth and coal, which they had been denied during the war. Investors poured capital into the traditional, staple industries: new cotton mills were built, shipyards extended. The trade unions successfully demanded higher wages and shorter hours. The 'national cake' was growing larger and everyone wanted his share.

By 1921 the boom had come to an end. The heavy demand for

*One of two posters issued by the Labour Party in 1923 for the general election of that year. The second is on page 99*

## Unfulfilled Expectations 1918–1929

British products in 1919 and 1920 had been part of the world-wide post-war elation, a reaction against wartime deprivation. The French and Belgians, for example, needed British goods because their own industries had been destroyed by the Germans. What had appeared in 1919 to be the return of normal prosperity was, in fact, highly abnormal. The chief characteristic of the remainder of the inter-war period, apart from revivals in the late 1920s and the late 1930s, was large-scale unemployment.

The heavy industries, which had been the basis of the country's prosperity, suffered most and unemployment was consequently concentrated in the coalmines of South Wales, south Yorkshire, and the north-east, in the Lancashire cotton mills, and in the shipyards of Tyneside and Clydeside. On the one hand there were places like Jarrow where, at the depths of the depression, virtually no one had a job, and, on the other, towns such as Watford and Luton which remained fairly prosperous. This uneven distribution of suffering heightened the distress of the unemployed and led to a division of the population into the 'haves' and the 'have nots', a division which was often deepened by contempt on one side and envy on the other.

The causes of the depression were not understood at the time and have remained a source of controversy ever since, but it seems clear that a combination of international economic factors and certain basic weaknesses in the British economy was responsible. The immediate cause was a decline in the total volume of world trade following the Great War. In a situation where nations traded less with each other, unemployment mounted, especially in those industries which had played a large part in the export trade.

There were several reasons for this post-war decline in international trade. First, industrial plant in Belgium and north-east France had been extensively damaged during the war and the Germans, when they retreated in 1918, had caused a great deal of destruction by dismantling factory machinery and flooding coalmines in the areas which they had occupied. In consequence, France and Belgium were unable to produce the same quantity of goods as before the war. Inevitably, they could export less and, therefore, could afford to buy less from other countries. Secondly, the peace treaty signed in 1919 compelled Germany to pay enormous sums as reparations, or damages, to the countries which had suffered from the war (see page 113). This meant that Germany was also prevented from buying foreign goods at the same rate as before 1914. A third consequence of the war was the creation of a number of new, small states in central and eastern Europe. Poles, Czechoslovaks, and Yugoslavs were proud of their new independence and eager to protect their own industries and agriculture. Most of the new states pursued protective tariff policies: duties on imported goods were high. This further discouraged trade.

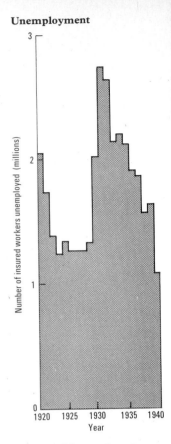

**Unemployment**

**Causes of depression**

# TO-DAY - UNEMPLOYED

The countries of Europe therefore traded less among themselves. This had far-reaching consequences: the contraction of European trade meant that European nations earned less money and were less able to buy food and raw materials from the rest of the world. The producers of food and raw materials (primary producers) in the Americas, Africa, Asia, and Australasia, since they could sell less to Europe, were not in a position to buy the manufactured goods which they had obtained previously from major exporters like Britain. One example will illustrate this point: as Germans could not afford to buy Brazilian coffee, the Brazilians could not buy British coal. Coffee beans were sometimes used as fuel for Brazilian railway engines while British pits were idle. Factors outside Britain caused a decline in world trade and British industry suffered.

The decline in trade, then, caused unemployment; and unemployment snowballed. Men who were out of work earned less than before, which meant that they had less to spend. This led to a reduction in the demand for every kind of commodity. Unemployed shipbuilders could not afford new shoes; this caused some unemployment among shoemakers. The depression, although concentrated in the heavy industries and therefore in particular areas, was to some extent passed on to the whole community. Justifiably, people all over the world looked with mystified outrage at the destruction of beef in Argentina and of corn in Canada and the empty factories in Britain, while everywhere there was hunger, cold, and misery.

Before 1914 Britain had been the world's leading shipping nation, transporting not only her own imports and exports, but also those of many other countries. With everyone trading less, there was a sharp reduction in the demand for shipping services and for new ships. Thus many of Britain's merchant seamen and shipbuilders had no work.

For several reasons unconnected with the decline in world trade there was less demand for British exports after 1920. During the war, exports of cloth and machinery to the Americas and Asia had been reduced, partly because of enemy submarine activity and partly because many of the mills and factories were producing uniforms and munitions. This had presented an opportunity to American and Japanese manufacturers to seize what had been a British preserve. After the war, these markets were difficult to recapture. Furthermore, countries like India and China, which had previously been among Britain's most important customers, were now beginning to develop their own textile industries. Cotton mills in Calcutta and Shanghai, with much lower labour and transport costs, often cut the Lancashire producers out of the market. Finally, there were technological changes, often accelerated by the war. Hydro-electric schemes were developed, especially in Scandinavia and Italy; also the world's oil reserves were being tapped as transport went through another revolution. Britain's only important natural asset, her plentiful supplies of coal, might no longer be the key to national prosperity.

The Great War not only affected international trade; it also had two harmful long-term effects on British industry. The steel, ship-building, and engineering industries had been the heart of the war effort: capital had been poured into them, new blast-furnaces and factories had been built, and shipyards extended, with the result that at the end of the war there was too much industrial plant. Factories built during the war to make shells could not change afterwards to producing bicycles if there was no demand for bicycles. Secondly, vast quantities of coal had been needed during the war to keep the essential industries running and many of the best seams had been rashly exploited. Now, in the 1920s, the coal-owners were left with worn-out machinery, only the more difficult and costly coal deposits, and a much contracted market.

The post-war boom had only made matters worse. Money was invested foolishly: for example, mills built in Oldham in 1920 never operated. Very few people recognized that the era of cotton and coal had passed and that Britain's future prosperity would depend on new industries demanding more intricate, specialized skills, such as motor manufacturing, radio, and a wide range of electrical industries. Technical advances (such as those employed by Henry Ford in America) had made possible the production of relatively cheap motor vehicles and electrical goods. These industries could have provided work for some unemployed miners and textile workers, who, through having more money to spend, would have stimulated further recovery.

It is untrue, of course, that Britain experienced a continuous depression from 1920 to 1939. Between 1920 and 1924 world trade declined. In the next five years, however, there was an improvement as the problem of German reparations was temporarily solved and large American loans, especially to Germany, encouraged an expansion of European trade. In Britain the newer industries, mostly located in the Midlands and the Home Counties, flourished. But the basic weaknesses in the British economy persisted: heavy industry still had an important role to play, but it could never recover its pre-war predominance. The long-expected revival failed to materialize, with the result that the number of unemployed in Britain never fell below one million even in the prosperous years of the late 1920s. The worst of the depression was to come in the 1930s (pages 134–142).

The internal political history of the 1920s is largely the story of the attempts of successive governments to solve the fundamental economic problem, and to lessen the suffering which accompanied it, and of the contest between employers and workers: few of them understood or sympathized with the others' position.

LLOYD GEORGE'S ADMINISTRATION 1918–1922—
DOMESTIC PROBLEMS AND ACHIEVEMENTS

Since 1916 Lloyd George had been at the head of a coalition government containing Liberal, Conservative, and Labour ministers. While the war had lasted there had been little formal opposition, although Asquith, the previous Prime Minister, refused to participate in the government and led a group of Liberals who were united in their dislike of the methods used by Lloyd George to displace Asquith in 1916. The Labour party had also been split: an anti-war section had remained in opposition. Lloyd George was in the strange position of being the head of a government supported by the fragment of the Liberal party which accepted his own leadership, by half of the Parliamentary Labour Party, and by the whole Conservative party. He remained Prime Minister, then, primarily through Conservative tolerance.

At the end of the war most Labour members of the coalition withdrew and the Labour party was soon reunited. Lloyd George and his Liberal and Conservative colleagues decided to preserve the coalition in order to deal with the domestic and foreign problems which would arise in the first years of peace, and, in particular, to present a united front at the Paris Peace Conference. They felt obliged, however, to appeal immediately to the voters for a vote of confidence. A general election was held in December 1918 and resulted in a massive victory for the coalition. Lloyd George's Liberals and their Conservative allies won 526 seats, Labour won 63, and Asquith's Liberals 28. Asquith himself and many other former Liberal ministers were defeated. The electorate, which for the first time included women, had agreed decisively that the wartime government should finish the job.

*Election Result 1918*

| Coalition parties | |
|---|---|
| Conservative | 383 |
| Liberal | 133 |
| Labour | 10 |
| Liberal (Asquith) | 28 |
| Labour | 63 |
| Irish Nationalist | 7 |
| Sinn Fein | 73 |
| Others | 10 |

The demobilization of the armed forces was one of the first tasks facing the government. The troops justifiably wanted to return to civilian life at once. But the largest army that Britain had ever assembled could not be disbanded overnight. One important stumbling-block was that the agreement of 11 November 1918 was an armistice, not a peace; if the Germans refused to accept the terms offered by the Peace Conference, hostilities would have to be resumed. The military situation was complicated by the government's decision to send troops to assist the anti-Bolshevik forces in Russia. Furthermore, if men were discharged from the services too rapidly it might not be possible to absorb them at once in civilian occupations and mass unemployment might result. The popular press took up the soldiers' cry for demobilization at the same time as it was insisting on a harsh peace. This is typical of the problems with which Lloyd George had to deal in the post-war years: whatever he did, he could not satisfy everyone. The War Office's original plan

**Demobilization**

*Lloyd George electioneering in his native Wales, 1919*

was to demobilize first the men most needed in industry. This caused grave discontent, for these were naturally the men who had been called up last. Military discipline, which had been excellent throughout the war, broke down in 1919. There were mutinies in the army camps at Calais, Folkestone, and Dover, troops demonstrated in the streets of London and Luton town hall was set on fire. The War Office plan was abandoned and Churchill produced the more acceptable formula of 'first in, first out'. By mid-1919 eighty per cent of the armed forces had been demobilized and the disturbances ceased.

Not only the troops caused trouble in 1919. The trade unions took advantage of the favourable conditions of the post-war boom to demand higher wages and shorter hours, and there were some serious strikes, especially among the coalminers of the north-east and the engineers of Clydeside. In most cases, however, the employers were willing to grant concessions rather than forfeit their share of the boom.

**Strikes**

103

During the war, the government had taken over the coalmines and the railways. Lloyd George's Cabinet decided that, after the war, the industries should be returned to private ownership but that the government should keep some control over industry so as to lessen hardship and, as far as possible, prevent industrial disputes. The Trade Boards Act of 1918 set up boards to prevent sweated labour. At the same time it proposed a system of Whitley Councils, which were to comprise representatives from both sides of industry, and which would negotiate wage rates and conditions of work. It was hoped that the relationship between employers and trade unions would become more cordial and disagreements would be settled peacefully, not through strikes and lock-outs. But suspicion on both sides prevented any real progress.

The railways were restored to private ownership in 1922; four regional amalgamations took the place of the former companies. The mines were a much more difficult problem. The miners, represented by their trade union, the Miners' Federation, wanted not only higher wages and shorter hours, but the nationalization of their industry. They thought that if the mines were under public ownership their wages and conditions would be improved. The owners, on the other hand, wanted to regain the rights to operate their own mines and to enjoy their profits, and the freedom to reach regional wage agreements with the miners. The government set up, in 1919, a Commission of Inquiry, under the chairmanship of Mr. Justice Sankey. The Sankey Commission, as it came to be known, suggested an increase in wages and a reduction in hours. A majority of the members (including all the miners' representatives) reported in favour of nationalization. The government acted indecisively and so won the respect of neither side. Arguing that the Sankey Commission had failed to agree, it refused to implement its recommendations. This provoked a miners' strike in 1920. The continuation of the boom (coal prices reached their peak in 1920) strengthened the miners' position and made the owners eager to reach a compromise. The miners were granted an immediate wage increase and a reduction of the working day to seven hours, but no promise of nationalization. The problem of the coal industry had not been solved and continued to bedevil industrial relations for the next six years.

One consequence of the miners' strike of 1920 was the passing of an Emergency Powers Act, which permitted the government to declare a state of emergency if essential supplies were threatened by a strike. This gave it the power to use troops to man the docks and railways and other vital services and to take extraordinary steps to maintain law and order and to ensure food supplies. The Act showed that Lloyd George and his Cabinet anticipated serious labour troubles and were determined to be forearmed.

The end of the war and the post-war boom led to two important

*Government poster during the miners' strike, 1920*

**Miners' strike 1920**

**Emergency Powers Act 1920**

developments in the trade union movement. First, there was a sharp rise in trade union membership: there were 4·1 million trade unionists in 1914, 6·5 million in early 1919, and 8·3 million by late 1920. Boom conditions have always led to a rise in trade union membership, but it is also possible that the demobilized soldiers wanted to carry the comradeship of the trenches into civilian life. Secondly, trade unions were reorganized and amalgamated. Two new large-scale unions appeared: the Transport and General Workers' Union and the General and Municipal Workers' Union. The general secretary of the former, Ernest Bevin, was to be a leading figure in the trade union movement in the 1920s and 1930s and, from 1940, a Cabinet Minister.

For over fifty years most trade unions had been loosely bound together in the Trades Union Congress, which had never seriously attempted to co-ordinate the industrial activities of its member unions. In 1920, however, the T.U.C. set up a General Council— a trade union 'general staff' which was to lay plans for industrial action and ensure that unions were not left to fight alone against employers and government. Also, the Triple Alliance was revived. This comprised the three largest unions, the Miners' Federation, the National Union of Railwaymen, and the Transport Workers, and was the backbone of potential union strength. Strikes by the three unions could paralyze some of the basic industries (coalmining, railways, docks, and road transport) and hold the government to ransom.

**Political victory for trade unions**

*Ernest Bevin*

The power of the unions to interfere in political affairs was demonstrated in 1920. Since the Bolshevik (Communist) Revolution of 1917, Russia had been involved in a civil war, in which the Bolsheviks' opponents, the Russian 'Whites', received support from various foreign states, including Britain. By 1920 the Bolsheviks had won and all the British forces had been withdrawn from Russia, but Lloyd George's government maintained contact with the area by sending arms to Poland, which had chosen this moment to attempt to extend its territories eastward at the expense of Russia. Interest in and sympathy for Soviet Russia was strong in the British trade union movement and in the Labour party, although the latter had refused a request for affiliation from the newly formed British Communist party. It was widely feared that Lloyd George's action might lead to war with Russia, and this was more than the unions, and the Transport Workers in particular, were willing to tolerate. For a time there seemed a real danger of a general strike. Among the trade union rank and file, determination to avoid another war was more important than sympathy for the Soviet régime. Eventually the Cabinet gave way and suspended the deliveries of arms, and the unions rejoiced in their victory. It was more than a question of arms for Poland, however; for the first time, the trade unions had achieved a purely political victory. Many people were worried by the thought that power lay perhaps not with the nation's elected government, but with the General Council of the T.U.C.

By the end of 1920 the boom was over: wages and prices fell and unemployment rose rapidly. There were more strikes, not now for higher wages, but to prevent decreases. Hunger marches and mass demonstrations by the jobless became commonplace and often led to violence as the police tried to control the crowds.

As usual, coalmining suffered most. Faced with falling coal prices in 1921, the owners demanded longer hours and lower wages. When the Miners' Federation resisted, the owners threatened a lock-out. It would suit them better to stop producing coal than to continue paying the high wages which they had conceded during the boom. The Miners' Federation appealed to the other members of the Triple Alliance, who agreed to begin a general strike on Friday, 15 April 1921. At the last moment, however, the Transport Workers and Railwaymen withdrew. To the miners, this was an act of treason and inter-union relations were embittered. The miners struck alone on the appointed day, 'Black Friday', and held out for four months until August, when, with their funds nearly exhausted, they had to admit defeat and accept the owners' terms.

**Miners' strike 1921**

*Miners' pickets; troops in Kensington Gardens; miners' soup queue*

The numbers of unemployed continued to rise: less than a million men were out of work in 1920, but the figure had reached nearly two million by 1922. Unemployment insurance had been introduced in 1911 for builders, engineers, and shipbuilders, and an Act of 1920 extended the scheme to most working people. But the benefit, which was intended as a safeguard against seasonal variations in trade, was paid for only fifteen weeks in any one year. This did not meet the needs of the men thrown out of work in 1921 and 1922 whose prospects of a return to employment were slight. Therefore, in 1921, a system of 'uncovenanted benefit', soon popularly known as 'the dole', was introduced. The original unemployment payments had been financed by contributions from the employers and the workers (see p. 30). Uncovenanted benefit was paid for by the government.

**The dole**

Another of the positive, although temporary, achievements of the Lloyd George government was its attempt to remedy the housing shortage, and thus to redeem the pledge made in the 1918 election campaign to build 'homes for heroes'. In 1921 Christopher Addison, the Minister of Health, began a scheme whereby the government authorized local councils to build houses to be let at low rents. Most of the cost was borne by the government. When the plan proved to be excessively expensive, the grants were reduced, Addison was dismissed and, in 1922, the scheme was abandoned. Nevertheless, more than 200,000 houses were built.

**Housing**

As the unemployment figures rose, of course, the government's income from taxes fell and the cost of supporting the jobless in-

*Council houses, Becontrees Heath, Essex, 1923*

creased. A committee presided over by Sir Eric Geddes recommended big reductions in expenditure, and consequently the government applied, in 1922, the 'Geddes Axe', cutting down sharply its spending on defence, the Civil Service, education, and unemployment benefit.

**'Geddes Axe' 1922**

Since hardly anyone at the time understood the causes of the depression, it would be unjust to blame Lloyd George's government for failing to foresee or prevent it. Nevertheless, the year 1922, which saw the beginnings of the slump, also saw the end of the Lloyd George coalition Cabinet. The coalition is often criticized and sometimes derided, but its achievements were not insignificant. Lloyd George had appeared as one of the world's great statesmen at the Paris Peace Conference, the Irish problem had finally been solved, some social reforms had been passed, but the ministers had run out of ideas on the central home issue. In addition, scandalous rumours circulated to the effect that honours and titles could be obtained in return for large payments into Lloyd George's 'political fund'. The immediate cause of the fall of the government, however, was the decision taken by a meeting of rank and file Conservative M.P.s that the coalition had lasted too long and that it was time that the party stood on its own feet again. Lloyd George relied very heavily on Conservative support and as soon as he learned of the withdrawal of his Conservative colleagues he resigned.

*The peacemakers: (left to right)*
*Clemenceau, Wilson, Lloyd George*

**Paris Peace Conference 1919**

LLOYD GEORGE'S ADMINISTRATION 1918–1922—FOREIGN POLICY

In many ways, the Paris Peace Conference, which met from January to June 1919, was the highlight of Lloyd George's career. For five months he sat with President Wilson of the United States, Clemenceau of France, and (intermittently) Orlando of Italy in supreme council. The world's four leading statesmen could be described as judges of the defeated nations or as architects of a new era; they and the millions who watched them were deeply conscious of their historic mission, their duty to make a just and lasting peace. To speak and think in these grand terms is, however, to forget that the statesmen were talented but nevertheless human, that none of them had supreme power in his own country, that they were subject to numerous, often contradictory pressures, and that many of their problems were virtually insoluble. They made a bad peace settlement, but perhaps they could not have done otherwise.

A vast task awaited the statesmen in Paris. The Allied and Associated Powers had fought and defeated an alliance of the empires of Germany, Austria-Hungary, and Turkey, and the kingdom of Bulgaria. As Austria-Hungary collapsed, the Hapsburgs' former subject nationalities demanded independence. At the same time military defeat, revolution, and civil war had thrown Russia into confusion. Most of Germany's neighbours naturally made territorial claims against her, while the defeat of Bulgaria and Turkey put the Balkans and the Middle East once more into a state of flux. The most pressing duty of the statesmen in Paris was, then, to redraw the maps of central, eastern, and south-eastern Europe, and the Middle East, while Germany's colonial empire presumably had to be confiscated and disposed of. Finally, and most important of all, the peacemakers had to devise a way of preventing a repetition of a disaster like the Great War.

The German government had agreed to an armistice in November 1918 in the hope that peace would be made in accordance with the Fourteen Points announced by President Wilson in January 1918 (see pages 82—83). The essence of the Fourteen Points was that justice, not revenge, should govern the peace settlement, that frontiers should be redrawn according to the principle of national self-determination, that there should be general disarmament, and that a League of Nations should be established to settle disputes between nations and to provide protection for all states against aggression. National self-determination meant that frontiers should correspond with national divisions, that all Poles should belong to a national Polish state, that the territories of Greece should include all those areas inhabited by Greeks, and so on. It was a death sentence for the Austro-Hungarian Empire, which, before 1918, had contained ten major national groups.

Lloyd George sympathized with Wilson's idealistic principles, but felt at the same time that he had a responsibility to uphold Britain's own interests. He wanted to eliminate the challenge of the German navy, and this aim was quickly realized. When the German fleet was escorted to Scapa Flow in the Orkneys the Germans scuttled their ships. He shared with the French and the British Dominion governments a desire to take over part of the German colonial empire and wanted to fortify British interests in the Middle East at the expense of Turkey. Lloyd George had no territorial claims in Europe and merely wanted a settlement which would guarantee peace. A just peace was the best way to avoid another war.

Anti-German feeling had been strong in Britain during the war and Lloyd George would, in any case, have had to pay attention to this during the Paris negotiations. All democratic politicians must respect, even if they do not always follow, public opinion. Lloyd George's task was made more difficult by the anti-German hysteria which was whipped up in Britain by the popular press, especially by the *Daily Mail*, immediately after the armistice.

Not only the press, but also the newly elected House of Commons kept pressure on the Prime Minister to exact the harshest possible terms. Contemporaries had a low opinion of the new members: Stanley Baldwin described them as 'hard-faced men who look as if they have done very well out of the war', implying that many of them were factory owners who had grown rich by manufacturing and selling munitions. Throughout the negotiations, they denounced every proposed concession to Germany.

Clemenceau, who had been a young man at the time of the Franco-Prussian War of 1870–1, wanted above all to ensure that France would not be invaded a third time. His central aim was to protect France by weakening Germany, if necessary by detaching some of her western territories. Orlando openly sought extra land for Italy. Like Lloyd George, the French and Italian Prime Ministers were in the grip of fiercely nationalist, anti-German public opinion. In these circumstances, strength and resolution were needed from the American President if the Fourteen Points and 'eternal justice' were to be rescued. But Woodrow Wilson could provide neither; he was repeatedly outwitted by his European colleagues and his position was gravely undermined when his party, the Democrats, lost their majority in both Houses of Congress to the Republicans in November 1918.

**Austria-Hungary**

There was no need for the Conference to carve up the Austro-Hungarian Empire. It had already disintegrated in November 1918. Czechs and Slovaks had united to form Czechoslovakia; a new Poland had emerged from former Austrian, German, and Russian territories; Rumania had seized Transylvania, the eastern part of Hungary; Serbs, Croats, and Slovenes within the Empire had joined Serbia and Montenegro in the new state of Yugoslavia; Italy had laid claim to the South Tyrol and parts of the Adriatic coastline; the remnants of the Empire became the separate republics of Austria and Hungary. The representatives of the Great Powers merely superintended the partition.

**Germany**

The German problem was more difficult and led to serious disagreements among the peacemakers. Wilson tried to observe the Fourteen Points, Lloyd George wanted a just settlement, but Clemenceau was obsessed by the fear that unless Germany was rendered incapable of waging a war of revenge, France might have to resist yet another invasion. One point was unquestioned: Alsace-Lorraine, which had been annexed by Germany in 1871, was restored unconditionally to France. But Clemenceau wanted to go further. Prompted by his generals, he suggested that the Rhine should become the frontier between France and Germany. Wilson and Lloyd George were unwilling to accept this transfer of several million Germans to French rule, or to agree with Clemenceau's compromise proposal that the Rhineland should become an independent buffer state. Agreement was finally reached on a plan to demilitarize the Rhineland (i.e. it would remain German, but German troops and military installations could not be kept there) and to station Allied troops in the area for fifteen years. Also, as partial recompense for the damage done to French industry, France would control the Saar coalmines for fifteen years; at the end of this time the people of the Saar would vote on their future status.

The debate over Germany's eastern frontier, her border with Poland, again saw Lloyd George taking the German side. Clemenceau, who wanted to weaken Germany wherever possible, proposed that Poland should have the rich coalfields of Upper Silesia and the city of Danzig. Lloyd George rightly claiming that Upper Silesia and Danzig were more German than Polish, would not consent to a settlement which the Germans would be unwilling to accept. Partially successful solutions were reached: Danzig became a free city, neither Polish nor German, but under League of Nations protection, while a plebiscite was held in Upper Silesia. Most of the inhabitants of Upper Silesia voted to remain German. Inevitably, the frontier did not correspond exactly to the national division, but Lloyd George had lessened the injustice.

Germany's frontier with Denmark was adjusted after another plebiscite. Northern Schleswig became part of Denmark, while the South voted to remain German. This was in keeping with the principle of self-determination, but the Conference's decision that the new republic of Austria must not unite with Germany could not be defended except in terms of military necessity. The seven million people of Austria were entirely German-speaking, but they were not consulted as to their future. Similarly, Czechoslovakia contained three million Sudeten Germans, living along the German frontier. The peacemakers decided to keep them under Czecho-slovak rule for military and economic reasons. The existing Czech-German frontier was mountainous and easily defended, but if Sudetenland went to Germany, Czechoslovakia would have to defend an open plain against the Germans*.

Germany's colonial possessions in Africa, New Guinea, the Pacific islands, and China had been conquered by the Allies, who showed no sign of being willing to give them up in 1919. The Fourteen Points spoke of a 'free and impartial adjustment of colonial claims', taking into account 'the interests of the populations concerned'. In fact, Germany's colonies were annexed by the victorious powers: France and Britain shared Togoland and the Cameroons in West Africa, Britain took German East Africa (Tanganyika), South Africa seized German South-West Africa, Australia assumed control of German New Guinea, and Germany's Pacific islands were shared between Australia, New Zealand, and Japan. In theory, these were not outright annexations, but man-dates to be held under League of Nations supervision. It is difficult to see the treatment of Germany's colonies as anything other than the distribution of spoils among the conquerors.

The arms race in which the Great Powers engaged before 1914 was undoubtedly one of the causes of the Great War and Wilson

* Sudetenland would also be the main industrial area of the new Czechoslovak state.

piously expressed the hope in 1918 that general disarmament would accompany the peace. Germany was disarmed. The fleet was surrendered and the Rhineland occupied (see page 111). The German army was to be restricted to 100,000 men, voluntarily recruited, Germany was forbidden to have tanks, military aircraft, heavy artillery, or submarines and the size and number of her warships was severely limited.

Of all the terms in the final treaty, perhaps the greatest controversy has surrounded the reparations clauses. When the Germans signed the armistice in November 1918 they agreed to pay the cost of damage to civilian property caused by military operations in Allied countries. This vague formula could be interpreted in dozens of ways; some people argued that Germany should even be responsible for the cost to the Allied governments of pensions paid to incapacitated soldiers and war widows. The essence of the anti-German hysteria in Britain in late 1918 and early 1919 was a demand for crippling reparations. Lloyd George was not against reparations altogether and could not swim against the tide of public opinion, but he did realize that absurdly high demands would prevent future reconciliation with Germany. He also probably foresaw to some extent the economic consequences of this proposed strangulation of the German economy (see page 98). At Paris, therefore, he demanded that Germany should pay as much as she could, but induced his colleagues to delay the fixing of the final sum.

**League of Nations**

The most ambitious act of the statesmen was to set up the League of Nations, a permanent organization comprising all the states which chose to take part. Its basic purpose was to secure the peaceful settlement of international disputes and to guarantee all nations against aggression. Subordinate bodies were to promote economic progress, watch over the rights of workers in all countries, and supervise the League of Nations' mandates. The League's principal promoter was Woodrow Wilson, and both Lloyd George and Clemenceau accepted the idea, although the latter was doubtful of its value. Almost from the beginning, the League had two fundamental weaknesses: its Covenant, or constitution, was very vague on what action member states might take in the event of aggression, and not all the Great Powers were members. The United States Senate, dominated by the Republican party, refused to ratify the peace treaties or to allow the United States to become a member of the League, and neither Germany nor Soviet Russia were invited to join at first. The task of making the League work fell therefore, almost entirely to Britain and France. Not unnaturally, they failed.

**The Treaties**

The Conference ended with the signing of formal peace treaties between the Allied and Associated Powers and their former enemies. There were five separate documents, the Treaty of Versailles (with

Germany), the Treaty of St. Germain (with Austria), the Treaty of Trianon (with Hungary), the Treaty of Neuilly (with Bulgaria), and the Treaty of Sèvres (with Turkey). The defeated powers played no part in the negotiations; they were faced with the option of accepting the terms dictated to them or resuming the war. In a rather pathetic ceremony in the Palace of Versailles on 28 June 1919, Dr. Müller and Dr. Bell signed the Treaty on behalf of the new German republic.

**The Middle East**

The former Turkish empire in the Middle East was partitioned, not at the Paris Peace Conference, but as a result of separate negotiations between the British, French, and Arab leaders. Lloyd George's government was again in a position where it could not satisfy everyone. During the war, Britain had made three separate agreements relating to the future of the Middle East and none of them could be fulfilled without breaking at least one of the others. Hussein, Sherif of Mecca, the spiritual leader of all Arabs, had been promised in 1914 and 1915 that if the Arabs helped the war effort by rebelling against the Turks, Britain would ensure that an Arab empire, with its capital at Damascus, was set up after the war. The Arabs duly revolted and were encouraged and advised by British officers, of whom Colonel T.E. Lawrence was the most famous. In May 1916, however, the British and French governments had reached a secret understanding (the Sykes-Picot agreement) to the effect that the Arab territories should be partitioned after the war: Syria (probably including Damascus) was to go to France, Mesopotamia to Britain, and the remainder was to form an independent Arab kingdom. The third commitment was the Balfour Declaration of 1917, in which Arthur Balfour expressed the British government's sympathy with 'the establishment in Palestine of a national home for the Jewish people'.

Hussein's son, Feisal, entered Damascus at the same time as Allenby's army in October 1918, and expected to become king. When the French asserted their claim to Syria, Feisal was thrown out and felt that the British had let him down. An Anglo-French agreement in 1920 laid down that Syria and the Lebanon should be held by France as League of Nations mandates, while Britain should control Palestine and Mesopotamia on the same terms. The remainder of Arabia became independent and was quickly conquered by Ibn Saud, the ruler of the central Arabian area; his kingdom became known as Saudi Arabia. Meanwhile, Winston Churchill, who had become Colonial Secretary, visited the Middle East in 1921 and decided that Feisal should become King of Irak (the new name for Mesopotamia), and that his brother Abdullah should rule in Transjordan, the eastern part of Palestine. Both would remain under British protection. The British government decided to maintain tighter control over western Palestine, and to admit limited numbers of Jewish immigrants. After a revolt against British rule, Egypt became substantially independent in 1922, although British troops were to remain to protect the Suez Canal. Harmony had been temporarily restored to the Middle East, but Britain had lost Arab goodwill and had sown the seeds of future conflicts between Arabs and Jews.

**Reparations and war debts**

The Treaty of Versailles declared Germany's obligation to pay reparations, but did not fix the amount. A Reparations Commission was set up and in 1921 it reached agreement on the figure of £6,600 million. There was still no agreement, however, on the rate of payment. The Genoa conference of April 1922 was intended to settle this question, and the complicated problem of war debts. Britain had borrowed £1000 million from the United States during the war, but had provided loans far in excess of this amount to her allies, principally Russia. A major difficulty was that the Soviet government refused to honour the debts of its Tsarist predecessor. Lloyd George proposed a general cancellation of debts, but the Americans would not even attend the Genoa conference. Faced with the prospect of repaying her debt to the United States, France insisted on the full payment of German reparations, and Britain had no alternative but to support this claim and to continue to demand the repayment of Russia's debts. The two principal sufferers from this round of failures were Germany and Soviet Russia, who proceeded to make a pact of mutual friendship at Rapallo. Defeated Germany and revolutionary Russia thus became even more estranged from the western democracies.

Wilson's Fourteen Points had spoken hopefully of all-round disarmament, which was also one of the objectives of the League of Nations. Apart from the harsh terms imposed on Germany in the Treaty of Versailles, the only real progress in this direction came

**Washington Naval Conference 1921–2**

about as a result of the Washington Naval Conference of 1921–2. Britain, the United States, and Japan (at the time, the world's leading naval powers) agreed to limit their total number of battleships so that Britain and the United States were equal, and Japan had three-fifths of their naval strength. This agreement removed any chance of a naval race between Britain and America. The Washington Conference also marked the end of the Anglo-Japanese alliance of 1902, as the Americans would agree to limit their number of battleships only if they could be sure that they would not have to face a combination of the British and Japanese navies.

The fall of Lloyd George was accompanied, and partly caused, by another foreign crisis. The Treaty of Sèvres had placed the Straits (the Dardanelles and the Bosphorus) under international control and had given the Smyrna region of Asia Minor to Greece. Patriotic Turks, who considered these terms humiliating, found a

**Chanak incident 1922**

leader in Mustapha Kemal, who rejuvenated the country, drove the

Greeks out of Smyrna in 1922 and, advancing on the Straits, threatened a British force at Chanak. Lloyd George decided to stand firm, but received no support either from his French and Italian allies or from the British Dominions, who resented the prospect of being dragged into war with Turkey. Fortunately, the generals on both sides avoided a clash and arranged a truce. The matter was referred for settlement to a conference of interested parties, which met at Lausanne in the following year. The Chanak incident cost Lloyd George prestige, and this was one of the reasons why the Conservatives withdrew their support from his coalition government. (See page 108).

LLOYD GEORGE'S ADMINISTRATION 1918–1922 — IRELAND

It is tempting to say that the Irish problem might have been solved peacefully but for the Dublin Rising of 1916 (see pages 92–93). The Home Rule Act, which became law in 1914 and was suspended for the duration of the war, might have provided a permanent settlement, but it is certain that tensions would have persisted between the Protestant North and the Catholic South, and that the republican extremists would have remained dissatisfied. The Easter Rising, or rather the execution of the Irish leaders, changed the climate of Irish public opinion, destroyed what little faith the Irish had in the British Liberal party, and played into the hands of the republicans.

*Michael Collins (left), reorganizer of the IRA, on the hurling field*

**The Dail**

In the 1918 election Redmond's Irish Nationalist party was totally eclipsed by the anti-British Sinn Fein, which won seventy-three Irish seats. Half of the Sinn Fein members elected to Parliament were serving sentences in British prisons and the remainder refused to take their seats at Westminster. They set up instead an Irish parliament, the Dail, in Dublin, and proceeded to organize separate institutions of government, complete with tax system, law courts, and local officials. Everywhere outside Ulster the agents of the Dail were obeyed, while the British administration with its headquarters in Dublin Castle was ignored. Eamonn de Valera, whose American birth had saved him from the firing-squad in 1916, was elected President by the Dail.

**The I.R.A.**

The Irish Republican Army was, according to one's point of view, either a gallant band of patriots or a ruthless gang of terrorists. Successor to the Irish National Volunteers, it was reorganized in 1919 by Michael Collins, using money donated in the United States and arms either smuggled from Europe or stolen from the British. It began immediately, without the Dail's authorization, a campaign of attacks on police stations and other government buildings and on individuals known to sympathize with British rule. The total strength of the I.R.A. is estimated never to have exceeded 15,000 and the only uniforms were trench coats and cloth caps. The police consequently found it virtually impossible to trace I.R.A. members.

The British administration in Ireland had at its disposal the

*De Valera (left) in 1948 inspects a guard of honour of old I.R.A. men, some of whom are wearing the uniform of trench coat and cloth cap*

10,000 policemen of the Royal Irish Constabulary and about 50,000 troops. Against the guerrilla tactics of the I.R.A. this force was inadequate. Police were withdrawn from the villages and concentrated in barracks, leaving the countryside to the I.R.A. and the agents of the Dail. The British forces were augmented by the Black and Tans, volunteer ex-soldiers from England whose khaki uniforms and black hats and belts were responsible for their name, and the Auxiliary Division, ex-army officers who had no profession other than war. There can be no doubt that the Black and Tans and the Auxies were responsible for numerous brutal murders during the Troubles, but it is equally certain that some of the atrocities for which they were blamed were in fact the work of the I.R.A. It is thought that the total Irish casualties were about 750 killed, while the British lost 500 police and 200 soldiers.

Lloyd George aimed at compromise, not outright victory. He had Parliament pass, in 1920, the Government of Ireland Act, which set up two Irish parliaments, one in Belfast for the six predominantly Protestant counties of Ulster and one in Dublin for the remaining twenty-six counties. Irish representatives would continue to sit at Westminster, and there would be a Council of Ireland, with members drawn from the two Irish parliaments. Ulster accepted the Act and, despite the real danger of assassination, King George V opened the Northern Ireland Parliament in Belfast in 1921. The South refused to accept the Act and the Troubles continued.

Lloyd George was advised that victory was possible in Ireland, but only if the British forces were doubled and martial law was proclaimed. As on many other occasions, he was subject to numerous pressures: many Conservatives wanted to preserve the United Kingdom at all costs, the Labour party wanted a settlement, the King was horrified by the thought of his troops shooting his Irish subjects. The I.R.A., which was also feeling the strain of two years' fighting, readily agreed to a truce in July 1921.

For the next five months Collins, Arthur Griffith, and other Irish leaders negotiated in London with Lloyd George's government. The Irish wanted an independent republic for the whole of Ireland, but Lloyd George was prepared to offer no more than Dominion status for the twenty-six counties. Southern Ireland, in other words, would have substantial independence but would retain the same ties with Britain as Canada. De Valera was opposed to these terms, but Lloyd George would go no further and when he threatened in December to renew hostilities the Irish leaders signed the Treaty. The agreement was approved by Parliament in December 1921 and by the Dail in January 1922.

There followed a tragic civil war in Ireland between the supporters and opponents of the Treaty. De Valera resigned as President and was succeeded by Arthur Griffith, who, with Collins,

*Arthur Griffith and Eamonn de Valera (right)*

**The Treaty 1921–2**

**Irish civil war 1922–3**

led the pro-Treaty faction. The war lasted until 1923, by which time Griffith was dead and Collins had been killed. Power was formally passed by the British government to the provisional government of the Irish Free State in March 1922. Henceforth, Southern Ireland would send no representatives to Westminster, but Ireland would have a Governor-General appointed by the King, and the members of the Dail would take an oath declaring that Ireland belonged to the British Commonwealth of Nations. Finally, the Royal Navy retained the right to use three Southern Irish 'treaty ports'.

The final solution was reasonable and not very different from that which might have been reached earlier by negotiation. Some Irish patriots thought that the national honour compelled them to fight for their country's freedom. Their idealism was simple and blind: it ignored the reality that a million Protestant inhabitants of Ulster were British, not Irish, patriots. The killings and destruction of the Troubles failed to achieve a united Ireland; they brought misery and fear to thousands of innocent people.

## THE EMERGENCE OF LABOUR 1922–1924

The general election which followed Lloyd George's resignation was a Conservative triumph: they won 345 seats, Labour 142, the Asquith Liberals 54, and Lloyd George's Liberals 62. This was a highly significant result, indicating the revival of the Conservative party, which had not won an election since 1900, the rise of the Labour party to second place and therefore the beginning of the modern two-party system, the confirmation of the Liberal collapse and the end of the ministerial career of Lloyd George. The new Prime Minister, Bonar Law, retained office for only five months (until May 1923), when he resigned for health reasons and was succeeded by Stanley Baldwin, who was to lead the Conservatives for the next fourteen years.

Baldwin, a solid Midland businessman, thought that Britain was importing too many foreign goods. The problem of unemployment could be solved, he believed, by raising customs duties, thus making imports more expensive and forcing people at home to buy British-made goods. If the home market was expanded in this way industrialists could be sure of selling more and would consequently take on more workers. In other words, he wanted to adopt a policy of

**Baldwin and Protection**

Protection. This measure would have achieved little, but its immediate importance was that Baldwin felt that he needed the voters' support for such a bold venture and asked for another dissolution of Parliament. Much to his surprise, his policy was rejected and his party beaten in the election of December 1923: the Conservatives won 258 seats, Labour 191, and the Liberals (united

119

again in opposition to Baldwin's Protection policy) 159.

The success of the Labour party, which increased its number of seats from 63 in 1918 to 142 in 1922 and 191 in 1923 is the most startling political fact of the early 1920s. Why did this happen? Undoubtedly, one of the main reasons was the rift in the Liberal party, torn between the Asquith and Lloyd George factions, not very harmoniously reunited in 1923 and no longer appearing to be a credible alternative to the Conservatives. Many people voted Labour in the 1920s, therefore, because they were against the Conservatives and had no confidence in the Liberals. But Labour also made a positive appeal: socialism, involving state control of the main industries and a wide-reaching system of social services, was a new idea to most British people and won many supporters in the years immediately following a war which had supposedly been fought to make the world a better place to live in. The onset of serious unemployment led thousands of working-class men and women, and a few middle-class intellectuals, to doubt the ability of the capitalists to deal with the problems of the twentieth century. Only in a few areas did the masses flock to the socialist banner, however. On Clydeside huge crowds listened attentively and enthusiastically to left-wing orators like Maxton, Kirkwood, Wheatley, and Shinwell, but elsewhere there was little more than a reticent feeling that, since the Liberals were split and the Conservatives had nothing but protective tariffs to offer, perhaps Labour should be given a chance. The Labour leaders reflected this lack of enthusiasm for socialism: although committed in principle to the ideals of their party's programme, they sought above all to be accepted as respectable statesmen. There was no British Lenin.

The political position after the 1923 election was confused: the Conservatives had lost 87 seats and Baldwin refused to remain Prime Minister, but no party had a majority. The problem was solved in January 1924 when Labour took office for the first time. The Liberals promised to support them in the House of Commons so long as they did not introduce any extreme measures. So, to the surprise of everyone, including the leaders of the Labour party, Britain had a Labour government with Ramsay MacDonald, a Scot of humble birth and compelling eloquence, as Prime Minister and Foreign Secretary. Who were these new men? They included the former engine-driver Jimmy Thomas, Sidney Webb, the Fabian intellectual, and George Lansbury, the Mayor of Poplar. One of their number, Arthur Henderson, had served as a member of Lloyd George's War Cabinet. The Cabinet contained no extremists; some ministers were not even members of the Labour party.

With no majority in the Commons, the new government faced the constant threat of overthrow if the Liberals should turn against it. In these circumstances it is not surprising that no attempt was

*Election Results 1922 and 1923*

|  | 1922 | 1923 |
|---|---|---|
| Conservative | 345 | 258 |
| Liberal |  |  |
| (L1 G) | 62 |  |
| (Asquith) | 54 | 159 |
| Labour | 142 | 191 |
| Others | 12 | 7 |

**The rise of Labour and first Labour Government**

*Working class support for Ernest Bevin who stood as a Labour candidate at the 1924 elections*

**Opposing economic ideas**

made to reorganize along socialist lines. In any case, 1924 was a year of comparative economic improvement and declining unemployment. Although there were numerous strikes, their objectives were higher wages, not resistance to reductions.

Many historians doubt whether, even with a parliamentary majority, MacDonald's government would have introduced any decisive new economic policies. Most members of the Cabinet, like everyone else at the time, took a conservative view of economic policy and followed the line indicated by Montagu Norman, the Governor of the Bank of England. Norman's answer to the depression was that taxation, and therefore government expenditure, should be kept to a minimum, so that people would have as much money as possible to spend, thereby stimulating industry and trade. But the economist J.M. Keynes argued that the government should spend money freely on large-scale public works such as major road-building schemes. This would give employment to men who could not find work in the traditional industries, with the result that they would have money to spend on food, clothes, furniture, and household goods. In this way, the demands of the road-builders etc., would give work to producers of consumer goods, who would in turn be able to buy other commodities. Keynes's novel and unorthodox ideas would have involved a high rate of taxation in order to pay for the public works, and for this reason they were rejected by the leading economists of the time and by politicians of

121

all parties, including most members of the Labour Cabinet. In the 1930s Roosevelt in the United States and Hitler in Germany successfully tackled the unemployment problem by using policies similar to those proposed by Keynes.

The one important domestic achievement of the first Labour government was Wheatley's Housing Act, which, like Addison's earlier scheme, gave the government power to offer high subsidies to local authorities for the building of houses to be let at low rents. Many thousands of these council houses were built in the years following and although often without architectural merit they helped to solve the housing problem.

**Wheatley's Housing Act 1924**

The Liberals withdrew their support in November 1924 and MacDonald's government fell. The subsequent general election became famous because of the 'Red Letter' affair. During the campaign, *The Times* published a letter supposedly from Zinoviev, the president of the Communist International, addressed to the British Communist Party, with instructions on how to prepare for a revolution in Britain. The implication that all left-wing parties, including the Labour party, were revolutionary was said at the time to have done Labour enormous harm in the election. More important, probably, were the electorate's dissatisfaction with an ineffective minority government and Baldwin's abandonment of his Protection policy. Whatever the causes, the results were decisive: the Conservatives won 419 seats, Labour 151, while the Liberals were reduced to 40. Baldwin thus became Prime Minister for the second time.

**'Red Letter' affair**

*Election Result 1924*
Conservative  419
Liberal         40
Labour         151
Others           5

*Labour leaders leave 10 Downing Street in a Morris car after the talks which brought the General Strike to an end*

### BALDWIN'S SECOND ADMINISTRATION 1924–1929

Winston Churchill, who had left the Liberal party on the fall of Lloyd George in 1922, had returned to the Conservatives and was included in Baldwin's new Cabinet as Chancellor of the Exchequer. Churchill was a man of outstanding ability in many fields, but finance was not one of them and he was apparently astonished by Baldwin's offer. His main answer to the economic crisis was to return, in 1925, to the gold standard, which meant that the foreign exchange value of the pound was firmly fixed at a high level. The move was an attempt to restore the prestige of the City of London as the world's leading banker. In this it failed, for New York had taken over London's role in international finance. The return to the gold standard had unexpected and undesirable consequences. Because the pound was now worth more, British exports cost more abroad and Britain had still greater difficulty in selling her goods in foreign markets. Naturally, one of the chief sufferers was coal, and the unemployment rate remained high in the mining industry.

Largely as a result of Churchill's mistaken policy, Britain did not share to any great extent in the economic revival which took place in Europe between 1924 and 1929. Although the years 1924 and 1925 were comparatively prosperous, the success was more marked in the newer industries located in the Midlands and the south. Three-quarters of the unemployed had worked in the old-style industries, such as coalmining, shipbuilding, and textiles.

The coal industry had done fairly well in 1924, but in the following year an increase in the production of cheap German and Polish coal caused prices to fall sharply. This coincided with Churchill's return to the gold standard. The coal-owners, trying to reduce costs, asked the miners to work longer hours for less money. The Miners' Federation resisted and appealed to the General Council of the T.U.C. for help. The owners announced that a reduction in wages would come into effect on 31 July 1925 and in retaliation, the General Council threatened a national embargo on all movements of coal. The government, which had previously refused to interfere, now gave in and offered to pay a subsidy to cover the difference between the miners' present wage and the amount the owners were willing to pay. The subsidy was to last for nine months, during which time a Royal Commission under the chairmanship of Sir Herbert Samuel would investigate the coal-mining industry. Because of this trade union victory, 31 July 1925 became known as 'Red Friday' in contrast to the Black Friday of 1921.

*J. M. Keynes, the economist whose ideas had too little influence during his lifetime*

The coal embargo, if put into effect, would have amounted to a general strike, since a suspension of coal supplies would soon have brought most industries to a halt. What would happen at the end

**Coal dispute 1925**

of the nine-month subsidy? Would the General Council bring the whole country to a standstill? The government made preparations in case a strike should come: the country was divided into regions, each under a commissioner, and plans were drawn up to maintain supplies of food and health services. At the same time, on the union side, local strike committees were organized, but there was little central planning by the T.U.C. Most members of the General Council dreaded a show-down.

The Samuel Commission reported in March 1926, proposing that the coal industry should be reorganized in the future, and that the miners' wages should be reduced immediately. Ignoring all comments on reorganization, the owners repeated their demand for longer hours and lower wages. A.J. Cook, the Miners' secretary, expressed his members' views bluntly and concisely: 'Not a penny off the pay, not a minute on the day.' Attempts by both government and General Council to reach a compromise failed and on 1 May 1926 (the day after the subsidy ended) the owners locked the miners out.

Reluctantly, the T.U.C. decided that a general strike was necessary. Its aim was to assist the miners in their contest with the coal-owners. The General Council had no weapons which could be used directly against the coal-owners, but it could, by means of a general strike, paralyze the whole nation. This, it was hoped, would force the government to take action, either to compel the coal-owners to moderate their demands, or to pay a further subsidy. What had been a struggle between the miners and the coal-owners thus became a war between the T.U.C. and the government.

The General Council began calling out other unions on 3 May. There was almost universal obedience to the strike summons: within two days there were no trains, buses, trams, or newspapers, all building work was stopped and all gas and electricity supplies were ended. On 11 May the shipyard workers and engineers were called out and they stopped work at once. Workers in the health and food services were not asked to strike. The emergency plans already mentioned were put into effect, although total confusion at T.U.C. headquarters was prevented only by the determined efforts of Bevin. Both sides published newspapers: the government's case was presented in the *British Gazette*, which was controlled by Churchill, while the unions issued the *British Worker*. The B.B.C., which had only recently come into existence, tried hard to remain impartial. There were some cases of violence, but they were rare, and the Russian observers who had come to watch what they expected to be the first stages of the British Revolution were dismayed to hear of strikers at Plymouth playing football against the police. Essential food supplies and transport services were maintained by volunteers—office workers and university students who

*The varying attitudes of the newspapers to the miners' cause*

*Below right* Miners and their
families gathering coal

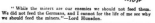

**The General Strike 1926**

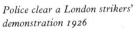

*Police clear a London strikers' demonstration 1926*

*Strikers versus police (in stripes), Plymouth 1926*

*May-Day procession in Glasgow, 1926*

generally enjoyed the break from routine.

Even though two and a half million men were on strike, the government's precautions and the activities of the volunteers prevented total breakdown. The General Council had not forced the government into immediate surrender, and its members were eager to end the strike, partly because of the drain on union funds, partly because they were afraid that extremist elements might take over and precipitate disaster. When the miners showed that they were unwilling to accept an apparently reasonable compromise suggested by Sir Herbert Samuel, the General Council decided that the strike must end. The other unions were prepared to help the miners avert total defeat, but they were not going to be bled to death in a quest for outright victory. The T.U.C. called off the strike on 12 May without securing Baldwin's acceptance of the Samuel compromise or any guarantee that strike leaders would not be victimized. The Prime Minister was thus able to speak on the radio of the unions' 'unconditional surrender'.

Baldwin and his Cabinet colleagues saw the strike as a challenge to the authority of the legally elected government and were determined to resist what they felt to be the T.U.C.'s blackmail. Some ministers, such as Churchill, wanted a fight to the finish with the unions, but Baldwin was more reasonable: he was resolute in resisting the strikers but would not allow the employers to exploit the government's victory. He said in Parliament: 'I will not countenance any attempt on the part of the employers to use this present occasion for trying in any way to get reductions in wages.'

The miners remained out until December, when, with their funds exhausted, they had to admit defeat. They accepted lower wages, longer hours, and district wage agreements, worse terms than they could have obtained in April.

Unlike the threatened general strike in 1920 over arms shipments to Poland, this had been an industrial dispute. Its purpose had been to resist a worsening of miners' working conditions and (probably) a similar deterioration in other industries. Its significance was that it showed the potential strength of the trade union movement, which could now bring the country to a standstill and challenge the authority of the government. It also showed that the general strike was a highly dangerous weapon: the General Council as well as the government drew back in alarm as Britain seemed to reach the brink of revolution. But the strike failed. The miners lost their battle. Members of the General Council such as Arthur Pugh, its president, and W.M. Citrine, were criticized for their apparent lack of courage, and the trade union movement as a whole was discredited. Trade union membership fell by half a million in the next year. Whereas after 1924 the unions seemed to offer more hope

# TO ALL WORKERS IN ALL TRADES.

## Additional Guarantees. Official.

**Every man who does his duty by the country and remains at work or returns to work during the present crisis will be protected by the State from loss of trade union benefits, superannuation allowances, or pension. His Majesty's Government will take whatever steps are necessary in Parliament or otherwise for this purpose.**

## STANLEY BALDWIN.

*Extract from the* British Gazette, *May 1926*

*A London bus, driven by a volunteer and escorted by a policeman, May 1926*

than the Labour party to the distressed and unemployed, the reverse now appeared to be the case.

**Trade Disputes Act 1927**

There was a postscript to the General Strike. In 1927 Baldwin's government had Parliament pass the Trade Disputes Act, which made general strikes and most sympathetic strikes (for example, dockers striking in sympathy with railwaymen) illegal, and imposed new restrictions on picketing. In addition, the Act weakened the financial connection between the trade unions and the Labour party. Previously, part of each member's union dues might, if the union chose, be donated to the Labour party. If a member objected to this political levy he could contract out, that is, not pay that part of his subscription. The new Act said that no one would pay the political levy unless he contracted in. In other words, individual trade unionists had to ask to be allowed to make this special contribution. The result was that fewer people paid the levy.

**Social reforms**

Apart from waging this protracted struggle with the trade unions, Baldwin's government carried out some important social reforms. The Minister of Health, Neville Chamberlain, was responsible for two of these measures. His Widows', Orphans' and Old-Age Pensions Act of 1925 established the principle of paying pensions to widows and orphans and provided that old-age pensions should be paid at the age of sixty-five. The Local Government Act of 1929 was even more far-reaching in bringing the structure of local government up to date. The Act was concerned above all with the care of the poor: it abolished the Boards of Guardians, which had administered the Poor Law since 1834, and transferred their powers to the Public Assistance Committees of county boroughs and county councils. Instead of a number of semi-independent bodies performing separate functions, the elected local councils were now responsible for a wide range of services such as education, public health, housing, police, roads, and public assistance.

*The TUC's strike newspaper,* The British Worker

Local authorities were also affected by the derating proposals made by Churchill in his 1928 budget. To stimulate industry and agriculture, rates (the taxes paid by occupiers of land to local councils) on industrial premises were reduced by three-quarters and agricultural land was entirely freed from the burden of rates. The small amount of money saved by industrialists and farmers, however, had little influence on the success or failure of their businesses. On the other hand, county councils and county boroughs suffered a serious loss of revenue, which had to be made up by the Treasury. This in turn led to closer control of local affairs by the central government.

An important political change was the passage in 1928 of an Act giving the vote to women on the same terms as men. By the Act of 1918 only women over thirty years of age could vote, but now everyone over twenty-one was enfranchised.

After the turmoil of the immediate post-war years, the international scene became much more placid in the mid and late 1920s. The treaty of peace with Turkey was revised; Germany's reparations responsibilities were satisfactorily defined, despite an acute crisis in 1923; even Soviet Russia was apparently accepted as an almost respectable newcomer. The United States continued its policy of isolation, but the states of western Europe, with the exception of Italy, had democratic governments and seemed glad to live in peace.

The Lausanne Conference of 1923 restored peace between Greece and Turkey and ended the threat of war between Turkey and Britain. The Turks recovered Constantinople and Smyrna, while Britain was promised control over the oil wells at Mosul on the frontiers of Turkey and the British mandate territory of Irak.

**Lausanne Conference 1923**

The problem of reparations continued to prevent international harmony. When the Germans fell behind in their payments in 1923 the French government sent troops into the Ruhr coalfield. This precipitated a general strike and financial chaos in Germany, where the mark quickly became worthless.

**Reparations and war debts**

A settlement was reached during MacDonald's brief first period of office. He persuaded the French and Germans to accept a reparations plan drawn up by a committee of international financial experts headed by an American, General Dawes. France's total bill was reduced, and for the next five years Germany paid regularly. A small share of German reparations came to Britain. This, plus the repayments of the wartime loan to France, allowed the British government to pay its debts to the United States.

MacDonald was an enthusiastic supporter of the League of Nations. He attended the League's Assembly in Geneva and spoke loftily of the importance of settling disputes by arbitration rather than war, about all-round disarmament, and in favour of resistance to aggression. Like most Labour politicians of the inter-war years, however, he placed too much confidence in the League without attempting to define what measures should be taken to stop aggression. He trusted men's decency and did not realize that gangster-statesmen will commit acts of aggression if they think they can succeed.

The other notable step taken by MacDonald's government was its recognition of Soviet Russia. This did not mean that he sympathized with the Communists; he merely accepted that they were effectively in control of Russia. On the other hand, he had no more success than Lloyd George in persuading the Soviet government to pay Russsia's pre-revolutionary debts.

**Recognition of Soviet Russia**

Baldwin did not share MacDonald's faith in the League of Nations. Nevertheless, the high point of international co-operation

**Locarno Treaty 1925**

in the inter-war years came in December 1925. The Locarno Treaty, negotiated for Britain by Austen Chamberlain (Neville's half-brother), was an agreement between France and Germany not to go to war, guaranteed by both Italy and Britain. In contrast to the Paris Conference, Germany was treated as an equal at Locarno; she was once more acceptable. Shortly afterwards, Germany was admitted to the League of Nations.

**Defence**

Britain's armed forces were neglected in the 1920s. Successive governments worked on an assumption that no major war need be expected within the next ten years. The Royal Navy, on which the defence of the Empire depended, was the exception. It remained equal to the American navy and kept a long lead over all other rivals. Despite the lessons of the First World War, the army was denied modern weapons: cavalry was preferred to tanks. Very little money was spent on the Royal Air Force. In a sense, this was fortunate, since when Britain rearmed in the late 1930s the Air Force had to be re-equipped almost from scratch and there was no temptation to rely on out-of-date aircraft.

*Stanley Baldwin in 1931*

*Preparations for the 1929 General
Election at the Liberal Party
Headquarters, London*

# Chapter 7
# Depression, Recovery and the Road to War 1929–1939

THE SECOND LABOUR GOVERNMENT 1929–1931

The late 1920s were a period of expansion and hope. European trade was recovering, relying heavily on American capital, and Britain shared in the improvement. More than a million men were still out of work, but unemployment was largely confined to the older industries; elsewhere there was full employment and brisk trade. There was no air of crisis or sense of emergency about the general election of 1929. Neither the Conservatives nor Labour put forward bold, adventurous proposals. Baldwin's appeal to the electorate was summed up in the phrase 'Safety first'. Lloyd George, on the other hand, advocated an extensive programme of public works (roads, houses, electricity supply, etc.), paid for out of a budget deficit. The government, in other words, would spend more than it received in tax revenue and borrow the remainder. It would use this money to create extra jobs for the unemployed. These ideas of Keynes were not generally understood by the voters or opposing politicians, and sometimes not even by the Liberal candidates who put them forward. The voters decided on a change, but rejected Lloyd George: Labour won 288 seats, the Conservatives 260, and the Liberals 59.

*Election Result 1929*
Labour 288
Conservative 260
Liberal 59
Others 8

Baldwin resigned and Ramsay MacDonald became, for the second time, head of a minority Labour government. He relied, as in 1924, on Liberal support in the Commons, and was therefore unable to carry out policies which both the Conservatives and the Liberals opposed. For the first time there was a woman, Margaret Bondfield, in the Cabinet, as Minister of Labour.

The second Labour government did attempt some reforms. The Coal Mines Act of 1930 reduced the miners' working day from eight hours to seven and a half and instituted a reorganization commission, which was to supervize the closure of inefficient pits and the amalgamation of others. Many miners were disappointed that a Labour government had not attempted to nationalize the industry. Wheatley's Act of 1924 was revived by the Housing Act of 1930, which also set in motion plans for slum clearance. J.H. Thomas, the Lord Privy Seal, was given the task of dealing with unemployment and began a modest programme of public works,

**Social reforms** but the £42 million which he spent was inadequate, and Snowden,

133

*Ramsay MacDonald 'puts the cart before the horse'*

the Chancellor of the Exchequer, would allow no more. The Chancellor of the Duchy of Lancaster, Sir Oswald Mosley, who was one of the three ministers assisting Thomas, put forward in 1930 a plan of action proposing to increase pensions, extend tariff protection of the home market, give help to British agriculture, and give the government more control over industry. When his plan was rejected by the Cabinet, Mosley resigned from the government and from the Labour party. He founded his own political party, the New party, and received some initial support from other Labour M.P.s. Mosley, however, who was an admirer of Mussolini, tragically drifted steadily towards fascism, with the result that responsible politicians abandoned him and his plans.

The Labour government's failures included its attempt to repeal the Trade Disputes Act of 1927 (prevented by the Liberals) and its Education Bill, raising the school-leaving age to fifteen (rejected by the House of Lords).

**Wall Street Crash, 1929, and depression**

International trade had flourished in the late 1920s, but a slight decline began in mid-1929. Then came the disaster known as the Wall Street Crash. During the 1920s American businessmen and many ordinary people had 'played the Wall Street market' (the New York Stock Exchange). Share prices rose continuously and it was easy to make money by buying and selling. At last people realized that the prices were absurdly high, and in October 1929 a selling panic began. Everyone wanted his money back before his shares lost their value altogether. Hundreds of investors were ruined. The story goes that the sun was obscured in Wall Street as scores of millionaires cast themselves from skyscraper windows. Americans withdrew their capital from overseas investments, and this sudden withdrawal led to a world depression.

Money does for trade what oil does for a car engine: it is a lubricant. Without oil a car engine seizes up; without a plentiful supply of money the machinery of trade operates more slowly: there are fewer transactions and prices are lower. Such were the consequences of the 1929 crash, and the worst sufferers were the primary producers. In 1933 the price of wheat stood at forty-two per cent of the 1929 level, that of copper at twenty-nine per cent. Because the primary producers were selling less, they were able to buy fewer manufactured goods. This inevitably led to unemployment in the industrial countries. In 1932 the unemployment figure reached 13·7 million in the United States, 5·6 million in Germany, and 2·7 million in Britain. Many countries introduced tariffs to protect their industries and agriculture. This further reduced the total volume of world trade and caused more unemployment.

In Britain the effects of the depression were threefold. In the first place, the balance of trade was upset. All nations must try to earn sufficient money to pay for their imports, and Britain was normally able to achieve this balance, partly by exporting coal and manufactured goods, partly by earning money through services such as shipping, banking, and insurance. In the abnormal circumstances of 1929–31 Britain continued to import food and raw materials, but could find few customers for her products. The cost of her imports exceeded the value of her exports. Secondly, the high rate of unemployment meant both that the government's revenue from taxes was reduced and that more money was being spent on unemployment benefit: the government was receiving less than it was paying out. This budget deficit alarmed the Treasury, whose officials demanded economies, and the cry for reductions in spending was taken up by the Conservatives in Parliament. Accordingly, in February 1931, Snowden appointed an Economy Committee under the chairmanship of Sir George May. Finally, there was a financial problem. International speculators in money and foreigners who sell goods to Britain can exchange any pounds they hold for gold or foreign currencies, usually dollars, at the Bank of England, which maintains a reserve fund (the gold and dollar reserve) to meet such demands. If foreigners are satisfied that pounds are worth having, they will keep them, but if they are alarmed by the state of the British economy, they will rush to exchange them for more reliable currencies or for gold. When they keep their pounds, the gold and dollar reserve will increase or, at any rate, remain static; when they sell, the reserves diminish. If the fund is exhausted, the nation has reached a state of bankruptcy: it can no longer meet its commitments. Such a calamity seemed imminent in the summer of 1931, when, following the collapse of several Austrian and German banks to which the Bank of England had made loans, foreigners holding sterling began a 'run on the pound', demanding that the Bank exchange their pounds for gold or dollars.

According to the Bank of England, a major cause of the panic selling was the foreign speculators' lack of confidence in the Labour government and, in particular, their alarm at the 'extravagant' rate of unemployment benefit which had produced a budget deficit.

Unless the Bank borrowed money, the reserves would soon be exhausted. In July 1931 it negotiated a loan of £50 million from the New York and Paris bankers. In mid-August MacDonald was told that this was spent, that a further £80 million was needed, and that the American and French bankers would provide this further loan only if they were assured of the British government's determination to deal with the crisis. In other words, the money was available only if the government would balance the budget. At the same time the May Committee reported, recommending sweeping economies, including a twenty per cent reduction in unemployment benefit. These proposals caused further alarm and more selling of sterling.

Two alternatives were open to the government in this situation. First, it could impose the economies necessary to balance the budget, raise the loan and ride out the storm. This was the traditional economic policy, the course favoured by Montagu Norman at the Bank of England, the May Committee, the Conservative opposition, the Civil Servants in the Treasury, and by MacDonald and Snowden. Secondly, it could abandon the gold standard; that is, devalue the pound. This, by making the pound less valuable, would have discouraged the selling of sterling by speculators, who would receive fewer dollars or less gold for their pounds, and, by making British exports cheaper in foreign markets, would have revived trade. The devaluation of currencies in central Europe in the early 1920s, however, had often had catastrophic consequences. In 1923, for example, the value of the German mark had disappeared altogether and the people had been forced to trade by barter. The government and the Bank, determined to avert a similar disaster in Britain, decided that the value of the pound must be preserved.

MacDonald and Snowden were prepared to balance the budget by raising taxes and imposing economies. This meant reducing the salaries of civil servants, the armed forces, teachers, and the police, and a cut in unemployment benefit. The Conservatives and Liberals were strongly in favour of the economies. Opposition came from within the Labour party. The General Council of the T.U.C., influenced by Ernest Bevin, rejected the policy of economies almost entirely, and in the Cabinet there was disagreement on the extent of the reductions. About half the members felt that a Labour government, supposedly acting on behalf of the working class, could not ask the unemployed to pay the price necessary to save the pound. A Cabinet split on 23 August convinced MacDonald that

*The National Government: Ramsey MacDonald with J. H. Thomas, followed by Stanley Baldwin and Lord Reading, and Philip Snowden (holding handrail)*

*Low had little confidence in the Governor of the Bank of England*

his government could not survive and he resigned on the following day.

Consultations took place during this crisis between the party leaders, MacDonald, Baldwin, and Sir Herbert Samuel (Lloyd George was recovering from an operation), and the King. When MacDonald reported the collapse of his government, Samuel suggested that MacDonald should become head of an all-party National Government, which would deal with the immediate problems, then dissolve itself. Baldwin and King George V approved of the idea and MacDonald agreed. The National Government took office on 24 August 1931. The Cabinet contained four Labour ministers, four Conservatives, and two Liberals.

The Conservative and Liberal parties welcomed the formation of the new government, but on 28 August the Parliamentary Labour Party, at a meeting which MacDonald did not even attend, decided to oppose it, and elected Henderson as leader in MacDonald's place. A month later, MacDonald and the handful of Labour members, including Snowden and Thomas, who followed him were expelled from the party.

THE NATIONAL GOVERNMENT 1931–1939

The National Government had been formed as a short-term measure to save the pound, but the pound was devalued within a month of its taking office.

The Labour government had fallen because the Cabinet disagreed over economies. Snowden, who remained Chancellor of the Exchequer, had no difficulty in persuading the new Cabinet to accept a series of severe cuts in the salaries of the Civil Service, the armed forces, the teachers, and the police, a ten per cent reduction in unemployment benefit, and an increase in income-tax. The economies balanced the budget, enabled the Bank to raise the £80 million foreign loan and, for a short time, halted the run on the pound. Within a few days, however, the spate of selling had re-commenced, partly as a result of a mutiny at the naval base of Invergordon in Scotland. When they heard about the intended reductions in pay, the sailors, without any violence, refused to obey orders to put to sea. Although it was a very mild and polite affair, the mutiny sparked off fears of a rebellion by the armed forces, which led to more selling of sterling. The government dealt leniently with the mutineers and moderated some of the wage cuts, but more important was the fact that the £80 million credit was now spent. Despite all the political manoeuvres of the past month and all the pledges to the contrary, the gold standard was abandoned on 21 September, and the value of the pound fell quickly from 4·86 dollars to 3·40 dollars. But it did not fall further. In fact, devaluation was successful. Because pounds were now worth less the rush to sell them subsided, and because British exports now cost less in foreign markets there was a slight improvement in trade.

Disaster had been averted, but an air of crisis still prevailed. MacDonald, Baldwin, who was now Lord President of the Council and in effect deputy Prime Minister, and almost everyone in the Conservative and Liberal parties believed that the National Govern-ment must remain in office, and this opinion won wide support in the country. Under strong pressure from the Conservatives, MacDonald reluctantly agreed to hold a general election in October. He appealed to the voters for a 'doctor's mandate' to cure the economic sickness. In other words, he did not commit himself to any particular policy, but merely asked the people to trust him. The Conservatives, most of the Liberals, and MacDonald's National Labour supporters fought on the same side in the campaign, although without a common policy, and were opposed by the remnant of the Labour party and a band of independent Liberals grouped round Lloyd George. The electorate overwhelmingly endorsed the National Government, whose supporters won 554 seats, while Labour was reduced to 52, and Lloyd George's group to 4. So pronounced was the swing in public opinion that Labour, which had won 19 seats in County Durham in 1929, could now hold only 2. Of the members of the Labour Cabinet who had not joined the National Government, all but one were defeated.

No less than 473 members of the new House of Commons were Conservatives, and although MacDonald remained Prime Minister his Cabinet was reconstituted to include 11 Conservatives out of 20. Snowden was elevated to the peerage and Neville Chamberlain took his place as Chancellor of the Exchequer. The two leading Liberals, Sir Herbert Samuel and Sir John Simon, held the offices

**Devaluation**

**General Election 1931**

*Election Result 1931*
National Government
| | |
|---|---:|
| Conservative | 473 |
| Liberal | 68 |
| National Labour | 13 |
| Independent Liberal | 4 |
| Labour | 52 |
| Others | 5 |

of Home Secretary and Foreign Secretary.

The events of August, September, and October 1931 were extraordinary. They caused passionate arguments and recriminations at the time and left a legacy of bitterness which is only now subsiding. In 1959, MacDonald's decision to collaborate with Baldwin and Samuel was described by Lord Attlee as 'the greatest political betrayal in our annals'. It was argued that MacDonald, in accepting the advice of the bankers, broke faith with the socialism of the Labour movement, and that he deliberately split the party and subjected it to a crushing electoral defeat merely in order to cling to office himself. This verdict is understandable but unfair. MacDonald may have been mistaken, he almost certainly overestimated his own importance, but his honesty and sincerity should not be questioned. He paid a high price for his faults: although he remained Prime Minister until 1935, he spent the rest of his life cut off from the party he had helped create.

**Trade policies**     Secure in its huge majority, the National Government set out to cure the country's economic ills. Only the Conservatives had any clear idea of how this was to be done. They turned again to the policy of Protection. This was an expression of faith rather than a proved formula for success. In February 1932 Neville Chamberlain introduced an Import Duties Bill, the eventual effect of which was that a quarter of Britain's imports, mainly food and raw materials, continued to enter the country duty-free, a further quarter paid between ten and twenty per cent duty, while the remainder paid higher rates. In theory, this meant that British industry would be encouraged as foreign manufacturers found it more difficult to sell their goods in Britain.

Joseph Chamberlain had tried unsuccessfully to persuade the Conservative government of 1902–5 to adopt Protection (see pages 19–20). Now, thirty years later, his son Neville had succeeded. He tried also to implement the other half of his father's programme, imperial preference or Empire Free Trade. Chamberlain and his colleagues hoped that the Dominions and colonies could be persuaded to abolish or reduce tariffs on trade between the various parts of the Empire. If this had succeeded Britain's lost foreign markets might have been replaced by colonial ones. To this end, an Imperial Conference was held in Ottawa in the summer of 1932. The plan did not work. The Commonwealth countries wanted to protect their own industries from British competition and Canada, in particular, resisted any interference with her growing trade with the United States. All that emerged from the conference was a number of agreements between individual governments. Over the next three years Britain signed trade treaties with several other states, including Argentina and the Soviet Union, promising to import an agreed quantity of their goods in return for lower tariffs on British exports. Protection and a modified form of imperial preference do not appear to have increased the total volume of trade, although there was a change in the pattern of trade, in that markets within the Empire became more important, while trade with foreign countries declined.

These policies caused the first cracks in the National Government. Ever since the mid-nineteenth century Free Trade had been one of the cardinal principles of the Liberal party, and when the government adopted Protection in 1932 its Liberal members were faced with the dilemma of resignation or the abandonment of one of their basic policies. The party split yet again. After the Ottawa conference Samuel and his supporters resigned from the government and went into opposition, while Simon's National Liberals remained loyal, becoming indistinguishable from Conservatives. Snowden resigned at the same time and over the same issue.

The government sought to overcome the budget deficit and to stimulate the economy by securing a low bank-rate. This meant that the government was able to save money by paying less interest on the National Debt. To a small extent, the low bank-rate encouraged house building, because it led building societies to charge lower rates of interest on mortgages. The low interest rates were intended to encourage investment in private businesses by making government bonds unattractive, but, like so many of the National Government's policies, this was not decisive enough and had little effect.

In the 1930s the government intervened in the affairs of all the major industries. In cotton, coalmining, and shipbuilding it encouraged schemes whereby owners' organizations bought up mills, mines, and yards and closed them. If only two hundred million tons of coal could be sold, there was no point in keeping open sufficient mines to produce two hundred and fifty million tons. This policy was to the advantage of those who remained in work, but did nothing to help the victims of the closures. Help was also given to the British Iron and Steel Federation, another owners' association, which constructed new steel plants in the Midlands and South Wales, but was refused permission to build a new steel works at Jarrow. Perhaps the most famous loan was that made to the Cunard Company for the construction of the *Queen Mary*, which was launched on Clydeside in 1936. Finally, in 1938 mining royalties (payments made to the owners of land on which mines were situated) were nationalized, although the owners were to receive compensation.

At the same time, help was given to British agriculture. A system of quotas limited imports of foodstuffs, government subsidies helped persuade British farmers to grow more barley, oats, and sugar-beet, and marketing boards were set up to maintain the price of milk,

**Economic policies**

*Steel produced*
(million tons)
| | |
|---|---|
| 1925 | 7·4 |
| 1930 | 7·3 |
| 1935 | 9·9 |
| 1940 | 13·0 |

*Coal produced*
(million tons)
| | |
|---|---|
| 1925 | 243 |
| 1930 | 244 |
| 1935 | 222 |
| 1940 | 224 |

*Raw cotton consumed*
(million lb.)
| | |
|---|---|
| 1925 | 1609 |
| 1930 | 1272 |
| 1935 | 1261 |
| 1940 | 1389 |

ARMAMENT FACTORY

HANDS WANTED

UNDERTAKER

HANDS WANTED

HANDS WANTED

Well done, sir, England is proud of you!

STATESMAN

ARMS RACKET

LOW

*Cynical, but accurate—rearmament did help solve the unemployment problem*

bacon, and potatoes. This helped the farmer, but not the unemployed miner and his family, since in most cases cheaper food could have been imported.

The government did try to help solve unemployment, but was largely unsuccessful. In 1934 the regions worst affected were designated as 'Special Areas' and £2 million set aside for their assistance, but attempts to attract new industries met with little success. By far the most effective contribution made by the government to the unemployment problem was the rearmament programme begun in 1935, which provided work and stimulated a wide range of other industries. The purpose of rearmament, of course, was not to create jobs but to prepare to meet the challenge of Hitler. It is perhaps typical that the National Government's most successful economic policy was unintentional.

Traditional economic opinion was on the side of the government, but it would be wrong to suppose that its policies went uncriticized. Sir Oswald Mosley put forward a novel plan of action in 1930; since 1929 Lloyd George and Ernest Bevin had been preaching investment in public works; Roosevelt, with his New Deal, had begun to operate such a policy in the United States in 1933; Harold Macmillan, a young Conservative M.P., expressed similar ideas in 1935; and J.M. Keynes provided the theoretical basis for the new approach with his publication of *The General Theory of Employment, Interest and Money* in 1936.

The most serious of the social problems of the 1930s was, of course, unemployment, which reached its peak early in 1933 and declined only slowly afterwards. It was concentrated in the older industries and therefore in the north of England, South Wales, and central Scotland.

**Unemployment**

It was government policy to keep the dole below the wage rates

of the lowest-paid employed workers. The cuts of 1931 reduced the benefit for a married man with two children from 30s. 0d. (£1.50) a week to 27s. 3d. (£1.36). At the same time, the average wage of coalminers was 45s. 11d. (£2.29½), and of agricultural labourers 31s. 4d. (£1.56½). Nevertheless, since the cost of living fell in the early 1930s and rose only slowly afterwards, the unemployed were better off from 1931 to 1939 than ever before. In 1931, however, a means test was introduced for those drawing uncovenanted benefit (see page 168). This hated device ensured that the dole was paid to only the neediest families. The income of the whole household was taken into account in calculating entitlement, with the result that if a son or daughter secured a job the father's dole might be stopped. This naturally sapped the self-respect of men forced to depend on their sons' and daughters' earnings. The means test condemned not only the unemployed but also their near relatives to a standard of living not far above starvation level.

The second half of the 1930s was for most people a period of economic recovery, but, for the areas of stubborn unemployment,

*Hunger marchers in Ayrshire in the 1930s, with their own version of U.A.B.*

the 'Hungry Thirties' were no myth. This was the time of the hunger marches, the most famous of which was the Jarrow March of 1936, when representatives of the town's unemployed, led by their M.P., Ellen Wilkinson, marched to London to publicize their plight. It was the time when grass grew in the shipyards and choirs of Welsh miners sang in the streets of London.

The government's unemployment policy was to mix economy and humanity. The cuts of 1931 were fully restored by 1936, and the dole kept pace with prices. Unemployment benefit and the means test, which had originally been administered by the Public Assistance Committees of local councils, were taken over in 1936 by central government bodies called Unemployment Assistance Boards, in an attempt to achieve greater uniformity, but the real problem was economic, not administrative: the number of men unemployed did not fall below the million mark before the outbreak of the Second World War.

**Housing**

Economy also influenced the government's housing policy. Subsidies to local authorities were suspended in 1932, but restored in the Housing Acts of 1933 and 1935, and in the second half of the decade council house building and slum clearance were resumed. The great building boom of the late 1930s, however, was confined to private building, which did not directly benefit the poorer sections of the community.

**Baldwin replaces MacDonald 1935**

In June 1935 MacDonald, whose health was failing, resigned as Prime Minister and was replaced by Stanley Baldwin. Although still in name National, the Cabinet was now overwhelmingly Conservative. Ramsay MacDonald, his son Malcolm, and J.H. Thomas were the only Labour ministers. The general election of

**General election 1935**

November 1935 confirmed the nation's confidence in the government: Labour secured 154 seats and the Liberals 21, but the 'coalition' won 432. Another political change took place in 1935 when George Lansbury, who had led Labour since Henderson's defeat in the 1931 election, gave way to Clement Attlee.

*Election Result 1935*
Conservative    432
Liberal          21
Labour          154
Others            9

**Abdication crisis, 1936**

Towards the end of 1936 the nation was suddenly involved in an unfortunate constitutional crisis. King George V had died in January of that year and was succeeded by his son, Edward VIII, who, as Prince of Wales, had been a popular national figure. The crisis arose because the King wished to marry a divorced American lady, Mrs. Simpson. Baldwin and his Cabinet were completely against the King marrying her and remaining on the throne and, since Edward would not change his mind, abdication was the only solution. The affair was kept from the public throughout 1936 and the news was not released until December, when the crisis had reached its height. There was a brief attempt to form a King's party, but public opinion, especially in the north of England, was against the King. Edward's brother ascended the throne as George

VI and the people quickly accepted him, his queen, and their family.

Baldwin's third ministry lasted until May 1937, when his place was taken by Neville Chamberlain, who had been a highly competent Chancellor of the Exchequer. The international tensions of the late 1930s meant that Chamberlain's attention in the next two years was focused almost entirely on foreign affairs.

When the Second World War began, the National Government had been in office for eight years. Born in financial panic, economic disorder, and political confusion, it gave the impression that there was a steady hand at the wheel. The brilliant statesmen like Churchill and Lloyd George were out of office; power was in the hands of safe, reliable, and unimaginative men, who did not solve the problems of 1931, but sat tight while the problems solved themselves.

ECONOMIC RECOVERY 1933–1939

Cotton, coal, and shipbuilding were the worst casualties of the depression. Industries concerned almost entirely with the home market, on the other hand, were never badly affected. These new industries expanded rapidly after 1933 and stimulated the economic revival which made the late 1930s, for most of the population, the most prosperous years of the inter-war period. Despite the million and a half unemployed, 1937 saw a record number of people in work and an unprecedented level of industrial production. Stable prices, rather than government policy, were responsible for this improvement. People had more money to spend on houses, cars, vacuum cleaners, wireless sets, and a wide range of other consumer goods.

**Growth of new industries**

Industries such as electricity supply, the manufacture of electrical equipment, and the motor industry expanded rapidly in the inter-war period, especially after 1933. Between 1923 and 1939 the number of men involved in the manufacture of electrical equipment increased by 160 per cent, and the number employed in the motor industry by 140 per cent. In 1939 six times as much electricity was generated as in 1920. The biggest boom in the late 1930s, however, came in building. Nearly three million private houses were built without government aid in the years after 1933.

*Hoover factory at Perivale, Middlesex; radio assembly; mass production of Morris cars*

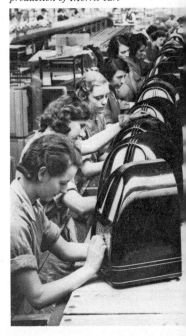

The boom was largely confined to southern England and the Midlands. Some attempts were made to introduce new industries to the rest of the country, but both investors and workers clung to the belief that the older industries would revive. Also, the decline of heavy industry between the wars was relative. The export market contracted, but the revival of the late 1930s meant, for example, that there was a strong demand from the power stations for coal. While there was an over-all increase of twenty-six per cent

in the number of workers employed in all industries between 1923 and 1939, cotton, coalmining, and shipbuilding all saw decreases of about thirty per cent in their labour forces. The mines, which had produced 267 million tons of coal in 1924, produced 222 million tons in 1935, and coal remained the country's leading industry in terms of the value of its output. But these older industries exported much less: cotton exports in 1935 were worth less than a third of those of 1924, while coal exports fell by about forty per cent between 1924 and 1938.

There was, then, in the inter-war period a definite, but not catastrophic, decline in heavy industry and a pronounced decline in traditional exports. Also, especially in the later 1930s, a notable expansion of light industry occurred, catering mainly for the home market. Foreign trade was much less important in 1939 than it had been in 1914. The balance of trade had been restored in 1935, but surpluses thereafter were small.

Following its own defeat in 1926 and the collapse of the Labour government in 1931, the trade union movement was comparatively docile in the 1930s. The total number of trade union members, which had stood at five and a quarter million in 1926, fell to under four and a half million in 1932, but rose again steadily after this, to reach six and a quarter million in 1939. The decline can be related to the failure of the General Strike and the depression, and the rise to the improved economic conditions of the late 1930s. Trade union leaders were more moderate and statesmanlike in their conduct: Bevin and Citrine dealt firmly with employers, but sought compromise solutions rather than outright victory. There were no major official strikes in the 1930s.

**Trade unions in the 1930s**

By 1939 an economic recovery had taken place: the standard of living was rising steadily, there was a plentiful supply of consumer goods, and many people lived in new houses. With bolder investment and more determined government assistance, the economic transformation might have taken place more quickly and gone further.

## BRITISH FOREIGN POLICY 1929–1939

Before Hitler's rise to power in Germany in 1933, few people in Britain doubted that they were in the middle of a long period of peace. Even the emergence of Hitler was not seen by many as a tragedy which would inevitably lead to war. Many observers thought that he would give Germany the stability, order, and prosperity which she so badly needed. Was the dictatorship of the Nazis in Germany any worse than that of the Fascists in Italy or of the Communists in Russia? Democracy was a frail plant, which had apparently failed to survive in central and eastern Europe, but no one thought that Britain should lead a crusade against foreign

Map 9 *Europe between the wars*

**Considerations influencing foreign policy**

tyrannies. A change came after 1935, when first Mussolini, then Hitler, began to reveal their aggressive intentions, and it is only from this date that one can justly speak of the 'road to war'.

Britain's leaders in the 1930s are often criticized for conducting short-sighted and misguided foreign policies. The critics, of course, have the advantage of knowing that the policies eventually failed and that a second world war broke out in 1939. They conveniently forget that MacDonald, Baldwin, and Chamberlain usually had the support of most of the British people and were honestly trying to solve peacefully a series of increasingly difficult problems. It is easy to say that in the early 1930s it was obvious that Britain would have to fight the dictators, but this is to ignore one of the fundamentals of British politics of the inter-war years: everyone, leaders and people, dreaded the thought of another war. To the horrors of trench warfare, with its machine-guns, artillery bombardment, and poison-gas, was now added the prospect of bombing from the air. Military experts seriously over-estimated the damage and casualties which aerial bombardment could cause, but the politicians cannot be blamed for believing them or for trying harder than ever to avoid war.

Several other important considerations influenced British foreign

147

policy in this decade. First, foreign policy is closely related to defence and economic policy. Britain could stand up to Hitler and Mussolini only if, in the last resort, she were able to fight them, and she could fight them only if she could afford to rearm. Between 1932 and 1935 Neville Chamberlain, the Chancellor of the Exchequer, resisted extra expenditure on the armed forces and, even after 1935, British rearmament was slow. The toothless British lion could not afford to prevent the dictators from twisting its tail. Secondly, no British government could commit its people to war, except in the defence of a vital national interest or on a major issue of principle. Many of Hitler's actions after 1933 were open breaches of the Versailles Peace Treaty, but what had seemed fit and proper treatment for Germany in 1919 appeared to many British people in the mid-1930s to be unduly harsh. Hardly anyone in Britain liked or trusted Hitler, but before resisting him the British had to be sure of their ground. Thirdly, among the population at large, and to a less extent among the politicians, there remained until about 1935 the hope that the League of Nations would make war unnecessary. Faith in the League was a substitute for national armaments. This partly explains why Britain was so slow to rearm. Finally, had Britain to carry the burden of resisting the aggressors alone? If the international affairs of the 1930s are seen in terms of cops and robbers, Japan, Germany, and Italy quickly identified themselves as robbers, while the American cop had handed in his badge in 1920. Baldwin and Chamberlain saw the Soviet Union as an enemy rather than a friend. This left France, whose numerous political crises made her a broken reed, not a pillar of support. The history of international relations in the 1930s is a tragic tale of failure, but it is difficult to see Britain's leaders as anything more than the victims of circumstance.

When Labour took office for the second time in 1929, MacDonald chose Arthur Henderson as his Foreign Secretary, although he himself continued to take a close interest in foreign affairs. Both men believed that, given trust and goodwill, all international problems could be solved by discussion and that friendly relations with most nations were possible. Accordingly, in October 1929 they resumed diplomatic relations, which had been broken off in 1927, with the Soviet Union. The London Naval Conference of 1930 extended the agreement with the United States and Japan which had been reached in the Washington Naval Treaty of 1922. The Young Plan of 1929 provided a new formula for German reparations, and by 1930 all Allied occupation forces had been withdrawn from the Rhineland. The Labour leaders' chief interest was the League of Nations, which both believed must be the foundation of peace and harmony. MacDonald impressed the League Assembly with his oratory in 1929 and Henderson earned a reputation as a states-

**Foreign policy of Second Labour Government**

man by his vigorous efforts in preparing for the League of Nations Disarmament Conference.

**Japanese invasion of Manchuria 1931**

The first serious act of aggression of the 1930s occurred in September 1931 when Japan seized the Chinese province of Manchuria. China had been in a state of intermittent civil war since before 1914 and Japan had strong commercial links with Manchuria, so there was a flimsy excuse for her action. Japan's attack was, of course, a breach of the League of Nations Covenant, and China appealed to the League in January 1932. This was the first time since the establishment of the League that a major power had been accused of aggression, and the case was therefore a test of the principle of collective security. Would the League be able to compel the aggressor, Japan, to give way? It did not even try. It sent to Manchuria a Commission of Inquiry, which found that some of Japan's grievances were justified, but that she was wrong to use force. In the face of this mild criticism, Japan resigned from the League in 1933 and later seized further Chinese territories. No one suggested that the League members should apply economic sanctions (that is, refuse to trade with Japan) and there was never the remotest chance that anyone would go to war on the side of China. Sir John Simon, the National Government's Foreign Secretary, tried to justify Britain's inactivity by saying that, although the Japanese were wrong to use force, they had at least restored law and order in Manchuria.

**Failure of Disarmament Conference**

The Disarmament Conference, which was intended to secure an all-round reduction in armaments as promised by the victors in 1919, finally met at Geneva in 1932. It soon reached deadlock. Germany, already rearmed beyond the limits set by the Treaty of Versailles, wanted equality with the French. The French, as in 1919, wanted security against Germany. There was never more than a slight hope that the Disarmament Conference would succeed; its failure became certain when Hitler was appointed German Chancellor in Janurary 1933. By October 1933 Germany had withdrawn from both the Disarmament Conference and the League of Nations.

Japanese expansion in the Far East, German rearmament, Hitler's rise to power, and the failure of the Disarmament Conference eventually persuaded the National Government that rearmament was necessary. The practice of informing the service chiefs annually that they need expect no major war within the next ten years was abandoned in 1932, but it was not until 1934 that the government began to rearm. Its aim was to create an efficient air force and to maintain the Royal Navy for the defence of the Empire. The army was neglected. Britain had no intention of providing an expeditionary force which could be used in a Continental war. Even **Rearmament** this modest and inadequate rearmament programme was opposed

*A portent of the future: Hitler reviewing Nazis in 1927*

by the Liberal and Labour parties. Winston Churchill, who was not a member of the National Government largely because he disagreed with its policies on India, was almost alone in demanding large-scale rearmament. He distrusted Hitler from the outset and argued that Britain must convince him that she could and would resist any act of aggression on his part.

Churchill had cause for alarm. The dictators made war-like noises, even if they did not yet dare to act. Hitler proclaimed the superiority of the German nation and denounced the 'inferior' Slavs and Jews. He openly demanded the revision of the Treaty of Versailles and announced that Germany needed *Lebensraum* or living-space in eastern Europe. Mussolini dreamt of a new Roman Empire and strove to turn the peace-loving Italian people into a nation of warriors: 'Better live as a lion one day than a hundred years as a sheep.'

The British public had more in common with Mussolini's sheep than his lions. They disliked what they learned about the dictators from their newspapers, radio, and cinema news-reels, but they hated the prospect of war even more. On the other hand, the mood of the nation was not pacifist: the man in the street did not prefer submission to resistance. The Oxford Union passed in 1933 the motion that 'This House will in no circumstances fight for its King and Country', but a few hundred students were hardly typical of public opinion. The Peace Ballot, organized by the League of Nations Union in 1934, the results of which were published in 1935, showed that an overwhelming majority of British people were in favour of the League of Nations and all-round disarmament. A

**Aims of Hitler and Mussolini**

**British public opinion**

150

*The Hitler Youth*

large majority thought that the League should enforce its decisions by economic sanctions if necessary, and nearly seven million of the eleven million votes cast were in favour of war as a last resort against aggressors. The public did not want peace at any price; it wanted peace and international order.

**Policy of appeasement**

Standing by the League meant, among other things, resisting any changes in the Versailles Peace Settlement, but by the mid-1930s it was widely felt that some of the Versailles terms were too harsh. The British and French governments began to think of negotiating some revision of the Treaty with Hitler, and in this they had the general approval of their peoples. Thus was born the policy of appeasement.

The 'era of appeasement' is perhaps an apt title for the years 1935–8. The last months of MacDonald's premiership, however, saw a final attempt to give collective security some real meaning. As yet, Hitler and Mussolini were mutually suspicious and Britain tried at the Stresa Conference of April 1935 to recruit the Italians to the League's side. Representatives of the British, French, and Italian governments agreed at Stresa to resist, through the League of Nations, any illegal attempts to revise the Treaties. Their declaration was a response to Hitler's admission earlier in the year that he had reintroduced conscription and his boast that the German air force already equalled Britain's. This was untrue, but it was believed at the time.

**Stresa Conference 1935**

**Anglo-German naval agreement 1935**

It is easy to see the confusion in the minds of British statesmen in 1935. Two months after they had pledged themselves to stand firm against treaty-breakers, they made a naval agreement with

Germany, allowing the Germans, despite the Treaty of Versailles, to have a naval strength equal to thirty-five per cent of the British. The appeasement of the naval agreement would presumably satisfy Hitler's ambitions and lessen the burden on the Stresa solidarity. At the same time, the expansion of the air force was speeded up and a target of 1,500 first-line aircraft by 1937 was set. The French showed how much faith they had in Stresa by making a defensive alliance with the Soviet Union in May 1935.

Mussolini's value as an ally was demonstrated when he launched his invasion of Abyssinia in October 1935. This was an act of unjustified and unprovoked aggression. There was a storm of protest in Britain and Sir Samuel Hoare, the Foreign Secretary, condemned Italy at the League of Nations. The League quickly called upon its members to employ economic sanctions against Italy: they were not to receive imports from her and to refuse to export to her commodities such as rubber, tin, and iron ore. Oil was omitted from the list of prohibited exports. The sanctions drew Mussolini closer to Hitler, but did not stop the conquest of Abyssinia. The British government was repeatedly urged to close the Suez Canal to Italian ships and to persuade the League to cut off Italy's oil supplies. Mussolini, who had hitherto been a slightly comic cartoon character in the eyes of the British public, had become a figure of scorn and contempt. But Baldwin and his Cabinet hesitated. Oil sanctions and the closure of the Canal might provoke Italy to war, and, as the French government was far from resolute, Britain would have to face Italy virtually alone. Further-

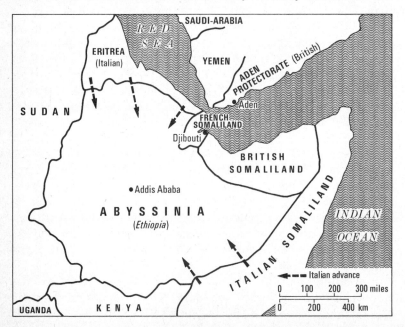

Map 10 *The Italian invasion of Abyssinia, 1935*

*Mussolini and Hitler in 1937*

**German occupation
of the Rhineland 1936**

more, the idea of detaching Mussolini from Hitler was still alive: appeasement over Abyssinia might, even now, make collective resistance to Hitler possible. With these thoughts in mind, Sir Samuel Hoare went to Paris in December 1935 and concluded with the French foreign minister, Laval, a plan whereby Italy was to take two-thirds of Abyssinia (the Hoare-Laval Pact). The British and French people received the plan with a howl of rage. It was hastily withdrawn and Hoare resigned, to be replaced by Anthony Eden. Still no decisive action was taken. By May 1936 the conquest of Abyssinia was complete, and in June the sanctions were withdrawn. Baldwin's government was, for a while, violently unpopular for giving in to Mussolini. It had backed down, however, not from cowardice but from uncertainty as to whether Mussolini would have stopped the invasion when faced with war with Britain, doubt over Britain's ability to defeat Italy, and alarm at the prospect of committing all the nation's forces in the Mediterranean when there was a growing menace on the Rhine. The question for every student of history is whether, if Britain had risked a limited war in 1935, she might have prevented a world war in 1939.

Apart from the empire of Abyssinia, the chief sufferer was the League of Nations. It was now worthless. Neville Chamberlain's comment in June 1936 may be taken as its epitaph:

The aggression was patent and flagrant, and there was hardly any country that it appeared a policy of sanctions could be exercised upon with greater chance of success than Italy. That policy has been tried out and it has failed. It failed to prevent war, it failed to stop war, it failed to save the victim of aggression.

The Italian invasion of Abyssinia made the British Labour party begin to rethink its foreign policies. George Lansbury, the party's leader since 1931 and a pacifist, had, like MacDonald and Henderson, trusted in the League of Nations and disarmament, but the anti-Italian feeling, which was especially strong in the trade unions, swept away the hope that war was obsolete, and, with it, Lansbury himself. He was succeeded as leader by Clement Attlee and henceforth the Labour party, although continuing to support the League, grudgingly assented to British rearmament.

In March 1936 the 'menace on the Rhine' crossed that river. Hitler sent troops into the demilitarized Rhineland, thus breaking the Treaties of Versailles and Locarno and defying the western powers. He could easily have been stopped by the vastly superior French army and he had assured his generals that he would withdraw at the first sign of French resistance. The French did nothing, partly because their army had no offensive plans and partly because they refused to resist Hitler without British support. Baldwin, still highly unpopular, had his eye on public opinion and the prevailing feeling in Britain was that it was no crime for the Germans to have soldiers in their own backyard. The public, and many politicians, had come to think that the demilitarization of the Rhineland was unjust; Baldwin would not run even this remote risk of war when the mood of the country was against it. The League could, and did, protest, but Hitler had learned not to fear harsh words from Geneva.

Churchill and his small group of sympathizers continued to warn that Britain was in danger of leaving herself undefended. More money was spent on the forces and, thanks to an over-estimate of the German air force, the aircraft construction programme was accelerated. Fortunately for Britain, there was more emphasis on fighters than bombers between 1937 and 1939, despite the common opinion that 'the bomber will always get through' and the view of most senior Air Force officers that Britain must build bombers to answer terror with terror. Two startling and, as it proved, crucial, technical developments belong to the mid-1930s: Mitchell's new fighter design, later known as the Spitfire, and Watson-Watt's invention of radar.

**Aircraft construction**

The Spanish Civil War, which began in 1936 and lasted until 1939, was another step down the slope of appeasement. When the rebel 'Nationalist' leader, General Franco, challenged the authority of the Spanish republican government, a bitter war began, with the army behind Franco and the trade unions with the government. Britain and France remained neutral and persuaded the governments of Germany, Italy, and the Soviet Union to agree not to send arms to either side. A Non-Intervention Committee was established in London to maintain this agreement but, despite their pledges to the Committee, Mussolini and Hitler backed Franco with men and arms and Stalin gave open support to the republic. Franco's eventual victory was another success for the dictators and an indication that the western democracies would always give in when faced with determined opposition. The war was also important for its influence on British Socialists and Communists. About two thousand Britons fought on the side of the Spanish republic. Most of them were young working men, but there was a minority of left-wing intellectuals, such as George Orwell, whose *Homage to Catalonia* is a moving record of his war experiences. The Spanish Civil War finally shook the British Left out of its pacifism and the Labour party became strongly anti-Hitler. Perhaps the most important result of the war was to give many western statesmen and military experts a false impression of the horrors of aerial bombing. The Nationalists bombed Madrid repeatedly, but the most notorious episode was the devastation of the Basque town of Guernica by the German Condor Legion. Neville Chamberlain concluded that, if war came, London would immediately become a huge

**Spanish Civil War 1936–9**

Guernica, and that casualties would have to be reckoned in hundreds of thousands. His pardonable ignorance of German air strength and of the effectiveness of bombing profoundly influenced his conduct of British foreign policy.

**Chamberlain**

Chamberlain's dealings with the dictators are usually described either as the attempts of an honest man to avoid war or as the desperate fumblings of a weakling. Both views are far too simple to be acceptable. Like many of his countrymen, he thought that some of Hitler's criticisms of the Treaty of Versailles were fair, and would have been happy to see the Treaty revised. When, in 1938 and 1939, Hitler became more aggressive and threatened to use the German army to achieve his aims, Chamberlain did not think he was bluffing. Stubborn resistance, in his opinion, would lead to a major war, for which Britain was not prepared and in which Britain's cities would be laid waste by German bombs. Perhaps Hitler might have been restrained by an alliance of great powers, but Mussolini's Abyssinian adventure demonstrated to Chamberlain that the League of Nations was valueless. France was Britain's friend and had the strongest army in Europe, but French governments were short-lived and insecure and Chamberlain doubted whether Britain could rely on her. Stalin's Russia was similarly undependable and British generals had a low opinion of the value of the Red Army. In any case, Chamberlain hated Russian Communism as much as German Nazism. It followed that the only way to approach Hitler was to try to reach peaceful settlements of what Chamberlain thought were often legitimate grievances. This could best be done by personal discussion. The British Prime Minister profoundly disliked what he knew of Hitler, but felt that if he could only meet him face to face he might begin to civilize him. At the same time, he could revive the policy of offering friendship to Italy in the hope that, even at this late stage, the dictators might be separated.

Such were the principles on which Chamberlain acted and, had he been given an accurate estimate of Germany's military strength, they would have been sound. His policies, however, had the disastrous effect of encouraging Hitler in the opinion that Britain and France would not resist him. Chamberlain's speeches and actions added weight to the opinion of Ribbentrop, Hitler's former ambassador in London, that Britain was soft and irresolute. Appeasement, far from preventing war, led the Führer to persevere.

**Resignation of Eden
1938**

Early in 1938 Chamberlain reopened negotiations with Mussolini, hoping to heal the breach in Anglo-Italian relations caused by the conquest of Abyssinia, and trying to weaken the Rome-Berlin Axis which had been formed in 1936. This led to the resignation of his Foreign Secretary, Anthony Eden, who insisted that Italian troops must be withdrawn from Spain. Chamberlain, however, was willing to sacrifice the Spanish republic and the principle of non-intervention in his pursuit of a common front against Hitler. Viscount Halifax took Eden's place at the Foreign Office and an almost meaningless Anglo-Italian agreement was reached in April 1938.

In March of the same year Hitler incorporated the Austrian republic in the German Reich. His army advanced into Austria and was met by cheering crowds. Churchill proclaimed that Europe was 'confronted with a programme of aggression, nicely calculated and timed, unfolding stage by stage', but Chamberlain offered only a mild protest, to which Hitler paid no attention.

**German annexation of Austria 1938**

Chamberlain's handling of the Czechoslovak crisis of 1938 was, according to one's view of appeasement, either a triumph of diplomacy or a disastrous surrender. The population of the new democratic state of Czechoslovakia, created in 1919, consisted of Czechs, Slovaks, Ruthenians, Hungarians, some Poles, and three and a half million Germans. The Sudetenland, in which the Germans lived, lay along the frontier of Czechoslovakia and Germany (see Map 10). The Sudeten Germans had long agitated for self-government and a pro-Nazi Sudeten party, led by Konrad Henlein and supported by Hitler, was in the forefront of the independence movement. As the map shows, Czechoslovakia was open to German attack, but she was well armed and had treaties of mutual defence with France and the Soviet Union. Britain had no special obligation to help Czechoslovakia, but was in theory bound to stand by all the Treaties of 1919.

**Sudeten problem**

Henlein and the Sudetens became more violent in the summer of 1938 and Hitler complained repeatedly of Czech 'atrocities'. Chamberlain urged the Czechoslovak government to grant concessions to the Sudetens and even sent a British mission to Prague under the leadership of Viscount Runciman. At the same time he warned the French that Britain would not fight for the present Czechoslovak frontiers.

The cauldron boiled over in September, when both Hitler and Henlein demanded the inclusion of the Sudeten territories in the Reich. Desperately trying to avoid war, Chamberlain flew three times to Germany in the second half of the month. At his first

*German troops are welcomed into the Sudetenland by Henlein's supporters, 1938*

Map 11 *Hitler's foreign policy*

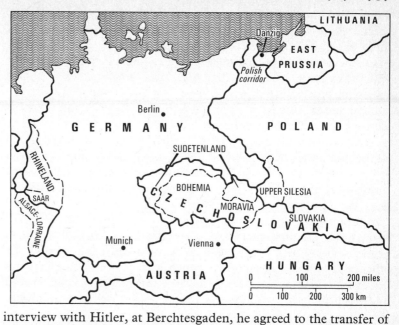

**Chamberlain's visits to Hitler**

interview with Hitler, at Berchtesgaden, he agreed to the transfer of the Sudetenland to Germany and later succeeded in winning over the British Cabinet and the French government to this appeasement policy. When, at the second meeting, at Godesberg, Hitler insisted on the immediate occupation of the Sudetenland by German troops, however, even Chamberlain resisted. Europe came very close to war. The British fleet was mobilized, schoolchildren were evacuated, gas masks were distributed, and slit trenches were dug in the London parks.

**Munich Conference 1938**

At the last moment, Hitler accepted a suggestion from Chamberlain that a meeting of the heads of the British, French, German, and Italian governments should try to find a compromise solution. On 30 September Chamberlain, Daladier, Hitler, and Mussolini met at Munich and reached an agreement which gave Hitler almost everything that he had asked for. On his return to London Chamberlain displayed a document signed by Hitler and himself which said:

We regard the agreement signed last night and the Anglo-German Naval Agreement as symbolic of the desire of our two peoples never to go to war with one another again. We are resolved that the method of consultation shall be the method adopted to deal with any other questions that may concern our two countries.

Later, he told the cheering crowds in Downing Street:

My good friends: this is the seond time in our history that there has come back from Germany to Downing Street peace with honour. I believe it is peace for our time.

The crowd cheered and sang 'O God our help in ages past'. The great majority of people in Britain were relieved and delighted that there was to be no war.

In the House of Commons most members reflected public opinion by congratulating Chamberlain enthusiastically. The few critics included Eden, Attlee, and Sir Archibald Sinclair, the Liberal leader. One member of the Cabinet, Duff Cooper, the First Lord of the Admiralty, resigned.

There can be no doubt that Chamberlain gave in to Hitler in September 1938. Was he right to do so? Against him it can be argued that he was wrong to give in to the threat of force, that he threw away the possibility of an alliance with the Soviet Union, and that Czechoslovakia would have been a valuable ally. The Czechoslovak army was large and well equipped and the strength of the fortifications on the mountainous frontier amazed the German generals when they subsequently occupied the territory. On the other side it can be said that the Sudetens were German and Czechoslovakia was not a country whose future was of vital concern to Britain. There was neither a great issue of principle nor were British interests directly threatened. *The Times* said on 15 September: 'The conviction is everywhere felt that war on this issue would be a folly and a crime.' Furthermore, the Soviet Union might not have helped Czechoslovakia and the breathing-space provided by Munich gave Britain a further chance to rearm. In the final calculation, of course, one has to set against the twenty extra squadrons of fighters which Britain produced in the year after Munich the entire Czechoslovak army and air force and the increase in German armed strength which Hitler achieved in the same period. Finally, Hitler was encouraged to pursue his aggressive policy in 1938 by Baldwin's and Chamberlain's earlier reactions to aggression and by the actions of the British Prime Minister and the opinions of the British press in 1938. It would not be unfair to say that Britain was partly responsible for the Czechoslovak crisis of 1938 or that her handling of it tempted Hitler to be even more daring in 1939. Chamberlain's motives were excellent: he wanted to save the world from war and (so he thought) to avoid the annihilation of the British population in mass bombing attacks. His military advice was over-pessimistic and his estimate of Hitler's sense of honour was over-optimistic; the result was failure.

In the tense atmosphere of September 1938, Chamberlain's government was aware that Europe was on the brink of a war for which Britain was ill-prepared. In the next year vigorous action was taken to bring the armed forces up to strength. The Royal Air Force was given priority: in September 1938 it had six squadrons of the new Spitfire and Hurricane fighters; by September 1939 it had twenty-six. The radar system, which had given protection

*The Munich Conference: Chamberlain at Munich; Chamberlain shows Londoners Hitler's written promise; while Berliners had no doubt about Hitler's triumph*

**Rearmament 1938–9**

only to the Thames Estuary in 1938, was extended, and by the outbreak of war there was a chain of radar stations from the Orkneys to the Isle of Wight. The army was also strengthened: a target of thirty-two divisions was set in February 1939, peacetime conscription (for a period of six months' service) was introduced in April, serious military conversations with France were begun, and plans for the dispatch of an expeditionary force to the continent were made. But it was the fear of bombing that was foremost in the politicians' minds. During 1939 an emergency fire-service was organized, 400,000 'Anderson shelters' (corrugated iron and earth structures which were the main feature of most back gardens in the war years) were ordered, and evacuation plans were completed. Many historians have pointed out that Chamberlain's government over-estimated the size of the German air force and wrongly assumed that the entire *Luftwaffe* would begin bombing British cities as soon as war began. On the other hand, the completion of the radar network, the extra fighters and, even more important, the modernization of the aircraft industry enabled the Royal Air Force to win the Battle of Britain.

The defence arrangements were an admission by Chamberlain that Hitler's peaceful promises at Munich might not be worth the paper they were written on. The suspicion became a certainty in March 1939 when Germany occupied the Czech provinces of Bohemia and Moravia and set up a puppet republic in Slovakia. Hitler paid no attention to Chamberlain's protest and moved on to his next objective, Poland. He demanded the return of Danzig to Germany and implied that he wanted to eliminate the Polish corridor (see Map 10). Even Chamberlain now saw that negotiation with Hitler was useless. Early in April the British government gave a guarantee to Poland and later made similar offers of support to Rumania and Greece. Mussolini, encouraged by Hitler's success, seized Albania in April and signed the 'Pact of Steel' with Hitler in May. War was not yet inevitable: Chamberlain had decided that since Hitler was not to be restrained by peaceful methods, he must be told that further aggression would lead to war. The tragedy of appeasement was that Hitler did not believe him.

Hitler's advance to the east naturally worried Stalin. The Soviet Union already had an alliance with France and it seemed for a while in 1939 that there was a prospect of a firm agreement between the British, French, and Russians to stop Hitler. But the British government had little confidence in the effectiveness or reliability of the Soviet Union as an ally. Chamberlain himself said:

> I must confess to the most profound distrust of Russia. I have no belief in her ability to maintain an effective offensive, even if she wanted to. And I distrust her motives, which seem to me to have little connection with our

**Hitler's occupation of the remainder of Czechoslovakia, March 1939**

**British guarantee to Poland**

**'Pact of Steel'**

**Soviet Union**

ideas of liberty, and to be concerned only with getting everyone else by the ears.

Slow, half-hearted negotiations went on between April and August 1939, full of mutual suspicion. There was, in any case, a serious strategic obstacle to a military alliance: neither the Polish nor the Rumanian governments wanted the Red Army on their soil. Stalin, who trusted no one, suspected that Britain and France wanted to see a war between Germany and the Soviet Union in which Nazism and Communism would destroy each other. He hated Hitler, but sought only security for the Soviet Union. Having no faith in the projected alliance with Britain and France, he instructed his foreign minister, Molotov, to hold talks with the Germans. The Non-Aggression Pact which resulted, and which was announced on 23 August, seemed to guarantee the Soviet Union against German attack. It also contained a secret clause which provided for the partition of Poland.

**Nazi-Soviet Pact, August 1939**

**German invasion of Poland and outbreak of war**

Secure in the knowledge that the Soviet Union would not resist him, Hitler was now free to attack Poland. Some historians believe that by invading Poland Hitler deliberately provoked war with Britain and France; others think that he was trying to repeat his success of 1938 and was sure that the western powers would again give way. Britain's policy, for once, was straightforward: an Anglo-Polish treaty was signed on 25 August. Hitler made a last-minute attempt to keep Britain neutral by promising to safeguard the British Empire if he were allowed a free hand in Poland, but Chamberlain stood firm. On 1 September German forces entered Poland and two days later Britain and France declared war.

Appeasement had failed. Chamberlain confessed to the House of Commons that he had set himself the task of preserving peace and that he had been defeated. There had been nothing weak or foolish about the attitude of Chamberlain and his predecessors to foreign affairs: they had tried to settle differences by discussion and conciliation, methods which had been highly successful in the 1920s. Their failure was due to the fact that Hitler and, to a less extent, Mussolini took conciliation for weakness and found that by blustering and threatening they could get their way. In the end, they had to be stopped, but by then the dictators had grown strong enough to wage a world war and almost to win. They could have been stopped earlier, but only at the risk of a war which the appeasers wanted above all to avoid. Discussion and conciliation were the methods of honourable gentlemen, which explains why MacDonald, Baldwin, and Chamberlain favoured them and why Hitler and Mussolini did not.

# Chapter 8

# Social Conditions between the Wars

'The lamps are going out all over Europe; we shall not see them lit again in our lifetime,' reflected Sir Edward Grey in 1914. He was wrong, of course. But when the lamps were relit they revealed a changed Europe. Britain was altered less than Germany, Austria, and Russia; but the war, its economic consequences, and a spate of technological developments prevented a return to Edwardian stability. Some people regretted this; most did not. For the wealthy there were losses and gains: most of them had more money, but they had to pay higher taxes; there was a shortage of domestic servants, but there were more labour-saving devices in the home; they were not accorded the same deference by their social inferiors, but they had an exciting new range of amusements and entertainments. It is even more difficult to generalize about the working class. Those who managed to stay in work throughout the twenties and thirties enjoyed a considerable improvement in their standard of living. But a very large proportion suffered from at least temporary unemployment. For them, the dole queues, the means test, and near starvation blighted these two decades. The twenties were gay for some; the thirties were hungry for others. Sir Edward Grey was thinking of Edwardian gas lamps; he did not visualize neon advertisements or traffic lights.

**Population**

Britain's population continued to grow after the war, but much more slowly than in the Victorian period. The main cause of this deceleration was a sharp fall in the birth-rate. This decline, due largely to the wider use of birth-control practices, meant that the size of the average family was much less. Families of between six and ten were common in 1900, but two was the average by the 1930s. To compensate for the lower birth-rate, the death-rate also fell as a result of improvements in medicine, hygiene, and housing and, in particular, a remarkable decline in infant mortality.

Another important population change was that the drift from south to north, which was characteristic of the Industrial Revolution, was reversed as heavy industry in the north declined and light industry in the south and Midlands expanded. Between the wars the number of people living in south-east Lancashire, Merseyside, west Yorkshire, and Tyneside hardly increased, while the west Midlands and London and the Home Counties grew rapidly. The other significant development was that fewer people lived in the

*Population* (millions)

| | 1921 | 1931 | 1941 |
|---|---|---|---|
| U.K. | 42·6 | 44·7 | 46·3 |
| S. Ireland | 4·3 | 4·2 | 4·2 |

*A miner's wife and the pawn-broker's sign, 1921*

163

centres of towns. Managers and professional people moved out to suburbs or dormitory towns like Leatherhead and Cobham, and many working-class families went to live in new council housing estates on the edges of towns.

As regards living standards, a distinction must still be made between the upper and middle classes on the one hand and the working class on the other, but there was an even more striking difference in standards between the employed and the unemployed. The economic causes of unemployment have been described in Chapters 6 and 7 and it should be clear that a working-class family's prosperity or poverty depended upon the breadwinner's job. The families of coalminers, shipbuilders, and cotton operatives experienced prolonged periods of hardship, while the dependants of workers in car factories had little cause for concern. As the worst-affected industries were concentrated in the north of England, South Wales, and central Scotland, these areas became depressed and many contemporary writers described the division between the stagnant north and the flourishing south. This explains the population drift.

There were some changes in the composition of the upper and middle classes after the First World War. At the top end of the scale, the ranks of the very wealthy were swelled by men who had made large profits out of the war, the 'hard-faced men' of whom Stanley Baldwin complained, the men to whom Lloyd George's government was suspected of selling titles and honours. Lower down the ladder, there was an increase in the number of clerical workers and professional men, a result of the expansion of individual firms and the complexity of the new industrial processes.

The chief complaint of wealthy people between the wars was the higher rate of taxation. Increased death-duties, in particular, led to the sale of many estates and a decline in the status of the landed aristocracy. Income-tax had also risen: it had stood at 1s. 2d. (6p) in the pound at the outbreak of war, but had risen to 5s. (25p) in the pound in 1918 and remained between 4s. (20p) and 5s. (25p) until 1939. It is estimated that a rich man paid eight per cent of his income in tax before the war, but over thirty per cent afterwards.

The comparative decline of the well-to-do is illustrated by the fall in the number of domestic servants. The main reason for this, however, was that men and women who would formerly have gone willingly into service now preferred to work shorter hours for higher wages in factories. Nevertheless, it is calculated that in the West End of London in the 1920s two families in every five still had at least one resident servant.

Evidence of middle-class prosperity is provided by the public school boom of the post-war years. Businessmen who had made sufficient money to qualify themselves for a higher social bracket sought to have their sons brought up as gentlemen. High fees did not deter them; there was such a demand that three new boys' public schools were founded in the 1920s. There was also a rapid expansion of private education for girls, an indication both that there was no shortage of money and that girls' education was at last being taken seriously.

Statistics of salaries and prices confirm that the middle-class standard of living rose between the wars. An average doctor in general practice would have earned about £400 a year in 1910. By 1924 his salary stood at £750, and by 1938 it had risen to £1,100. A bank clerk, at the lower end of the middle class, earned £140 in 1910, £280 in 1924, and £370 in 1938. Prices, of course, had risen, but not steadily. In the early 1920s they stood at about twice the pre-war level, but by the mid-1930s they had fallen to sixty per cent above those of 1914. Judging from the salaries of doctors and bank clerks, then, one can conclude that although professional people were no better off in the early 1920s than before the war their standard of living had risen by about seventy per cent by 1938.

**Working class**    For workers in regular employment the inter-war years saw an improvement in living standards which was not quite so marked as that of the middle class. Employees in the new industries naturally benefited most, while the conditions of miners and textile workers actually deteriorated. There was, of course, fluctuation of wage rates according to the state of trade. Wages had risen rapidly during the war and continued to rise in the post-war boom. They then fell, although not at a constant rate, between 1920 and 1932. A slow improvement ensued, and most wages had reached the 1924 level again by 1937. Earnings were appreciably higher than before the First World War, although in the mid-thirties three-quarters of all families had weekly incomes of less than four pounds. The following table gives some idea of typical weekly wages at this time.

|  | 1906–1913 | 1922–1924 | 1935–1938 |
|---|---|---|---|
| Foremen | £2 4s. 0d. | £5 4s. 0d. | £5 4s. 0d. |
| Coalface workers | £2 2s. 0d. | £3 9s. 0d. | £2 18s. 0d. |
| Fitters | £1 15s. 0d. | £3 2s. 0d. | £4 1s. 0d. |
| London bus drivers | £2 0s. 0d. | £3 13s. 0d. | £4 5s. 0d. |
| Agricultural labourers | 19s. 0d. | £1 11s. 0d. | £1 15s. 0d. |
| Women typists | £1 11s. 0d. | £3 9s. 0d. | £3 2s. 0d. |

Wage rates, of course, are meaningless unless related to the cost of living. Rises and falls in price levels during and after the war generally kept pace with wage fluctuations, with some significant exceptions. Real wages in the early 1920s were broadly comparable to those of 1910: that is, a fitter could buy the same goods with his £3. 2s. 0d. (£3.10) in 1923 as he could with his £1. 15s. 0d. (£1.75) in 1910. For coalminers and other workers in heavy industry, however, there had been a decline, and this fact helps to explain the series of strikes in the coal industry leading to the General Strike of 1926. The fall in prices up to 1932 was sharper than the fall in wages, with the result that there was a rise in living standards for employed workers. This favourable trend continued in the later 1930s, when wages rose faster than prices. Most employed workers, then, were very much better off in the late thirties than in the early twenties or before 1914. Again, miners were the exception: their £2. 18s. 0d. (£2.90) of 1935–8 would not buy the goods which could be obtained for £2. 2s. 0d. (£2.10) in 1910.

The improvement in living standards for the majority is undeniable, yet few working-class families were in a state of comfort. Abnormal expenses, such as new clothes or shoes, put a strain on the budget, which explains the popularity of clothing clubs, whose agents would collect a few coppers a week from each family and supply them with the required suits and dresses. The hire-purchase system was extended to cover such items as furniture, sewing-machines, and wireless sets.

The inter-war period also brought more leisure for the working people. By 1935 the average working week had been reduced to forty-eight hours, but perhaps more important was the increasingly common practice of firms allowing their employees a week's holiday with pay. Not many lower-paid workers, however, could afford to stay in seaside boarding-houses, and most had to be content with day trips.

It must be stressed that the improvement in the working-class standard of living between the wars was enjoyed only by those people in work. For the unemployed there was misery, idleness, and often abject poverty. The unemployed, of course, were never more than a minority, although their number did on one occasion exceed three million. There were unemployment peaks in the early 1920s and the early 1930s, and the rate of unemployment was always higher in the coalmining, shipbuilding, iron and steel and textile industries than in the motor, chemical, and electrical industries. As a result, the incidence of unemployment varied from region to region (see page 98).

For far more than the two to three million workers out of work in the early 1930s, unemployment was a threat, a nagging uncertainty. Even when he was in work, the mill-hand knew that 'bad times' might come again, bringing the prospect of weeks or months of enforced leisure. For some, the long-term unemployed, work became a faint memory. Some young men had never worked. In 1936, 205,000 men had not worked for two years; 53,000 had been unemployed for five years and more. This problem was especially acute in South Wales: formerly sturdy, robust miners

*Unemployment: this Durham miner had been 'on the dole' for nearly 15 years in 1938; Right the unemployed did not starve, but there were no luxuries; Bottom right unemployed men in the public library*

**Unemployment and poverty**

*A dole queue in 1924*

grew soft and flabby and lost their self-respect. They spent their time lounging at street corners, shuffling in the dole queues, huddling for warmth into the reading-room of the public library, or trying to dig a few lumps of usable coal from the pit-heap.

From 1921, of course, the unemployed were entitled to the dole. This in itself was an improvement on the pre-1911 situation, but the huge numbers of unemployed imposed a serious burden on the government's resources and one of the first actions of the National Government in 1931 was to reduce unemployment benefit (see pages 137–138). The prevailing principle at the time was that the money provided for the unemployed should be less than the wages of the lowest-paid workers. From 1929 to 1931, for example, agricultural labourers' wages averaged £1. 11s. 4d. (£1.56½) a week and the dole for a married man with two children was 30s. (£1.50) a week. After the economies of 1931 the same man received £1. 7s. 3d. (£1.36).

The means test, introduced at the same time as the 1931 reductions, was the main grievance of the unemployed. It took into account all the family's sources of income including wages, pensions, and savings, and if the total earnings were deemed to be adequate dole might be withheld from the unemployed members. Many people realized the meaning of the change only when they went to sign on at the Labour Exchange. The clerks' refusal to give them their accustomed pittance caused bewilderment, then resentment, then fury. There were angry demonstrations in many parts of the country, and in Birkenhead demonstrators and police fought a pitched battle for three days. Walter Greenwood, in *Love on the Dole*, a novel about unemployment in a Lancashire town, describes the experience of a typical applicant:

168

The man, grey-haired, middle-aged, a stocky fellow in corduroys, clay-muddied blucher boots and with 'yorks' strapped about his knees, exclaimed: 'What d'y' mean? Nowt for me. Ah'm out o' collar ain't Ah?'

The clerk put aside his pen and sighed, wearily: 'Doan argue wi' me,' he appealed: ''T'ain't my fault. If you want to know why, go'n see manager.'

The indignant man duly sought out the manager, who, after consulting the relevant documents, addressed him:

'You've a couple of sons living with you who are working, haven't you?'

'Aye,' the man answered: 'One's earnin' twenty-five bob an' t'other a couple o' quid, when they work a full week. An' th'eldest . . .'

'In view of this fact,' the manager interrupted: 'The Public Assistance Committee have ruled your household's aggregate income sufficient for your needs; therefore, your claim for transitional benefit is disallowed.'

The fact that the man's eldest son was about to be married was irrelevant. There was, in fact, much ill-informed resentment among the employed population at the thought of recipients of the dole marrying, or even going to the cinema.

That there was acute poverty was proved by Seebohm Rowntree, who repeated in 1935–6 his survey of the working population of York. He calculated that a married couple with three children needed an income, after paying the rent, of £2. 3s. 6d. (£2.17½) a week, and that thirty-one per cent of the working population was below this poverty line. This figure would obviously include all the unemployed. Half the working population, said Rowntree, were likely to be below the poverty line at some stage during their lives, probably in childhood and old age. There had been a thirty per cent decrease in the incidence of poverty since 1899, but there was still an appreciable section of the community which just did not get enough to eat.

After the butchery of the two wars, the unemployment of the 1920s and 1930s was the most appalling phenomenon of the first half of this century. It was not an all-consuming monster, but it was big enough to cast a shadow over most people's gaiety. Few starved, but many went hungry. Surprisingly few turned to crime. Some spent their time profitably in reading, 'improving their minds'. Most stood sullenly and dejectedly in shabby groups on the corners of streets whose shop windows were boarded up for lack of business, not talking much, slowly growing older and more hopeless.

A family's standard of living obviously depends above all on the income of the breadwinner and the cost of living. It is also affected by the kind of housing available. It was in housing that the most important social improvement of the inter-war years took place. By no means the whole population was rehoused, but local authorities did take steps to clear the worst of the slums and to provide their former occupants with new and healthy, if plain, houses.

**Housing**

Except during periods of economy, the government encouraged local councils to clear slums and to build new council houses with low rents, specifically for working-class families (see pages 106–7 and 143). This in itself was a significant change from pre-war practice and was one of the most important indications that the *laissez-faire* principle had been abandoned. Eleven thousand slum houses were demolished during the 1920s and by 1939 over a million people had been rehoused from the slums.

The council houses were built with cheap materials and their design was usually unimaginative, often ugly. They were small, normally semi-detached, with two rooms downstairs and two or three bedrooms, but they had features which were entirely novel to most of their occupants: gas and electricity, bathrooms, indoor lavatories, gardens at front and back. Some of the new residents were bewildered by such luxury and there were plenty of jokes about families who kept coal in the bath, but for the lucky minority they marked an end to overcrowding, dirt, and squalor.

Life on housing estates was different. For some the change was a mixed blessing. Families who had lived for generations in the tightly-packed city-centre streets, where there was a genuine sense of community, suddenly found themselves uprooted and deposited in new, characterless, unfriendly surroundings. Many longed for a return to the cosy intimacy of the back streets. There were other problems: there were often few shops and no cinemas on the new estates and transport to the town centre was sometimes inadequate. Some local authorities sought to avoid these difficulties by building blocks of flats on the sites of the demolished slums. But the social problems were gradually overcome and there can be no doubt that council houses contributed substantially to the improvement in

*The building boom: privately owned suburban housing*

the nation's health.

As well as the local authorities' housing programmes, there was also a boom in the building of houses for private purchase in the later 1930s (see page 143). This benefited primarily the middle-class families who could afford mortgage payments, but they moved from older houses which were in turn occupied by working-class people. As a result, there was no longer a housing shortage by the end of the thirties. For the most part, the privately owned houses followed the same semi-detached pattern as the council houses, although their rooms and gardens might be bigger, and they often had refinements such as garages, bay windows, and mock-Tudor, half-timbered fronts. They too were built either in estates, devouring the green fields at the edge of every town, or along the sides of main roads, so as to provide a view of open countryside from the back windows. This ribbon development added to traffic and transport problems.

The new building was socially useful, but only a beginning. By the mid-thirties overcrowding had been almost eliminated in England and Wales—although not in Scotland—but most working-class people still lived in old houses without baths or indoor lavatories. Not unnaturally, conditions were worse in the north than the south. George Orwell, in *The Road to Wigan Pier*, wrote:

As you walk through the industrial towns you lose yourself in labyrinths of little brick houses blackened by smoke, festering in planless chaos round miry alleys and little cindered yards where there are stinking dustbins and lines of grimy washing and half-ruinous W.C.s. The interiors of these houses are always very much the same, though the number of rooms varies between two or five. All have an almost exactly similar living room, ten or fifteen feet square, with an open kitchen range; in the larger ones there is a scullery as

171

*Slum housing in a northern town, 1936*

well, in the smaller ones the sink and copper are in the living room. At the back there is the yard, or part of a yard shared by a number of houses, just big enough for the dustbin and the W.C. Not a single one has hot water laid on.

The picture was changing between the wars, but at any time before 1939 Orwell's description was accurate and typical.

In many ways the period between 1918 and 1939 was one of bright hopes, high expectations, and modest achievements. Just as the housing policies of successive governments had provided a minority of the people with attractive new houses, but left the majority in old-fashioned, seedy dwellings, so in education their ideas were new and interesting, while their performance was halting. Ever present economic crises and the prevailing view that government spending must be kept down prevented the fulfilment of progressive programmes.

A bold beginning was H.A.L. Fisher's Education Act of 1918, which at last made full-time education compulsory for all children up to the age of fourteen, and which further suggested that all local authorities should provide day continuation schools for all school leavers between the ages of fourteen and sixteen. The idea was that

**Education**

172

education should not cease when the pupil left school, but should continue for at least two more years on a part-time, day-release basis. A few such continuation schools were set up, but government financial support was withdrawn during the 'Geddes Axe' economies of 1922 and the scheme foundered.

Since 1907 the secondary schools had been compelled to offer at least a quarter of their places free to former pupils of the elementary schools. An important improvement in the 1920s was an increase in the number of these secondary school scholarships and consequently more opportunities for children from working-class homes to pass on to higher education. It is calculated that in 1914 one elementary-school pupil in forty would win a free place in a secondary school, but that by 1929 the proportion had become one in thirteen. Even so, an intelligent boy or girl from a poor home was often prevented from taking advantage of a scholarship because parents could not afford the secondary-school uniform and textbooks, and because the child would be expected to leave school as soon as possible to earn a wage.

An important landmark in the history of English education was the publication in 1926 of the Hadow Report. An advisory committee of the Board of Education, under the chairmanship of Sir Henry Hadow, recommended that in future elementary education for all pupils should cease at the age of eleven. There should then follow a variety of courses in different types of school according to the abilities and aptitudes of the pupils: secondary schools, junior technical schools, or central (modern) schools. Hadow also proposed that the school-leaving age be raised to fifteen. Although reorganization was seriously impeded by lack of money, some progress was made and central or modern schools (the predecessors of secondary modern schools) were built by many authorities. The Labour government of 1929 to 1931 tried unsuccessfully to implement the other main point in the Hadow Report, the raising of the school-leaving age to fifteen. The National Government which followed finally decided in favour of this step and planned to make the change in September 1939; but the outbreak of the Second World War caused a further eight years' delay.

The number of university places also increased and a new university was founded at Reading, while university colleges were established at Swansea, Leicester, and Hull. By the mid-1920s there were about 30,000 university students in England and a further 3,000 in Wales. The fact that Scotland, with a much smaller population than England, had 10,000 students was an indication that educational opportunities were still much brighter north of the border. The most important development was the introduction in 1920 of state scholarships, which allowed students from poor homes to attend universities. Although on a modest scale at first and subject, like everything else, to curtailment in times of financial crisis, the scheme was supplemented by grants from local authorities and helped to reduce the inequalities of the education system. It is necessary, however, to maintain a sense of proportion: out of every thousand children who began their education in elementary schools only four eventually went to universities.

Half of the population needed no help to carry out a social revolution. The suffragettes had been a minority of campaigners for women's rights before the war. They had fought gallantly, often ferociously, but unsuccessfully, to breach the ramparts of male privilege. During and after the war these defences tumbled down of their own accord and, if women still failed to achieve equality in all respects, at least the principle of man's natural superiority was destroyed forever.

The suffragettes' immediate aim had been votes for women. In recognition of the splendid contribution which women had made to the war effort, this was granted by the Parliamentary Reform Act of 1918, although only women over the age of thirty who were householders or the wives of householders were given the vote, whereas all men over twenty-one were enfranchised. Women had to wait until 1928 for full equality of voting rights. The same Act of 1918 allowed women to be elected to the House of Commons. Only one woman was returned in the 1918 election, however. This was Countess Markiewicz, who, as a Sinn Feiner, one of the Dublin rebels of 1916, refused to take her seat at Westminster. The first woman to sit in the House of Commons was Lady Astor, who was returned at a by-election in 1919. She was joined by two other women in 1921, but there were never more than twenty women M.P.s in the inter-war years. This was mainly a result of the political parties' reluctance to select women as candidates. The only woman to hold Cabinet office before 1945 was Margaret Bondfield, who was Minister of Labour from 1929 to 1931.

The entry of women into politics was only a symptom of a bigger change. The role and status of women were changing. Married women, freed from the drudgery of large families, usually enjoyed a much higher standard of living: they could make their homes more comfortable, dress more fashionably, and take advantage of a new range of labour-saving devices in the home. Few of them went out to work, partly because of the shortage of jobs and partly because the married woman's place was still thought to be in the home.

The change was perhaps greatest for unmarried women and girls from working-class homes. Before the war they had gone into domestic service or the sweated trades, such as millinery or laundry work, as soon as they left school. Now there were far more attractive opportunities: they worked in shops or offices or took jobs as

**Western Electric**
Modernised
Housekeeping

**Status of women**

unskilled or semi-skilled workers in the new light industrial factories. Girls had always worked in the Lancashire cotton mills, but as a result of the First World War factory work for women became commonplace throughout Britain.

For a minority of intelligent 'career girls' there was the chance of university education and entry into the professions. The newer universities gave women students equal rights to men and Oxford followed suit in 1919. Women were admitted to Cambridge on slightly less favourable terms in 1921. Teaching and nursing, of course, were the traditional vocations of women, and a few lady doctors had qualified before the war. Now most professions opened their doors to women, although they were still excluded from the Church and the Stock Exchange. They seldom reached the top ranks, however: the first woman barrister qualified in 1921, but there were no women judges; there were very few women university professors, and no directors of large companies. In the professions, as in business and industry, women were paid less than men, and the next stage in the campaign for women's rights was the attempt to secure equal pay for equal work.

Married or unmarried, 'career girl' or shop assistant, the young woman of the 1920s was much freer, much more self-confident than her Victorian or Edwardian predecessor. The term 'flappers' was applied, somewhat disparagingly, to this new breed of young women, who wore their hair and skirts short, smoked in public, went out without chaperones, and rode on the pillions or 'flapper-brackets' of their boy-friends' motor cycles. The older generation, brought up under a stricter code, deplored their careless, empty-headed gaiety and, in 1928, wondered what would happen when the 'flappers' got the vote.

Critics of the 'flappers' were appalled more by their clothes than their behaviour. Certainly women's fashions are a good illustration of their new-found freedom. Skirts which did not quite reach the ground first appeared during the war as a means of saving material and caused little comment at the time. In the early 1920s dresses

**Fashion**

*'Flappers'*

remained fairly long, but their most striking feature was their
tubular shape which concealed all the curves. This and the bobbed
or shingled short hair-styles were in complete contrast to Edwardian
convention. The mid-twenties, the age of the Charleston, was the
time of really short, knee-length skirts, but by the early thirties
longer skirts and feminine curves had come into vogue again. Hair
had remained short in the mid-twenties with the Eton crop, but by
the thirties it was being worn longer, curled at the back and waved
on top. The greatest change in women's clothes was the increased
use of new materials, such as rayon. Clothes were not only lighter
and more colourful, but also cheaper. As dress factories copied the
latest Paris fashions it at last became possible to mistake a housewife
for a duchess.

Men's fashions usually change more slowly than women's and
to a great extent it remained true that a man's clothes were a clear
guide to his social class and even occupation. Dark suit, rolled
umbrella, and bowler hat were as much the uniform of the City
businessman as overalls and greasy cloth cap were of the shipyard
worker. There were a few changes: lighter-coloured suits might be
worn by car salesmen or commercial travellers, many men took to
wearing soft felt hats (few went hatless), and a minority wore
coloured shirts with soft, attached collars. The only entirely novel
men's garments to appear between the wars were the wide-
bottomed grey flannel trousers, popularly known as Oxford bags.

Since early Victorian times men's dress had been conservative and until the 1960s it remained so. Apart from the unemployed, the mass of the population was better dressed between the wars than ever before. This was due partly to the new cheap materials, but also partly to the fact that most people, especially by the mid-thirties, had more money to spend.

**Newspapers**    As a result of having more money, people could afford a few little luxuries, such as daily newspapers. Serious, 'quality' newspapers like *The Times*, the *Daily Telegraph*, the *Morning Post*, and the *Manchester Guardian* had always been read by the educated minority, while the Harmsworth brothers had opened up the mass-circulation field at the turn of the century (see Chapter 3), but the boom in the sales of popular dailies did not come until the 1930s.

Lord Northcliffe, the creator of the *Daily Mail* and the owner, since 1908, of *The Times*, died in 1922. His interest in *The Times* passed to J.J. Astor and John Walter, who appointed Wickham Steed as editor. Under Steed *The Times* retained its traditional character: the first three and last three pages consisted entirely of small advertisements and it concentrated mainly on political news and comment in closely-printed columns with small headlines and very few photographs.

Northcliffe's popular newspaper, the *Daily Mail*, was taken over by his brother, Lord Rothermere, who shared his views and enthusiasm, but lacked his business flair. The main competitors were the Liberal *Daily News* and *Daily Chronicle*, the Conservative *Daily Express*, which had recently been acquired by the Canadian Lord Beaverbrook, and the Labour *Daily Herald*. Rothermere's was the most successful of these journals in the 1920s, but only in the mid-1930s did they make massive increases in readership. Their styles were similar: they reported political events, but also gave prominence to stories of crimes, railway crashes, shipwrecks, and similar disasters. They paid more attention to sport than *The Times* and its rivals, appealed to the snobbery of their readers by featuring articles on Mayfair society, and ran stunts, such as offering prizes for aeroplane flights. In appearance, however, they were still far removed from the American yellow press: the day of the banner headline had not yet dawned in Fleet Street. Nevertheless, their aim was to sell and they knew what their public needed. Their sentences were short. They used no difficult words. The news was pre-digested.

A substantial, and soon the most important, part of each popular newspaper's income was advertising revenue. Firms naturally were readiest to advertise in the newspapers with the biggest circulations. Hence the 'circulation war' of the 1930s, in which the popular dailies feverishly competed for new readers, each striving to reach the magical figure of two million daily sales. The competitors were the *Daily Mail*, the *Daily Express*, the *Daily Herald*, and the *News Chronicle*, an amalgamation of the *Daily News* and the *Daily Chronicle*. They began with prize competitions and went on to offer free life insurance to each new reader, then to bribe the public with gifts of kettles, handbags, cameras, encyclopaedias, and complete sets of the works of Dickens. A bewildered public was bombarded with the 'press barons' ' bounty; by changing regularly from one newspaper to another a family could accumulate an impressive hoard of more or less useless paraphernalia. The race to the two million mark was won by the *Daily Express*, which then admitted that each new reader was costing it 8*s.* 3*d.* (41p). The war was brought to an end by mutual agreement, much to the relief of the owners and their unfortunate door-to-door canvassers, and to the regret of the gift-receiving public.

Newspapers were almost the only means of mass communication before the First World War. They were supplemented in the 1920s by the development of radio broadcasting. The wireless, as everyone called it, was not a new invention: it had been used in 1912 to summon help to the scene of the *Titanic* disaster and had been employed extensively by the Royal Navy during the war. The Marconi Company's first experimental broadcasts of entertainment programmes in 1919, however, were a novelty in Britain. The public was intrigued and enthralled, not so much by the quality of the programmes as by the apparent magic of picking up sounds out of thin air. Most receivers were home-made crystal sets, assembled from ready-made parts bought for a few shillings. Many a family sat in awed silence as Father, adorned with headphones, minutely adjusted the cat's-whisker. The sudden movement of a newspaper would disturb the delicate mechanism and earn the guilty party a harsh rebuke. The smile of triumph on the listener's face when he was at last successful was slight recompense, for only he was able to listen in. It was some years before mass-produced sets with valves and loudspeakers were plentiful.

The popularity of wireless broadcasting and the prevailing confusion in the United States, where numerous commercially-sponsored stations competed with each other, led the government to grant a monopoly to the British Broadcasting Company in 1922. This became a public corporation, the British Broadcasting Corporation, in 1926. Its revenue came from licence fees and its governors were appointed by the government, but great care was taken that it should never become the mere mouthpiece of the ruling party. The B.B.C. set up a string of transmitting stations and by 1927 the country was divided into five regions, each putting out the two programmes, the Regional and the National. The Corporation was under the direction of John Reith, a high-principled Scot, who declared his belief that broadcasting 'should

**The B.B.C.**

bring into the greatest possible number of homes . . . all that is best in every department of human knowledge, endeavour and achievement'. The first headquarters of the B.B.C. was at Savoy Hill in the Strand. It broadcast mainly news bulletins and concerts, but for most of its listeners the chief thrill was still to hear the introductory '2 L.O. calling!'

By modern standards the early B.B.C. programmes were dull. Reith saw himself as an educator rather than an entertainer. In this he was highly successful and, as the quality of reception improved, the B.B.C.'s coverage of serious music reached a very high standard. Talks and plays completed the diet, but neither were allowed to be controversial. George Bernard Shaw on one occasion refused to give a wireless talk because he would not obey the instruction not to be provocative.

By the mid-1930s the sombre tone was beginning to lighten in response to listeners' demands. Dance music was provided by the bands of Jack Payne and Henry Hall and the Saturday night *Music Hall* soon had a large following, but by far the most popular programme was *Band Wagon*, a light variety programme broadcast every Wednesday evening. Clubs and societies could no longer arrange to meet on Wednesdays—everyone stayed at home to listen to *Band Wagon*. By 1939, when nine out of ten homes had a wireless set, broadcasting had profoundly changed leisure habits. People did not sit huddled round the set every night, but when the B.B.C. succeeded in capturing the nation's imagination it could stop the traffic and empty the streets.

There were two other significant B.B.C. innovations. Broadcasts to schools were quickly welcomed by teachers as a useful supplement to ordinary lessons and were being used regularly by 11,000 schools in 1939. Secondly, King George V began a series of regular Christmas broadcasts in 1932. Besides bringing King and people closer together, these fireside talks had the effect of inducing a cosy, family spirit in the nation and the Empire, at Christmas at least.

When our own age takes so much for granted it is hard to realize how miraculous the wireless seemed in the twenties and thirties. The chimes of Big Ben were heard by a crofter in the Hebrides before they reached a pedestrian in Whitehall; the news of the King's death was flashed in seconds to every part of the Empire in 1936; supporters who had been unable to get Cup Final tickets could listen to a running commentary; most of the nation waited eagerly every Sunday evening for the next instalment of *The Count of Monte Cristo* or *The Cloister and the Hearth*. Television was in its infancy: a service began in 1936, but never extended beyond the London area and had to be abandoned at the outbreak of war. Surely one miracle was enough for the inter-war generation!

The change-over from horse transport to motor vehicles was

*Dame Nellie Melba broadcasting from the Marconi works in Chelmsford in 1920, two years before the foundation of the BBC*

another feature of this period. But it was much more gradual than the broadcasting revolution, mainly because of the difference in cost. There was no broadcasting service in 1918, yet nearly every household had a wireless set in 1939. There had been motor cars, buses, lorries, and electric trams on the roads since the turn of the century, but the era of horse-drawn vehicles had not entirely passed when the Second World War broke out. The reason for the difference is obvious: cheap mass-produced wireless sets quickly became available, while only a wealthy minority could afford to run cars. Everyone was affected by the growth in the volume of motor traffic, however; town-dwellers in particular had to cope with a new menace to their personal safety.

The number of private cars on Britain's roads in 1920 was 200,000. By 1930 it had passed the million mark, and in 1939 it reached two million. Motor cycles and commercial goods vehicles swelled the totals. The number of horse-drawn vehicles, in contrast, fell from 233,000 in 1922 to 52,000 in 1930 and continued to decline thereafter.

Before the First World War motor cars had been rich men's toys. A large number of firms, each employing a handful of highly skilled engineers and coach-builders, had produced vehicles which were expensive, beautifully finished, and often mechanically unreliable. The early 1920s saw the intrusion into the British market of the first mass-produced car, the American Model T Ford. Henry Ford's assembly-line process reduced the need for skilled labour, accelerated production, and brought down costs. Many people laughed at his 'Tin Lizzies', which were all exactly the same, like boxes on wheels. Ford himself commented that Model Ts were available in 'any colour, so long as it's black'. As well as being cheap, the 'Tin Lizzies' were also reliable, and soon they were being assembled in Britain from parts shipped over from the United States and Canada. The British manufacturers had to copy Ford or go out of business. In 1923–4 Morris and Austin both went over to mass-production methods, and in 1924 appeared the Austin Seven and the Morris Minor. They were small family cars costing well under £200 and therefore within the price range of many middle-class families. It was Ford's initiative and the retaliation of his British competitors which caused the explosion in car sales in the 1920s and created the traffic problem of the 1930s. Mass production, of course, was possible only in big factories and the new techniques forced many of the smaller companies out of existence. Others joined together in amalgamations such as the Rootes Group, which comprised the Humber, Hillman, and Commer companies.

The commonest form of public transport in the towns was the electric tram-car, which was only gradually replaced by the motor

**Motor vehicles**

*Motor vehicles produced in Britain—cars, motor cycles, buses, lorries* (thousands)

| | |
|---|---|
| 1925 | 1523 |
| 1930 | 2208 |
| 1935 | 2261 |
| 1940 | 2332 |

*A Model T Ford*

bus and, in some places, by the trolley-bus. The development of the motor bus was particularly helpful for people living in country areas. Previously they had relied on branch railways and villagers remote from railway stations had been very isolated. Now they were able to travel much more easily and frequently to neighbouring towns for shopping and entertainment. Their children could be sent by bus to school in the towns, and it became possible to close many old, small, and inefficient country schools. Furthermore, the motor coach and its predecessor, the charabanc, revolutionized working-class holiday habits. Working-men's clubs, Sunday schools, or merely groups of neighbours clubbed together and chartered charabancs or coaches for day trips to the seaside or into the country. Everyone enjoyed the friendly atmosphere, the sing-song and fish and chips on the return journey, the occasional stop for refreshment *en route*; they even tolerated with good humour the not infrequent breakdowns. Day trips were cheap: all but the unemployed could afford them.

The original charabancs were uncomfortable and notoriously unreliable. They resembled large open motor cars and had rows of bench seats behind the driver, with a door at the end of each bench. By the 1930s they were being superseded by motor coaches, whose standard of performance and comfort often astonished their passengers.

Britain's roads were not immediately improved to cope with the

*A charabanc trip in 1913*

# VACANCIES
## FROM NOW UNTIL
## OCTOBER AT
# BUTLIN'S

### SKEGNESS HOLIDAY CAMP

*A GOOD TIME—WET OR FINE!*

Everything in full swing, including—
organised Sports, Cabarets, Dancing,
Orchestra, etc.

*FOUR GOOD MEALS A DAY*

# £2.12.6 PER WEEK PER PERSON

**(ABSOLUTELY INCLUSIVE)**

WRITE NOW FOR BOOKLET
AND APPLICATION FORM

C O U P O N

Please send me a
copy of the FREE
ILLUSTRATED
BUTLIN Booklet

To MR & MRS S. COOKSON
8 LYNGROVE COURT MOOR PARK

BUTLIN'S HOLIDAY CAMP, Dept. D.E.A., SKEGNESS, Lincs.

*Advertisement for Butlin's holiday
camp, 1936*

**Traffic problems**

extra volume of motor transport. Country roads were often narrow and badly surfaced and in many cases were enclosed between high hedges, which made every corner a major hazard. There were bottle-necks in villages, whose inhabitants, human and animal, did not take kindly to invasion by noisy, fast-moving motors. In some places there was open warfare between motorists and villagers: the latter encouraged their children to throw stones at passing cars and to line the roads with glass and tin tacks. Until 1930 there was a general speed limit of twenty miles per hour on all roads, but this was naturally ignored by most motorists. The police set up speed traps and in a few areas the local magistrates became notorious for the severity of the sentences which they imposed on offenders.

In the towns the situation was far worse. The press and government expressed concern at the number of road casualties: 7,000 people were killed on the roads in 1934 and 100,000 were injured. These figures are roughly the same as those for the mid-1960s, when there were six times as many cars. Reasons for the high accident rate are not hard to find: speed limits varied from one town to another, there was no standard procedure at cross-roads and, worst of all, there was no driving test—anyone over the age of seventeen could obtain a licence to drive. In 1934 the Minister of Transport, Mr. Leslie Hore-Belisha, took a number of decisive steps, which were resented by motorists but which had the desired effect. New road signs, such as 'Roundabout', 'Major Road Ahead' and 'One Way Street' were brought in; a thirty-miles-per-hour speed limit was enforced in all built-up areas; pedestrian crossings, marked by metal studs and orange beacons, called Belisha beacons after the Minister, were established; all new drivers were compelled to take a driving test. Even though many motorists were reluctant to obey the new rules, the death rate fell and never again exceeded 6,500 a year before 1939, despite the continuous increase in the volume of traffic.

**Railways**

Motor vehicles took trade from the railways which experienced the beginnings of a decline in the inter-war years. This was not at first appreciated by the railway companies, which had been grouped into four great amalgamations (London and North Eastern, London, Midland and Scottish, Great Western, and Southern) in 1921. With the exception of the Southern Railway, which electrified some of its main lines, the companies continued to depend upon steam locomotives and some of the designs, such as the L.N.E.R.'s Pacific class and the G.W.R.'s Castle and King classes, were highly successful. Express services provided the companies with small profits, but local branch lines were a liability and some of them were closed in the 1930s. The inadequate state of the main roads meant that trains were still unchallenged on long journeys, but bus services were cutting deeply into the railways' local trade.

Air transport did not present a serious challenge to either the railways or the steam ship companies at any time between the wars. Flying was still generally regarded as a sport; aviators, as they were still called, were foolhardy young men and women who risked sudden death in competing for huge newspaper prizes. Operating independently or backed by small business syndicates, the pilots vied for the honour of achieving aerial firsts: the first flight across the Atlantic, the first flight to Australia, etc. In their rickety machines, these daredevil pioneers faced the elements on equal terms and were deservedly welcomed as national heroes if they arrived safely.

Within six months of the end of the war the Atlantic was flown. Two young British officers, Captain John Alcock and Lieutenant Arthur Whitten-Brown, flew from Newfoundland to Western Ireland in a Vickers-Vimy biplane in June 1919. Their flight of 1,880 miles took just under sixteen hours and ended in a crash-landing near Clifden. They received tremendous public acclaim, obtained a *Daily Mail* prize of £10,000 and were knighted by King George V. Even more celebrated was the solo flight from New York to Paris of the young American, Charles Lindbergh, in 1927. Ross and Smith flew from England to Australia in twenty-eight days in 1919, and two young Australians, M'Intosh and Parer, made a similar flight in the following year. The latter pair had a series of hair-raising adventures: having made a forced landing in the Arabian desert, one tinkered with the engine while the other used his revolver to frighten off the Bedouin tribesmen. Alfred Cobban's achievement in flying to Cape Town and back in May 1926 and to Australia and back in October was technically superior but not so dramatic. Amy Johnson, the first woman to fly solo to Australia, also received £10,000 from the *Daily Mail* and for a time received the kind of publicity normally reserved for film stars.

The courage and skill of the aviators was undeniable. The practical value of their flights seemed slight. Some people thought that only airships would be capable of transporting large numbers of people by air over long distances. A British hydrogen-filled airship, the R.34, did make the east-west Atlantic crossing in 1919, but it took 108 hours and North Atlantic weather conditions obviously made the journey unsafe. Experiments with lighter-than-air machines continued, however, until 1930, when the R.101, *en route* from England to India, crashed with appalling loss of life in northern France.

Regular passenger-carrying aeroplane services were slowly established. The first commercial flights between London and Paris were made in 1919 and by the mid-twenties Imperial Airways was carrying passengers from London to Paris, Cologne, and Zurich. Ten years later one could fly to India, Singapore, and Australia,

*The Charleston*

although the Atlantic had not yet been mastered. Flying therefore lagged a generation behind motoring: the motorists of the inter-war years benefited from the achievements of the pre-war pioneers, while the full commercial exploitation of flying had to wait until after the Second World War.

**Dancing**

The aviators were more enterprising than the rest of their generation. After the First World War most young people were intent only on enjoying themselves. The 'flappers' and the 'bright young things' of Evelyn Waugh's novels are good examples of this carefree spirit. One of the most popular activities among the young was the hectic dancing which accompanied the new musical craze, American jazz. Dances such as the tango, the one-step, and the foxtrot were quickly replaced in popular favour by the wilder shimmy, Charleston, and black bottom. The kill-joys, who disapprove of everything new, especially if it is popular among the young, had to carp, of course. One clergyman wrote: 'If these up-to-date dances, described as "the latest craze", are within a hundred miles of all I hear about them, I should say that the morals of a pig-sty would be respectable in comparison.' The Charleston and the black bottom soon fell out of favour, perhaps because they were too energetic, and were superseded by the revived foxtrot and one-step.

By the 1930s swing was the most favoured form of dance music and, as a result of the film successes of Bing Crosby, every swing band had to have its crooner. Whereas in the early twenties dancing had been most popular among the wealthy and leisured young people, it was now the regular Saturday evening pursuit of most of the nation's youth. Lavish new dance-halls were built in working-class areas. Each one was officially called a 'Palais de Danse', but was soon known as 'the Pally'.

Dancing was mainly for the young. The other great popular entertainment, the cinema, was for everyone. The early films of the pre-war days had been short and jerky, but technical developments during and after the war made feature films possible. Admission prices were low and in the early post-war years the whole nation was able to take advantage of a new form of recreation. In the early 1920s almost half Britain's population went to the pictures at least once a week. There were 94 cinemas in London in 1911, and 266 by 1921. Performances normally began at eight o'clock, but it was common to see a queue beginning to form at six o'clock.

**The cinema**

The films were all silent and nearly all American. Most of them were sentimental and many were almost childish. The stories were all too obviously written by Hollywood hacks, taking advantage of an uncritical audience. The dashing hero and the demure, wide-eyed heroine would fall in love, but the heroine was usually carried off by a scheming villain, who would subject her to the indignity of

185

being tied to a railway track in the path of an express train. 'In the nick of time', as the captions ran, she would be rescued by her sweetheart, who had overcome all manner of obstacles to reach her. The villain normally met his just deserts, often after another breath-taking chase. But the silent film was more than cheap entertainment; it was a new art form. The studios of the 1920s produced a great deal of rubbish, and a few masterpieces. The audiences absorbed them all. They flocked to the 'picture palaces' to see their idols, the film stars. Actresses like Mary Pickford, Gloria Swanson, and Greta Garbo attracted the male customers, while the handsome young Italian, Rudolf Valentino, star of *The Sheikh* and *Son of the Sheikh*, was the hero of the women picture-goers of all nations. An icy chill gripped many a fluttering heart when the news of Valentino's premature death was announced.

Even more popular than the romantic heroes and heroines were the comedians. Fatty Arbuckle, Harold Lloyd, and the unsmiling, brilliantly acrobatic Buster Keaton were surely among the greatest clowns of all time. In a class of his own was Charlie Chaplin, a touchingly sentimental actor as well as an inspired comic, who conveyed an enormous range of emotions with a shrug of the shoulders or the raising of an eyebrow. Chaplin's *The Kid* and *The Gold Rush* were probably the most popular films of the 1920s.

The essence of the silent film's plot was revealed in the captions which were flashed onto the screen at regular intervals: 'Came the dawn', 'Spare my child!', etc. The audiences were kept in the right mood by the pianist who accompanied the films. Better-class cinemas had full orchestras and, by the end of the twenties, some of them had expensive but unmusical electric organs.

At the end of the 1920s came a major breakthrough. Al Jolson's *The Singing Fool*, shown in Britain in 1929, was the first talking picture. Silent films, apart from Chaplin's, were dead. The advent of the 'talkies', of course, brought problems: cinemas had to be wired for sound and, more serious, the film producers had to find actors who could speak—most of the silent stars had very poor speaking voices. New techniques of film-making had to be learned also, and the early 1930s saw very few films of any real merit. A further result of the coming of 'talkies' was the dismissal of cinema pianists and orchestras. At a time of rampant unemployment these unfortunate performers had great difficulty in getting new jobs.

During the middle and later thirties the British film industry began to achieve some success. British film-makers in the early 1920s failed through lack of money and talent. A law passed in 1927 had obliged cinema owners to exhibit a quota of British made films, but this was widely evaded. In 1935, however, the Hungarian-born director, Alexander Korda, made a highly successful film in England, *The Private Life of Henry VIII*, in which Charles Laughton played

*The 'silver screen' of the twenties and thirties:* clockwise *Fatty Arbuckle; Greta Garbo; Rudolph Valentino; Buster Keaton; still from* The Skeleton Dance, *Walt Disney's first feature cartoon; poster for Al Jolson's* The Jazz Singer, *the first talking film; and still of Charles Laughton in* The Private Life of Henry VIII.

RUDOLPH
Valentino
again a
Sheik

WARNER BROS. SUPREME TRIUMPH
AL JOLSON
IN
"The JAZZ SINGER"

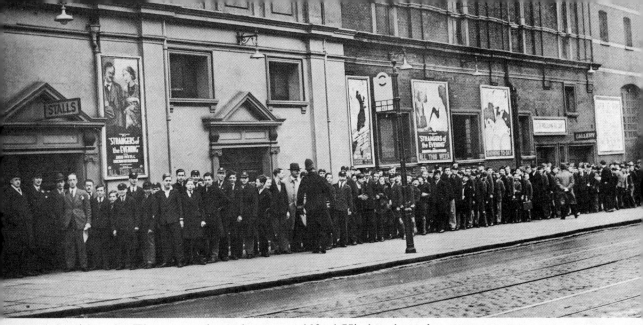

the title role. Three years later the young Alfred Hitchcock made his name with *The Lady Vanishes*. British studios were at last beginning to make a noteworthy contribution to the cinema, even though many of the best directors and actors were still lured away to Hollywood. Significantly, the best British films were cheaply made documentaries, of which type *Night Mail* is an outstanding example.

The cinema's popularity had only a slight effect on the fortunes of the live theatre, although some music-halls were forced to close. The cinema appealed not to the former theatre-goers, but to a new audience. Many of the people who queued to see Valentino, Chaplin, and Al Jolson had just not gone to places of public entertainment before the cinema boom. In particular, working-class men now for the first time went out for the evening with their wives. Curious though it may seem, this was a new social phenomenon.

A Liverpool docker or a Geordie shipyard worker might condescend to take his wife to the pictures, but he would not take her to the football match. And watching professional football was by far the most popular leisure pursuit among working-class men. Most of them apparently thought that a Saturday afternoon on the terraces was good value for a shilling (5p), for they flocked in their thousands to give noisy and loyal support to their favourites, teams such as Huddersfield Town, who won three First Division championships in a row between 1923 and 1926, and Arsenal, who were five times League champions between 1930 and 1939. The largest crowd recorded at a match in England attended the first Wembley Cup Final in 1923. No less than 126,000 paid to watch Bolton Wanderers beat West Ham United, but a further 70,000 or so broke through the gates and saw the game free.

*New methods in education: children queuing for an educational film matinee in London, 1932*

**Sport**

188

Cricket, for obvious reasons, was never so popular as football, although attendances in the 1920s and 1930s were much higher than in recent years. The game is slower and less exciting than football, and first-class matches last for several days, so that only a leisured minority of enthusiasts can watch matches from start to finish. Nevertheless, people were always interested in the exploits of the great players and in the outcome of Test Matches. Their concern was encouraged and exploited by the popular press, especially in the summer months, when there was usually very little 'hard' news. Thus there was great excitement in 1925 when Jack Hobbs passed W.G. Grace's record of 126 centuries in first-class matches, and during Test Matches, headlines such as 'England in Peril' and 'Can We Avoid Disaster' would confound non-cricketing foreigners. Cricket did, in fact, provoke an international crisis in 1932 when the M.C.C. team touring Australia became involved in the 'bodyline bowling' controversy. The Australian protest against Harold Larwood's intimidating bowling reached Cabinet level.

Lawn tennis also enjoyed a boom, although this was a sport for players rather than spectators. It was especially popular among women, whose game was no longer impeded by their dress. Tennis clubs sprang up all over the country and most local councils provided tennis-courts in their public parks. As well as improving the nation's health this helped to break down class barriers, for previously tennis, like golf, had been very much a middle-class sport.

So long as one remembers that there were never less than a million unemployed between 1920 and 1939, it would be safe to conclude that the British people were more prosperous between the wars than ever before. Most of them had a much higher standard of living; some had motor cars; almost everyone could afford a wireless set; their newspapers were bright and entertaining; and there was a wide variety of amusements and distractions, ranging from the 'Palais' and the 'Odeon' to Highbury Stadium and The Oval. In addition, 1924 saw the British Empire Exhibition at Wembley, at once a trade fair, a demonstration of Britain's imperial might, and an amusement park. There were two further occasions for public celebration and rejoicing: the Silver Jubilee of King George V in 1935 and the Coronation of King George VI two years later. As well as the grand parades and enormous crowds in London there were lesser carnivals in every town and village in Britain. The frenzied preparations and demonstrations of loyalty were evidence of the popularity of the Royal Family, but they were also expressions of relief as the 'bad times' of the early 1930s receded. 'I can't understand it, I'm really quite an ordinary sort of chap,' said King George V in 1935. This was true; perhaps it is also why the people loved him.

**British Empire Exhibition**

Over a wide field, the 1920s and 1930s saw change and development, some of it gradual, some astonishingly rapid. In many ways the social changes were more significant than the political events and economic currents described in Chapters 7 and 8. The central fact remains, however, that social progress depends upon economic and political forces. A picture of the life of the British people between the wars must be a kaleidoscope: there were bright and dark patches. J.B. Priestley's accounts of Coventry and Jarrow in *English Journey* demonstrate the contrast.

Coventry seems to have acquired the trick of keeping up with the times, a trick that many of our industrial cities find hard to learn. It made bicycles when everyone was cycling, cars when everyone wanted a motor, and now it is also busy with aeroplanes, wireless sets, and various electrical contrivances, including the apparatus used by the Talkies. There are still plenty of unemployed here, almost twelve thousand, I believe. But as I write, this place has passed its worst period of depression and unless this country reels back into a bottomless pit of trade depression, Coventry should be all right. Factories that were working on short time a year or two ago, are now in some instances back on double shifts. I saw their lights and heard the deep roar of their machinery late that night.

Of Jarrow, he wrote:

One little street may be rather more wretched than another, but to the outsider they all look alike. One out of every two shops appeared to be permanently closed. Wherever we went there were men hanging about, not scores of them but hundreds and thousands of them. The whole town looked as if it had entered a perpetual penniless bleak Sabbath. The men wore the drawn masks of prisoners of war.

# Chapter 9
# The Second World War
# —Military Events

The British government and its French ally went reluctantly to war in September 1939. War, it seemed, was the only way to prevent Hitler from acting as the rogue elephant of Europe. It was a war which the western powers had tried desperately to avoid and for which they were ill prepared. Faced with a ruthless German government and a brilliant military machine, they suffered defeats far worse than those of 1914. A series of staggering victories gave Hitler control of most of Europe and only the stubbornness of the British government and people denied him the final victory which seemed to be within his grasp. Then ambition drove Hitler and his Japanese ally to attack the Soviet Union and the United States, so condemning themselves to eventual defeat and destruction. But the westward march of the Red Army and the eastward advance of the Americans and their British allies not only crushed the life out of German Nazism; it also heralded the domination of the world in the second half of the twentieth century by the two super powers. By standing alone in 1940 Britain made a vital contribution to victory, but the cost of the war was such that she had finally to abandon her claim to equality of status with the United States.

The Second World War probably changed the lives of the British people less than the First: many of the Edwardian barriers had been broken down between 1914 and 1918 and had not been rebuilt in the twenty-one years of peace. In two senses, however, the Second World War was more popular than the First: nearly everyone agreed that it had to be fought and, even in the darkest days, very few thought of giving in; secondly, government controls, conscription, rationing and, above all, air raids brought everyone into the firing-line. Politicians talked glibly in 1939 of fighting to defend democracy; by 1945 the British people had won a great democratic victory.

### DEFEAT IN EUROPE 1939–1940

As in 1914, a British Expeditionary Force was quickly sent to France. The four divisions which Lord Gort commanded were the first of the thirty-two divisions which had been promised within twelve months of the outbreak of war. Trying to avoid some of the mistakes of 1914–18, the governments had already agreed on a

*Conscription introduced, 1939*

single Allied commander, the French General Gamelin. Gamelin ordered the B.E.F. to defend the Franco-Belgian frontier, in case of a repetition of the Schlieffen Plan, while the bulk of the French army remained behind the Maginot Line.

**B.E.F. sent to France**

**The Maginot Line**

It may be argued that Gamelin missed a great opportunity in the autumn of 1939, for only a third of the German army was on the Western Front while the remainder was dealing with the Poles. The French army, however, although it outnumbered the Germans, had no offensive plan. In direct contrast to 1914, French military thinking was dominated by the idea of defence: the Maginot Line, so it was thought, was impregnable. Had the French advanced, they would have been open to German counter-attack as soon as the Polish campaign was over and the advantage of the Maginot Line might have been thrown away.

While all was quiet on the Western Front and the first British soldier was not killed until 13 December, the Germans had been winning the expected victory in Poland. Despite the opinion of some old-fashioned British optimists that the Polish cavalry would soon be in Berlin, the panzer divisions and the *Luftwaffe* quickly eliminated Polish opposition. Within a month Polish organized resistance was at an end and the promised partition of Poland between Germany and the Soviet Union had taken place. Hitler offered peace to Britain and France, but the suggestion was firmly rejected.

**Defeat of Poland**

Still no one made a move in the west, although the Germans began moving divisions to the Western Front in October. British aircraft bombed German cities with leaflets urging the Germans to overthrow Hitler, but it was decided that anything more dangerous might provoke retaliation. This 'Phoney War' lasted until the spring of 1940 and prompted Neville Chamberlain to announce to the House of Commons that Hitler had 'missed the bus'.

*Recruiting poster*

In April and May 1940 it quickly became obvious that Hitler had not, after all, missed the bus, or that he had decided to travel by express train instead. He began by moving into Denmark and Norway in order to secure his supplies of iron ore from northern Sweden. The Danes capitulated immediately and, although the Norwegians resisted, their main ports and airfields were soon in German hands. The Allies readily came to Norway's assistance, but the operation was badly planned and ineptly conducted. German air superiority was decisive and the Allies had to withdraw. The Norwegian fiasco convinced the British public and many members of the House of Commons that Neville Chamberlain was not the man to conduct the war. Chamberlain resigned on 10 May (see pages 215–216) and was succeeded by Winston Churchill.

Churchill's assumption of power coincided with the beginning of the biggest Allied disaster in either World War. Without

Map 12 *The German victory in Western Europe, 1940*

gun

warning, German armies invaded Holland and Belgium on 10 May and forced the Dutch into surrender within five days. This was the long-anticipated German offensive in the west; its success was due partly to the efficiency of the German armies and the skill of their commanders, and partly to two fatal mistakes by Gamelin. His first was to fritter away France's superiority in tanks by deploying them thinly throughout his armies instead of concentrating them in specialized armoured divisions; his second was to send the French reserves forward into Holland to meet what turned out to be a German feint.

The massed tanks of the panzer divisions, supported by fighter aircraft and dive-bombers, advanced unexpectedly through the Ardennes and broke through the weakest part of the French line at Sedan on 14 May. With no more available reserves, Gamelin could not prevent them from racing forward to Amiens and reaching the sea at Abbeville, thus cutting the Allied armies in two (see Map 12). This was a perfect example of the German *Blitzkrieg*, or 'lightning war'—an overwhelming concentration of power at a vital point, a decisive victory, and a rapid breakthrough which so disrupted the enemy's forces that he was unable to recover.

Lord Gort's B.E.F., the Belgian army, and a large part of the

*German troops entering Paris*

French army were now cut off in northern Belgium and the north-east corner of France. Gort was unable to counter-attack southwards and on 27 May he was told 'to evacuate the maximum force possible'. Churchill and his War Cabinet were forced into the heart-breaking decision to desert their French allies, hoping desperately that the now inevitable defeat of France might not be followed by the conquest of Britain. One of the most fateful decisions of the war had already been taken: the Commander-in-Chief of R.A.F. Fighter Command, Air Chief Marshal Dowding, had persuaded the War Cabinet to break Churchill's promise to the French government and to send no more fighters to France. By thus conserving his strength, Dowding made possible Fighter Command's victory in the Battle of Britain.

The evacuation of the B.E.F. was not expected to succeed. Calais was already in German hands and the Belgian army surrendered on 28 May. Only the port of Dunkirk and the neighbouring beaches were available. Fortunately for the Allies, the panzer divisions had been ordered to halt on 23 May, possibly in order to allow the *Luftwaffe* the honour of finally eliminating the British army. This German decision gave the B.E.F. the breathing-space which it needed. In eight days, between 27 May and 3 June, over 300,000 Allied troops, a third of them French, were ferried across the Channel—eight times as many as the most optimistic estimate.

Destroyers of the Royal Navy transported most of the troops from Dunkirk, but they were assisted by a flotilla of small craft, including cross-Channel steamers, fishing boats, Thames barges, and private pleasure craft. The *Luftwaffe* kept up almost continuous attacks throughout the operation and succeeded in sinking about a

**Dunkirk evacuation**

194

*The evacuation of Dunkirk*

quarter of the 800 craft involved, but the destroyers and small boats scurried to and fro, day and night, until the evacuation was complete. The B.B.C., in the last days of May, had cautiously prepared the British people for the news that most of the B.E.F. had been lost; when it became clear that the armies had, in fact, escaped, a thrill of pleasure and relief swept the country. Dunkirk, so it seemed, was a military and naval triumph, a miraculous deliverance.

There was a more sombre side to the Dunkirk story. Most of the men had been saved, but all the B.E.F.'s tanks, field-guns, and transport had been abandoned. If the Germans had succeeded in landing an army in southern England in 1940, the British would no doubt have fought bravely, but they would have had no chance of success. The nation rightly rejoiced that a quarter of a million of its young men had escaped death or captivity, but Churchill wisely remarked in the House of Commons on 4 June: 'Wars are not won by evacuations.'

The remaining French armies were still in the field, but their defeat was certain. The Germans poured south, occupied Paris and, streaming into eastern France, cut off the retreat of the defenders of the Maginot Line, who suddenly found themselves facing the wrong way. Churchill visited France frequently in the hectic days of June and on 16 June went so far as to propose to Reynaud, the French Prime Minister, a permanent union of Britain and France, so that their combined forces might continue the war. The offer was rejected, Reynaud resigned, and the new government, under Marshal Pétain, signed an armistice with the Germans on 22 June. 'The Battle of France is over,' said Churchill. 'I expect that the **French capitulation** Battle of Britain is about to begin.'

*Spitfires*

For most of the First World War aircraft had merely been auxiliaries for the armies. The creation of the Royal Air Force in 1917 indicated their growing importance, but all the decisive fighting was still done on land and at sea. Technical developments between the wars revolutionized the situation. By 1939 military aircraft were much larger, faster, more heavily armed, and able to carry far bigger bomb loads than at the end of the First War. Politicians and senior officers realized this and, indeed, were apt to over-estimate the effectiveness of bombing (see Chapter 9). The first year of the Second World War proved the importance of air power. The *Luftwaffe*'s fighters swept the Polish air force from the skies, while its dive-bombers destroyed communications and terrorized the Polish army and civilian population. German air superiority had been one of the main reasons for the Allies' failure in the Norwegian campaign. The *Luftwaffe* had played an important, but this time not decisive, part in the Battle of France.

The lesson of the Norwegian campaign was that fighters and bombers in complete control of the air could overcome even British sea power. When, therefore, the British government did not sue for peace after the French armistice, Hitler ordered the preparation of plans for the invasion of Britain and decreed that the first step must be the destruction of British air power over the Channel, so that the *Luftwaffe* could neutralize the Royal Navy.

**Battle of Britain**

The Battle of Britain lasted from mid-August to mid-September 1940. Its heroes were a few hundred British, Commonwealth, and Allied fighter pilots, but the architects of the Royal Air Force's victory were Air Chief Marshal Dowding and the commander of Number 11 Group, Fighter Command, Air Vice Marshal Park. Although the *Luftwaffe* had many more aircraft than the R.A.F., there was not much difference in their respective fighter strengths, for the British Spitfires and Hurricanes were generally superior to the German Messerschmitts and Fighter Command had the advantage of a chain of radar stations around the coast, so that the

British fighter squadrons need take off only when the enemy approached. During the vital summer of 1940 British aircraft factories were working non-stop and managed to make good all the R.A.F.'s losses. Trained and experienced pilots, however, were impossible to replace, and in the critical days of the battle it was the loss of pilots which caused Dowding most concern.

Fleets of German bombers, protected by fighter escorts, began to attack south-east England on 13 August. Having lost twice as many aircraft as the R.A.F. in the first two weeks, the *Luftwaffe* turned its attention to the British fighter bases in Kent at the beginning of September. During the next week extensive damage to the airfields and losses almost as great as the Germans' led Dowding to doubt his ability to continue. Hitler then rescued the R.A.F. Infuriated by British bombing of German cities, including Berlin, he ordered the *Luftwaffe* to retaliate by bombing London, hoping perhaps to break the public's will to resist. The bombing of London caused many casualties and a great deal of damage, but it saved the Kent airfields. Fighter Command licked its wounds and returned to the attack, inflicting heavier losses than ever on the daylight raiders. In mid-September the Germans gave up their attempt to annihilate the R.A.F. and dispersed the fleet of invasion barges which had been assembled in the French Channel ports. Fighter Command's victory guaranteed Britain against invasion and Churchill was expressing the thanks and relief of the whole nation when he said: 'Never in the field of human conflict was so much owed by so many to so few.'

'The few' numbered little over a thousand; 414 of them lost their lives in the battle and many others survived after having been shot down. All of them were young, many hardly more than schoolboys. Veterans of the battle relate that their dominant feelings in that critical month were fear and fatigue, not the hearty exuberance of the hunting-field so falsely depicted in many a third-rate film. They were fighting for their lives, and only the most skilful of them could survive. They were forced to go almost without sleep for a month and yet had to react like lightning and perform amazing acts of dexterity. They have been very properly immortalized in Churchill's tribute. On the other hand, their chief, Dowding, was removed from his command in November 1940.

The Battle of Britain not only compelled Hitler to postpone indefinitely his plan to invade Britain; it also showed both sides that daylight bombing raids were too costly in aircraft and crews to be worthwhile. Bombers were an easy prey for fighters and anti-aircraft batteries, and fighter escorts, operating far from their home bases, could not provide adequate protection. Both the *Luftwaffe* and the R.A.F. decided, therefore, to concentrate on bombing by night. Attacking under the cover of darkness, bombers were more difficult to detect, but they also had the problem of locating targets in enemy territory where strict black-out regulations were applied. The high commands soon realized that precision bombing of bridges, railway junctions, military camps, and munitions factories was impossible by night and gradually turned instead to the policy of area bombing of key towns and cities, in the hope that massive raids would seriously harm the enemy's war production and destroy the morale of the civilian population.

German bombers attacked London every night between 7 September and 2 November 1940 and carried out spasmodic, but less regular, raids until the spring of 1941. Their mixture of incendiary and high-explosive bombs caused extensive damage, particularly in the East End and the City, rendering thousands of families homeless. Civilian casualties were high, but far short of the pre-war estimates. The Londoners withstood the Blitz, as they called it; they did not 'grin and bear it', but they bore it nevertheless. In mid-November the *Luftwaffe* turned to the provincial cities. In a ten-hour raid on Coventry on 14 November the centre of the city was completely destroyed and 544 people killed. The heart of Southampton was devastated on 30 November and 1 December, and Plymouth, Bristol, Sheffield, Liverpool, Hull, Birmingham, and Clydebank received similar treatment.

The Royal Air Force could not prevent the Germans from bombing Britain, but it could retaliate. Indeed, after the fall of France, the bombing of German cities was one of the very few ways in which Britain could strike at Germany at all. Like their German counterparts, the senior officers of Bomber Command firmly believed that they could destroy the enemy's capacity and will to fight. Abandoning its pre-war promise not to permit the indiscriminate bombing of civilian populations, the British government, in mid-1940, ordered Bomber Command to begin night attacks on German cities.

Bombing proved to be a far less effective weapon than anticipated. After even the heaviest of raids communications were soon restored and work resumed. The destruction of Coventry was unprecedented, yet the city's factories were back in full production within five days. Some civilians were killed, many more lost their homes and all their possessions, but they found alternative accommodation and continued to go to work. If anything, Britain's will to resist was increased by the Blitz. The same was true of the R.A.F.'s raids on Germany. Until 1944 they had little or no effect on the German war economy and cost the lives of more R.A.F. crews than German civilians.

German munitions production actually doubled between early 1942 and late 1943, despite extremely heavy raids on the Ruhr towns and on Hamburg and Berlin. Area bombing reduced the

**The Blitz**

**Bombing of Germany**

*St. Paul's in the blitz, 1940*

centres of many German towns and cities to rubble and destroyed large numbers of houses and old factories, but by this stage of the war most of the vital armament factories had been dispersed to remote parts of the country. One of the few positive results of the heavy bombing of Germany was to bolster British morale: at the end of May 1942, when most of the war news was gloomy, the people were cheered to hear that a thousand bombers had just attacked Cologne.

Only in the last months of the war, when the Allies were in sight of victory, did bombing have a pronounced effect. Daylight raids by American 'flying fortresses', protected by the newly developed Mustang long-range fighters, destroyed sufficient German oil supplies to immobilize some of the army's tanks and transport vehicles. The most notorious of all the Allied raids on Germany, however, the R.A.F.'s devastation of Dresden in February 1945, probably contributed nothing to the war effort and cost the lives of between 60,000 and 250,000 German civilians, many of whom were refugees fleeing before the advancing Red Army.

Really heavy German bombing of British cities was suspended in the spring of 1941, when Hitler ordered the *Luftwaffe* to prepare

**Flying bombs**

for the invasion of Russia. Thereafter, most urban areas suffered

199

occasional raids, but nothing of the intensity of the Blitz. Then, in June 1944, London and the south-east came under fire again when the first flying bombs or V1s began to fall. These were jet-propelled, pilotless aircraft, carrying high-explosive war-heads. Six thousand people was killed by V1s, but by August the menace had been overcome: fast fighter aircraft could keep pace with them and were able to shoot down a high proportion. Far more sinister were the rockets, or V2s, which began to fall in September. Travelling much faster than the speed of sound, they gave no warning—they simply exploded. Fortunately for Londoners, V2s were apt to go astray and were expensive to produce. Also, as the Allied armies advanced through northern Europe their launching sites were overrun. The V1s and V2s were terror weapons, directed solely against the civilian population. Had the bombardment continued, the British government might have had to order the abandonment of London, but Hitler's new secret weapons could not have won the war.

The events of the Second World War showed that control of the air was vital to the success of any military operation. Armies and navies could not function effectively if subject to continuous air attack. On the other hand, it should have become obvious that air power alone could not win a war. High-explosive and incendiary bombs, except on the Dresden scale, were ineffective unless used with precision on strategic targets. Precision bombing, however, was possible only in daylight, and daylight raids were practicable only if the enemy's fighter force were neutralized. Not until the advent of nuclear weapons did it become possible to terrorize an enemy into submission.

THE WAR AT SEA

Naval strategy in the Second World War followed broadly the lines laid down between 1914 and 1918. The Royal Navy used its superior strength to impose a blockade on German ports, while German U-boats and surface raiders tried to cut off Britain's overseas trade. The techniques were more advanced, but the aims and the outcome were identical.

Germany's ports were blockaded as soon as the war began. Disregarding the lessons of the First World War, Chamberlain's government confidently predicted that a shortage of oil and essential raw materials would quickly cause economic collapse in Germany and that Hitler would have to make peace. In the first two years of war, in fact, the necessary supplies continued to enter Germany via Italy and the Soviet Union, and German chemists developed sufficient synthetic materials to replace most of the lost imports. The blockade was doubtless an inconvenience to the Germans, but it was no more a war-winning weapon than was heavy bombing.

*Vera Lynn, 'the Forces' sweetheart'*

**Failure of British blockade**

**Battle of the Atlantic**

Britain depended to a far greater extent than Germany on imports, and the attacks on British merchantmen by U-boats and surface warships which began in September 1939, were an immediate challenge to the national survival. There was no 'Phoney War' at sea. Over three-quarters of a million tons of merchant shipping were lost in the first nine months of the war and one daring U-boat commander even penetrated the defences of Scapa Flow. The convoy system was adopted as soon as the war began, however, and although sinkings continued, an adequate supply of food and raw materials was brought in. The Royal Navy had one striking success in the first winter of the war: the German pocket battleship *Graf Spee*, which had been causing havoc in the South Atlantic, was cornered in Montevideo harbour, where she scuttled herself.

The fall of France in June 1940 could have turned the naval balance in Germany's favour. The armistice signed by Pétain's government included the provision that the French fleet was to be handed over to the Germans and the Italians, but that they would not use it. Churchill did not trust Hitler's word and, with great reluctance, ordered the Royal Navy to destroy the French vessels at Oran in Algeria in July 1940. Churchill was acutely distressed to think that British guns were sinking the warships and killing the sailors of his recent ally, but could not afford to risk the alternative.

The main theatre of naval warfare was now, and remained, the North Atlantic convoy routes, and the contest which lasted until the end of 1943 is often referred to as the Battle of the Atlantic. British losses reached a peak between March and July 1941, but the immediate crisis was overcome when aircraft in R.A.F. Coastal Command began assisting the escort destroyers in tracking down U-boats. British losses might have been far worse had the German battleship *Bismarck*, the most heavily-armed ship afloat, managed to evade her pursuers when she broke out into the Atlantic in May 1941. But she was damaged by torpedo-carrying aircraft from the carrier *Ark Royal* and subsequently sunk.

Heavy shipping losses continued throughout 1942 and into 1943, when they reached another peak of half a million tons in March. Hunting in packs, the German submarines found abundant targets, for the convoys were now swelled by vessels carrying American soldiers and armaments to Europe and others transporting military supplies to northern Russia. The Allies redoubled their efforts to protect the convoys: the United States provided 260 extra destroyers and some aircraft carriers for escort duty, while Coastal Command aircraft, now equipped with short-wave radar, kept up constant patrols. In the second half of 1943 the battle was won. The number of sinkings fell dramatically and fifty-three U-boats were destroyed in the last quarter of the year. By the end of the year Admiral Doenitz, the German submarine commander-in-chief, had withdrawn his fleet from the Atlantic.

The naval victory was completed when Germany's remaining battleship, the *Tirpitz*, was put out of action by British midget submarines in a Norwegian fjord in September 1943 and the battle-cruiser *Scharnhorst* was sunk in December. The Allies were now able, without fear of molestation, to build up their supplies for the imminent invasion of Europe. The naval war had been won at the cost of the lives of 30,000 British merchant seamen. Thousands of others were torpedoed and rescued, some of them several times. Victory was due not to any brilliant tactical stroke, but to the watchfulness, patience, and fortitude of the seamen and crews of the British and American escort ships and aircraft.

WAR IN THE MEDITERRANEAN

The miracle of Dunkirk and victory in the Battle of Britain guaranteed the British Isles against invasion, but some parts of the Empire were highly vulnerable. The entry of Italy into the war meant that the Mediterranean was closed to British merchant shipping and that British bases at Gibraltar and Malta and her position in Egypt and Palestine were threatened. With the Italians in Libya and Abyssinia, there seemed to be some prospect that the Axis Powers might try to take over the whole of the Middle East and thus cut off a major source of Britain's oil. As soon as the immediate danger of invasion had passed, therefore, the War Cabinet decided to augment British and Commonwealth forces in Egypt.

A further important consideration in the autumn of 1940 was that, having been driven out of Europe, the British army's only chance of engaging the enemy at all lay in north Africa. Even here the outlook was not bright: Wavell, the British commander in the Middle East, had only 100,000 troops at his disposal, as against 300,000 Italians in Libya and a further 200,000 in Abyssinia. With apparently justified confidence, the Italians advanced from Libya into Egypt in September 1940. They made some progress at first, but when Wavell counter-attacked in December, Italian resistance suddenly collapsed. At the cost of only a few hundred casualties, the British and Commonwealth forces drove the Italians right back to Benghazi (see Map 13) and took more than 100,000 prisoners. One British officer, in his report to Headquarters, confessed that he was unable to count the prisoners, but estimated that there were 'five acres of officers and two hundred acres of other ranks'. Meanwhile, half the Italian fleet had been put out of action by a British air raid on the naval base at Taranto.

The ambitious Mussolini had hoped to impress his German ally by conquering Greece as well as Egypt, but the Greeks also resisted

**Fighting in north Africa**

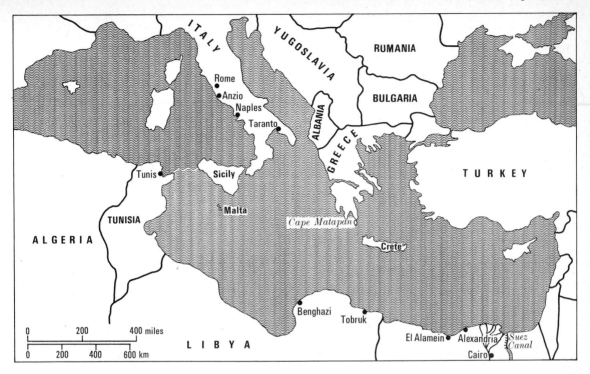

Rome
Anzio
Naples
Taranto
Tunis
Sicily
Malta
*Cape Matapan*
Crete
Benghazi
Tobruk
El Alamein
Alexandria
*Suez Canal*
Cairo
ALGERIA
TUNISIA
LIBYA
ITALY
YUGOSLAVIA
RUMANIA
BULGARIA
ALBANIA
GREECE
TURKEY

0    200    400 miles
0   200   400    600 km

*Map 13 The Mediterranean and the Second World War*

**German conquest of Greece**

successfully and pushed the Italians back into Albania. Angry that his partner had let him down, but anxious lest Axis authority should be undermined by Italy's failures, Hitler decided to help Mussolini in both north Africa and Greece. Rommel's Afrika Korps arrived in Libya early in 1941 and drove the British back into Egypt in March. In April the Germans invaded and quickly conquered Yugoslavia, then, having induced Bulgaria to join the Axis camp, began an invasion of Greece. Despite the worsening position in north Africa, Churchill decided to honour the pledge of support given to Greece in 1939 and ordered Wavell to send a large part of his forces across the Mediterranean. British reinforcements arrived too late to help the Greeks, and German control of southeast Europe was soon complete. The most startling feature of the campaign was the capture of Crete by German parachutists and airborne troops, demonstrating another of the applications of air power in modern warfare.

The only British successes in these early months of 1941 were a naval victory over the Italians in the Battle of Matapan in March and the conquest of Abyssinia in May. The unlucky Wavell, who had been asked to do too much with very limited resources, was somewhat unjustly removed from his command in June 1941.

Between mid-1941 and the autumn of 1942 the Germans had the better of the north African campaign. General Auchinleck, Wavell's successor, forced Rommel to retreat to Benghazi again in November 1941, but German offensives at the beginning of 1942 and in the summer drove the Eighth Army back to El Alamein, a mere sixty miles from Alexandria. The loss of Tobruk in June 1942 was bitter news for the British people and even led to some criticism of Churchill's leadership. But Rommel never penetrated beyond El Alamein. His supply lines were now stretched for hundreds of miles across the desert and the British were beginning to receive substantial supplies of American arms, notably Sherman tanks.

The United States had been drawn into the war by the Japanese attack on Pearl Harbour in December 1941, but American troops took no part in the fighting against Germany in the first half of 1942. Churchill and President Roosevelt decided in the middle of the year that a joint Allied offensive was necessary and agreed that north Africa offered the best prospects of success. Accordingly, an Allied invasion of north-west Africa was planned for the end of the year, and was to coincide with a British attack in Egypt. At the same time, Churchill came to the conclusion that Auchinleck's conduct of the campaign was not sufficiently vigorous. He was replaced as commander-in-chief in the Middle East by General Alexander, while Montgomery took over command of the Eighth Army.

Montgomery built up a massive superiority in tanks and guns during the autumn of 1942 and attacked at El Alamein on 23 October. After a bitter twelve-day struggle Rommel was at last decisively beaten and began a retreat which did not end until the whole of Libya was in the hands of the Eighth Army. Anglo-American forces had meanwhile landed in Morocco and Algeria— 'Operation Torch'. The Germans and Italians were caught in Tunis between the jaws of the Allied pincers: the 'Torch' forces advanced from the west while the Eighth Army advanced from the east. On 12 May 1943 the Axis armies in north Africa surrendered and a quarter of a million prisoners, a third of them German, fell into Allied hands.

**Axis defeat in North Africa**

By the spring of 1943 the grand alliance of Britain, the United States, and Soviet Russia could be sure of eventual victory. At the same time as the British and Americans were driving the enemy out of north Africa, the German advance into the heart of Russia was being turned into a retreat. The main strategic problem was to decide where the western Allies should attack next. Ever since Hitler's invasion of Russia in mid-1941 Stalin had been demanding the opening of a second front in France. While Britain had been alone this had clearly been impossible, and the slow build-up of American troops in Europe had prevented a cross-Channel invasion in 1942. Now, in 1943, not only Stalin, but also Roosevelt pressed Churchill to agree to a second front. The British Prime Minister objected, however, that there were still insufficient Allied troops and landing craft for such an enterprise and proposed instead an invasion of Sicily, to be followed by an attack on Italy. By thus striking at what he called the 'soft under-belly of Europe', Churchill hoped to win the war without incurring the heavy casualties which an invasion of France would involve. In meetings with Roosevelt at Casablanca in January 1943 and in Washington in the summer, Churchill persuaded the President to agree to the invasion of Sicily and an attack on the mainland of Italy.

**Invasion of Sicily and Italy**

Sicily quickly fell to the Allies in July 1943 and when Italy itself was invaded in September the Italians overthrew Mussolini, signed an armistice, and declared war on Germany. The southern part of the peninsula was soon in Allied hands, but the Germans now moved troops into Italy and stopped the Allied advance between Naples and Rome. Here the position remained static during the winter of 1943–4. An attempt to break the deadlock by landing a force behind the German lines at Anzio in January was unsuccessful and the Anzio troops were rescued only when the Allied armies resumed their advance in May 1944. Rome itself was taken on 4 June, but by this time the Italian campaign had been eclipsed by the Normandy invasions. The Allies continued to advance into northern Italy, but Italy was not the 'soft under-belly' of which Churchill had dreamed. The attack on Italy certainly engaged large numbers of German troops and had the effect of reopening the Mediterranean to Allied shipping, but the diversion of Allied forces probably delayed the invasion of France by almost a year.

THE RUSSIAN FRONT

Hitler's armies attacked the Soviet Union on 22 June 1941, thereby ending Britain's isolation. For the next three years the Red Army bore the brunt of the fighting against Germany and throughout the remainder of the war more than half Germany's divisions were engaged on the Russian Front.

During the inter-war years no British statesman had been well-disposed towards the Soviet Union and Churchill, in particular, had been an outspoken critic of Communism. Nevertheless, he realized immediately that any enemy of Hitler must be a friend of Britain. He remarked in private: 'If Hitler invaded Hell I would make at least a favourable reference to the Devil in the House of Commons.' Stalin accepted the British alliance and later gladly received very large quantities of British and American armaments, but he was never a friendly comrade-in-arms. He repeatedly demanded that the western Allies should open a second front in France to take the pressure off the Red Army and complained bitterly that Britain and the United States expected Russia to do

**Churchill and Stalin**

all the fighting for them.

At first the German attack was as successful as the earlier *Blitzkriegs*. The German armies overran the Russian positions, took hundreds of thousands of prisoners and advanced deep into the Ukraine. By Christmas 1941 the Germans were almost in the suburbs of Moscow, but here the Russian winter and a counter-attack by the Red Army stopped them. In the following year the Germans turned south-eastwards, heading for the Caucasian oil-fields. Again they made spectacular progress and were only halted by resolute Russian resistance in the streets of Stalingrad. **German advance into Russia**

The Battle of Stalingrad in the last months of 1942 was the turning-point of the war in the east. When the Red Army counter-attacked in November Hitler forbade a German retreat, with the result that a German army of 300,000 men was surrounded. Only 22,000 prisoners were taken by the Russians. The Germans never recovered from Stalingrad. Early in 1943 they began a retreat which was not to end until the Red Army was in the streets of Berlin. The Soviet Union itself was almost cleared of invaders by the end of 1943, and in the following year the Russians advanced into the Baltic states, then into Poland, Rumania, Czechoslovakia, Hungary, and Yugoslavia. After a halt at Warsaw in the autumn of 1944 they continued their progress into Germany itself in early 1945, linked up with the Allies advancing from the west and compelled the Germans to surrender. **Battle of Stalingrad** **Russian advance into Germany**

The Soviet Union played a major part in the war against Germany. Russia suffered more casualties, military and civilian, than any other nation, and her people underwent far greater hardships. The citizens of Leningrad, for example, were subjected to bombardment and starvation in a siege which lasted for two and a half years. The two great Allied victories of Stalingrad and El Alamein almost coincided, but there can be no doubt that the former was the bigger blow for Hitler. On the other hand, the Soviet Union was at war only with Germany, whereas from the end of 1941 Britain and the United States also had to face the Japanese. This must not, however, detract from the Soviet achievement: the Russian people contributed more to the defeat of Nazi Germany than either the Americans or the British.

## THE GRAND ALLIANCE—VICTORY IN EUROPE

'So we had won after all!' Such was Churchill's reaction when the United States entered the war. Nazi Germany, with the resources of most of Europe at her disposal, would no doubt be able to hold out for several more years, but the final issue was no longer in question. The main problems were to co-ordinate Allied efforts and to decide upon a proper time-table of operations.

*The Teheran Conference, 1943—Stalin, Roosevelt and Churchill*

**Teheran Conference**

Anglo-American military co-operation began immediately after Pearl Harbour. Churchill visited Washington in December 1941 and agreed with Roosevelt that there should be single Allied commanders for all joint operations, that a Combined Chiefs of Staff Committee should co-ordinate British and American activities, and that British military secrets, including the details of the research work on the early stages of the atomic bomb, should be handed over to the Americans. Their most important decision was to give first priority to victory in Europe.

Of the three Allies, the Soviet Union was under the greatest pressure in 1941 and 1942. Stalin repeatedly complained that Britain and the United States were not playing their part in the war against Germany and called time and again for an Anglo-American invasion of occupied France.

Although Churchill had visited Stalin in Moscow in 1942, the 'Big Three' did not meet until November 1943, when they conferred at Teheran in Persia. At Teheran, Stalin demanded that the western Allies should invade France in 1944. Roosevelt supported him, Churchill had to concur, and 'Operation Overlord' was fixed for May 1944.

An Anglo-Canadian raid on Dieppe in 1942 had demonstrated just how difficult an assault on a heavily defended coast would be.

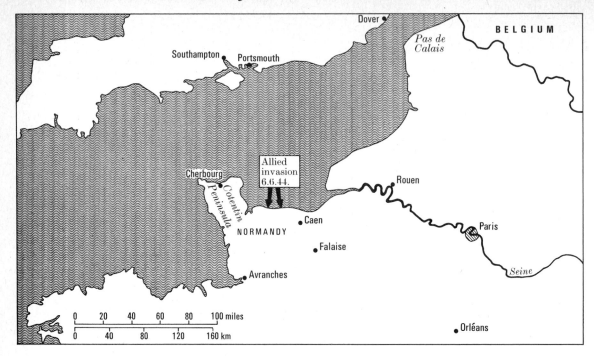

Map 14 *The Normandy invasions, 1944*

If 'Overlord' was to succeed, massive forces and meticulous preparation were necessary. Over-all command had to go to an American, for the United States would contribute more troops than Britain, and the choice fell upon General Eisenhower, who had commanded the 'Torch' operation. Montgomery was to be in charge of the actual landings. The obvious target-area was the Pas de Calais, but, partly for this reason, the Allies chose Normandy instead. Although the sea crossing would be longer, Normandy was less heavily defended and offered better port facilities. Until the last moment, the Germans were deceived into expecting an invasion in the Pas de Calais by a build-up of forces in Kent and the assembly of hundreds of imitation landing craft in Dover and neighbouring harbours.

In size, the invasion force exceeded all previous armadas. Three and a half million men were made ready for eventual transport to France, 3,000 ships and 4,000 landing craft were assembled to convey them or protect their crossing, while no less than 13,000 aircraft would sweep the *Luftwaffe* from the skies. With great ingenuity, Allied engineers devised and constructed two artificial harbours ('Mulberries'), to be towed across the Channel and used until a port was captured, and a submarine oil pipeline ('Pluto'). Strict security was maintained throughout the spring and early summer of 1944: southern England was virtually cut off from the rest of the world.

**Normandy invasion: victory in France**

*One of a series of photographs by Robert Capa of the Normandy invasion*

The invasion began on 6 June 1944. Once ashore, the British were given the task of advancing on Caen and engaging the mass of German armour, while the Americans, further west, occupied the Cotentin peninsula and seized the port of Cherbourg. The fighting around Caen was bitter and the casualties heavy, but the Americans broke out southwards from Avranches at the end of July and, swinging north-eastwards, inflicted a crushing defeat on the Germans near Falaise (see Map 14). Victory in Normandy was complete and there followed a total collapse of German resistance in France and Belgium. Allied forces were landed in southern France on 15 August, but they did little more than pursue the already retreating Germans. Paris was liberated on 25 August and by the end of September no German troops were left in France.

At this point, Eisenhower, who had taken over command of the land forces, disagreed on strategy with Montgomery, now in charge of the British army group in the north. Montgomery wanted the British to act as the Allied spear-head, to advance ahead of the other armies through Belgium, over the Rhine, and into the Ruhr industrial area, thus destroying Germany's ability to continue fighting. Eisenhower, who was afraid that the British might extend their supply lines too far, rejected the idea and ordered a steady advance over a broad front. He did, however, allow Montgomery to try to establish a bridge-head over the lower Rhine at Arnhem

**Arnhem**

in Holland. Although paratroops captured the bridge at Arnhem, the supporting ground forces were not able to reach them and the ambitious project failed—the Allies' first set-back since D Day.

For the Germans, the war was now lost, but they nevertheless managed to postpone the inevitable for a further seven months. They regrouped their remaining armies behind the Rhine and prepared to defend the Fatherland, and at the same time kept the Russians at bay on the frontiers of Poland. In December 1944 they even counter-attacked against a weakly held American position in the Ardennes (the 'Battle of the Bulge'). After advancing forty-five miles in three days, their tanks and transports ran out of petrol so that they had to withdraw once more. **Battle of the Bulge**

The Allied leaders, meanwhile, were more concerned with the post-war settlement than with how to win the war. Roosevelt, like Woodrow Wilson before him, hoped that international co-operation would outlast the war and that all future disputes would be settled peacefully. He was mainly responsible for a meeting of representatives of the three Great Powers at Dumbarton Oaks in the United States in September 1944, at which the constitution of the future United Nations was drawn up. More important still was the second meeting of Churchill, Roosevelt, and Stalin at Yalta in southern Russia in February 1945. At Yalta the Allies drew up final plans **Yalta Conference** for the defeat of Germany and agreed that Germany should be divided into zones of occupation after the war. Stalin also pledged the Soviet Union to declare war on Japan three months after the end of the war in Europe. Roosevelt, unlike Churchill, was hopeful of good relations with Russia after the war, but the slight chance of post-war harmony between the Soviet Union and the United States probably vanished when Roosevelt died suddenly on 12 April.

Victory in Europe came quite suddenly in the spring of 1945. **German surrender** British and American forces crossed the Rhine in March and began a swift advance into the heart of Germany. The Red Army meanwhile resumed its westward march and at last even Hitler admitted defeat. He committed suicide on 30 April and on 7 May Eisenhower received the unconditional surrender of all the German forces.

THE WAR AGAINST JAPAN

Although Japan had been at war with China since 1937, she did not become involved in the World War until 1941. By the middle of that year Japanese forces had gained control of much of eastern China and had just taken over French Indo-China (see Map 15). In protest against this expansion Britain and the United States had cut off almost all trade with Japan, who had consequently become short of oil and vital raw materials. These shortages tempted the Japanese to seize Malaya and the Dutch East Indies, which were rich in tin, rubber, and oil. The Japanese government **Japanese expansion**

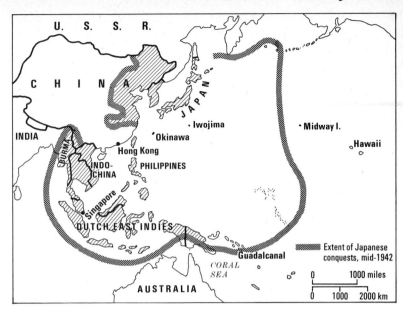

Map 15 *The war against Japan*

hesitated to make such a bold move, however, for it would clearly amount to an attempt to make Japan dominant throughout south-east Asia and would lead to war with Britain and, almost certainly, with the United States.

**Admiral Tojo**

Cautious policies were finally rejected when Admiral Tojo came to power as Japanese Prime Minister in the autumn of 1941. Tojo decided to strike a crippling blow against the American fleet in the Pacific, thus depriving the United States of the capacity to retaliate for several years to come, to seize Malaya and the East Indies, and to assert Japanese control over the whole of south-east Asia and the Pacific. It would, of course, be beyond Japan's power to defeat the United States, but Tojo hoped that he would be able to negotiate a favourable peace from a position of strength.

**Pearl Harbour**

Without any declaration of war, Japanese carrier-based aircraft attacked the American naval base at Pearl Harbour in Hawaii on the morning of Sunday, 6 December 1941. Five battleships and nearly two hundred American aircraft were destroyed. Even before the American Congress could approve the declaration of war against Japan, Hitler, dragging his Italian ally behind him, made the war global by declaring war on the United States. The Anglo-American alliance for which Churchill had so long hoped was made complete when Britain went to war with Japan. Only one link was missing from the chain: until August 1945 the Soviet Union and Japan remained at peace.

Pearl Harbour was a terrible blow for the United States. Furthermore, the destruction of a large part of the American Pacific fleet enormously harmed the whole Allied cause. Yet from the purely

211

British point of view it was almost a blessing: Churchill was distressed that his American friends should have been so treacherously attacked, but was relieved that, at last, the United States was in the war.

December 1941 and the first months of 1942 saw a series of astonishing Japanese victories. Mastery of the air enabled the Japanese to destroy another American fleet in the Philippines and to sink two British capital ships, the *Prince of Wales* and the *Repulse*, which had been sent hurriedly to the Far East. Hong Kong fell almost immediately, the Philippines were conquered in the first four months of 1942, and the seizure of a large number of small islands gave Japan control of the whole of the western Pacific. Worst of all for Britain was the lightning Japanese conquest of Malaya in January 1942, culminating in the loss of Singapore and the surrender of 60,000 troops on 15 February. By May, all of Burma was in enemy hands and the British government feared for the safety of India, although this does not appear to have been one of Japan's objectives.

In mid-1942 the Japanese advance was halted by the British and Australian army in Burma, by the Australians and Americans in New Guinea and, most important of all, by the United States fleet in the Pacific. The naval battles of the Coral Sea and Midway were the turning-point of the war against Japan. In both, carrier-based aircraft were the decisive weapon, proving that the battleship had been outmoded by the aircraft carrier.

The Allies then took the offensive in the Pacific. The United States began a submarine campaign against Japanese merchant shipping, for Japan was as dependent as Britain on imported raw materials. American submarines were much more successful than the German and, by the end of the war, ninety per cent of Japan's merchant fleet had been sunk. Then, in late 1942, American, Australian, and New Zealand forces began the reconquest of the numerous Pacific Islands which the Japanese had seized in the first months of the war. In a series of bitter land, sea, and air battles, the most famous of which was that for Guadalcanal in the Solomon Islands, the Allies moved slowly forward from one group of islands to the next. The Japanese fought fiercely; few of them surrendered, for death was preferable to capture for the Japanese soldier.

The British Fourteenth Army was stationary in Burma for almost two years between mid-1942 and early 1944. The Japanese then attempted to penetrate Assam in an attempt to cut off the supplies which the Allies were sending over the Himalayas to China. At the Battle of Imphal, however, the British won their first decisive victory over the Japanese and turned their advance into a retreat. Under its outstanding general, Sir William Slim, the Fourteenth Army drove the enemy back through Burma,

**Japanese advance halted 1942**

**Allied offensive**

retook Mandalay and, by May 1945, had reached Rangoon.

Meanwhile, the Americans pressed on in the Pacific, although Japanese resistance never relented and each small gain cost hundreds or thousands of casualties. Between late 1944 and early 1945 General MacArthur's army reconquered the Philippines, while the capture of Iwojima and Okinawa in February 1945 brought Japanese cities well within the range of American bombers. The capture of these islands, however, showed just how costly would be the conquest of the Japanese homeland. Twenty thousand Americans were killed in the battle for the eight square miles of Iwojima; the 23,000 Japanese defenders fought to the last man.

In the summer of 1945, with her European allies defeated, most of her fleet destroyed, and her cities subject to very heavy Allied bombing, Japan also faced defeat. The government wanted peace but would not submit to the humiliation of the unconditional surrender which the Allies demanded. In particular, the Japanese were prepared to risk everything to preserve the imperial throne: all Japanese politicians and soldiers were fanatically loyal to the Emperor.

Although the Allies were bound to win in the end, they still had to drive the Japanese out of south-east Asia and China and, ultimately, invade Japan itself. Furthermore, there was no doubt that the enemy would resist vigorously at every point; Allied commanders calculated that the war would last for another eighteen months and that their armies would sustain another million casualties.

Two developments changed the situation. On 8 August the Soviet Union at last declared war on Japan and began an invasion of Manchuria, thus rendering Japan's military position even more hopeless. Secondly, and more important, American scientists, profiting from the earlier researches of British physicists, perfected an atomic bomb. The city of Hiroshima was totally devastated on 6 August and three days later Nagasaki met a similar fate. The nature of warfare and the course of history were changed. A single aircraft, carrying a single bomb, could now cause intolerable destruction.

Not even the heroic Japanese could withstand the atomic terror. Fearing, wrongly, that the Americans had further stocks of bombs and that other cities would be obliterated, they rushed to make peace on the best possible terms. Breaking all precedent, the Emperor broadcast to the nation on 15 August:

> The war situation has developed not necessarily to Japan's advantage ... We have resolved to pave the way for a grand peace for all the generations to come by enduring the unendurable and suffering what is insufferable.

**Japanese surrender**

The Japanese threw themselves upon the mercy of the Allies, who

*Hiroshima*
**The atomic bomb**

did, in fact, allow the Emperor to retain his throne. The final surrender was received by General MacArthur on board the American battleship *Missouri* in Tokyo harbour on 2 September 1945.

CONCLUSION

In the last two years of war Britain was eclipsed by her two great allies. British forces played an important part in the Allied victory, both in Europe and in south-east Asia, but they were heavily outnumbered by the Russians and the Americans. Britain's main contribution was to keep alive resistance to Nazi Germany until such time as the Soviet Union and the United States were drawn in.

# Chapter 10
# The Second World War
# —Domestic Events

**Chamberlain's war cabinet**

Serious observers at the beginning of the Second World war had little doubt that, as in the last two years of the First War, the government would have to assume extensive powers over manpower, industry, and individual liberty. When the controls were enforced they caused little resentment. The people realized that the restrictions were necessary and that they were being fairly applied. The population was united and resolute in face of danger and hardship and this, after 1940, was very largely due to Winston Churchill's inspiring leadership.

Success, of course, depended on the efficiency with which the nation was mobilized for total war. In the First War, an all-party coalition had been formed in May 1915, but it was not until Lloyd George replaced Asquith in December 1916 that the machinery of government was effectively geared to the demands of twentieth-century warfare. On the outbreak of war in September 1939, however, Chamberlain immediately instituted a small War Cabinet on Lloyd George's lines, brought into his government the talented but rebellious Churchill and Eden and established ministries of economic warfare, food, shipping, information, and home security. But the administration remained overwhelmingly Conservative since the Labour leaders refused to serve under Chamberlain.

The vital transformation in the central command came in May 1940 when a Commons debate on the failure of the Norwegian campaign turned into an attack on Chamberlain's leadership. The most violent criticism came from Conservative back-benchers. L.S. Amery concluded his assault on the Prime Minister with a quotation from Cromwell's final speech to the Rump Parliament:

Depart, I say, and let us have done with you. In the name of God, go!

Chamberlain appealed for the support of 'his friends', but the aged Lloyd George demanded from the Prime Minister an example of sacrifice,

. . . because there is nothing which can contribute more to victory in this war than that he should sacrifice the seals of office.

The government's majority fell from the normal 240 to 81 as a result of the back-bench rebellion. After some hesitation,

215

Chamberlain's place as Prime Minister was taken by Churchill, who had secured promises of Labour and Liberal support.

Churchill placed the supreme command in the hands of a War Cabinet of five, containing two Labour representatives and two Conservatives in addition to himself. The original members were Churchill, Chamberlain, Halifax, Attlee, and Greenwood. Whereas Asquith had refused to join Lloyd George's War Cabinet, Chamberlain was quite willing to accept Churchill's leadership. Churchill appointed men to other ministerial positions, outside the War Cabinet, irrespective of their political backgrounds, looking always for drive, determination, and proven administrative ability. Thus Lord Beaverbrook, the newspaper magnate, became Minister of Aircraft Production, Lord Woolton, a successful businessman, was chosen as Minister of Food, and Ernest Bevin, the leading figure in the trade union movement, was persuaded to join the government as Minister of Labour. Churchill himself took the additional title of Minister of Defence, showing that the final military responsibility was to be his. Although he continually insisted that he could be overruled by the War Cabinet, Churchill, in fact, took all the main military decisions himself. The service chiefs were sometimes angered by his detailed instructions and advice, for this self-styled military expert was often wrong, but they admired him and worked for him as they would for no one else.

Churchill's energy and enthusiasm were apparently boundless. He drove his subordinates ruthlessly, expecting devotion to duty and loyalty to himself, and refusing to tolerate inefficiency or indolence. He was liable to interfere unexpectedly in any department on matters of major principle or minor detail. In this way he sought to keep ministers and civil servants alike on their toes. He rightly maintained that Parliament could remove him from office whenever it chose. While in power, however, he behaved not unlike a dictator. Of the War Cabinet, he said: 'All I wanted was compliance with my wishes after reasonable discussion.' This is what total war demanded.

Popular morale is of the utmost importance in wartime, especially when, as in 1940, invasion and defeat seem possible. In this respect, Churchill's speeches in the House of Commons and on the radio were among his main contributions to the war effort. They had the effect of instilling a spirit of determination and self-sacrifice. Shortly after taking office he outlined his policy:

I have nothing to offer but blood, toil, tears and sweat. You ask, What is our policy? I will say: It is to wage war, by sea, land, and air, with all our might and with all the strength that God can give us . . . You ask, What is our aim? I can answer in one word: Victory—victory at all costs, victory in spite of all terror; victory, however long and hard the road may be.

In the middle of the disastrous Battle of France, he proclaimed:

We shall not flag or fail, we shall go on to the end, we shall fight in France, we shall fight on the seas and the oceans, we shall fight with growing strength and confidence in the air, we shall defend our island whatever the cost may be, we shall fight on the beaches, we shall fight on the landing grounds, we shall fight in the fields and in the streets, we shall fight in the hills, we shall never surrender, and even if, which I do not for a moment believe, this island or a large part of it were subjugated and starving, then our Empire beyond the seas, armed and guarded by the British Fleet, would carry on the struggle, until, in God's good time, the New World, with all its power and might, steps forth to the rescue and liberation of the Old.

This wonderful summons to battle was also a realistic statement of policy. The British Empire would not give in to Hitler, but alone it could do no more than survive. The liberation of the continent of Europe was possible only if the New World (that is, the United States) entered the war.

Churchill hit just the right note, and the public responded magnificently. Hardly anyone contemplated defeat. One Scotsman remarked to another: 'Aye, Jock, if the English give in this is going to be a long war.' The 'Dunkirk spirit' was abroad. Munitions workers undertook ten hour shifts, seven days a week. The entire nation faced the same hardships: black-out, bombing, rationing and, possibly, invasion.

Speeches alone did not win the war. The most important of the national resources which had to be mobilized was manpower. The conscription of men into the forces was begun in the summer of 1939 even before the war started; there were no illusions this time about being able to fight a major war with a volunteer army. As soon as war was declared Parliament passed a National Service (Armed Forces) Act, which made all men between the ages of eighteen and forty-one liable to conscription. As in the First World War, there was a table of reserved occupations: key workers, such as munitions engineers and coalminers, would not be called up. By the spring of 1940 over a million and a half men had joined the forces. Shortages of uniforms, weapons, and training facilities prevented a more rapid mobilization.

When a German invasion seemed probable in mid-1940, men between the ages of seventeen and sixty-five who were not already in the forces were invited to join the Local Defence Volunteer force, later known as the Home Guard. In two months, over a million men volunteered and further recruits had to be discouraged. Arms and uniforms were not available for so large a number and a common sight was a Home Guard detachment drilling with broom handles instead of rifles.

**The Home Guard**

An almost military approach was adopted towards industrial workers, who were directed from non-essential pursuits to vital war work. This potentially dangerous policy worked smoothly because of Bevin's tactful administration. Total involvement was carried a stage further late in 1941 when the conscription of unmarried women into the women's forces or other war work was inaugurated.

The manufacture and supply of munitions had been one of the biggest problems of the First World War. Under Churchill a committee of four ministers, including Beaverbrook and Bevin, was responsible, and although these two forceful personalities were often in conflict, armaments were produced at a highly satisfactory rate. In 1940 aircraft production was Beaverbrook's special concern and, thanks to his business efficiency and skill in cutting through red tape, the R.A.F. had more fighter aircraft at the end of the Battle of Britain than at the beginning. Beaverbrook launched a national appeal for scrap metal, which resulted in miles of garden railings being converted into Spitfires and Hurricanes. He also demanded extra work from the factories, and, with Bevin's co-operation, persuaded the unions to suspend rules governing the length of the working day.

In the summer of 1940 the army was desperately short of weapons. All the B.E.F.'s armour and heavy equipment had been abandoned at Dunkirk, and there were not even enough rifles to go round. One veteran recalls an incident from his basic training at that time:

> We drilled at first with broomsticks owing to the dearth of rifles, then an actual rifle appeared and was handed round the square, though our platoon hadn't much time to learn its mechanism before a runner came to attention in front of our sergeant saying: 'Please sar'nt our sarn't in No. 8 says could we have the rifle for a dekko over there 'cause none of our blokes so much as seen one yet.'

Early in the war Churchill secured President Roosevelt's agreement to sales of surplus American arms. Such transactions quickly led to currency difficulties as Britain was not exporting enough to pay for these imports from the United States. The obstacle was overcome when Churchill and Roosevelt agreed late in 1940 on 'lend-lease', a scheme whereby the United States government would pay the manufacturers for the war materials supplied to Britain; those not used could be subsequently returned. There was no immediate and dramatic increase in imports of arms from the United States, for the American armaments industry was not yet mobilized. But the important principle had been established. Addressing the American people in February 1941, Churchill said: 'Give us the tools and we shall finish the job.' By 1944 the United States was supplying half of Britain's tanks, two-thirds of its transport aircraft, and nearly all of its landing craft.

PLOUGH NOW! *by day and night*

GROW FOOD FOR THE NATION
FEEDING STUFFS FOR YOUR FARMS
KEEP OUR SHIPS AND MONEY FREE
FOR BUYING VITAL ARMS

WOMEN OF BRITAIN! ARM HIM

ISSUED BY THE MINISTRY OF LABOUR AND NATIONAL SERVICE

**Munitions and Armaments**

WOMEN OF BRITAIN
**COME INTO THE FACTORIES**
AT ANY EMPLOYMENT EXCHANGE FOR ADVICE AND FULL DETAILS

ERNEST BEVIN
SAYS –
"We must have exports"

YOU ARE WORKING FOR
**EXPORT**
YOU ARE WORKING FOR
**VICTORY**

As in the First War, the government directed the basic industries. Government commissioners co-ordinated transport, taking over general control of the docks and railways. The mines remained under private ownership, but a Ministry of Fuel and Power was set up to deal with a coal shortage in 1942. Coal production was declining, partly because too many miners had gone into the forces. From 1943 Bevin directed a scheme whereby some young men ('Bevin boys') went into the mines instead of the army.

The cost of the war was, of course, enormous, and although taxes were increased, extra borrowing was also necessary. The main increase was in income-tax, which rose to 7s. 6d. (37½p) in the pound in 1939 and eventually to 10s. 0d. (50p) in the pound. There was also a heavy purchase-tax on luxury items. These measures led to a general levelling-out of wealth, to the satisfaction of most of the population.

One main aim of government policies was to keep prices down, to prevent the appalling inflation of the First War. Prices, in fact, rose by no more than fifty per cent during the war, and since wages increased by slightly more and unemployment vanished, the general standard of living was higher. The main hardship was shortage, of houses, clothes, and food. Most housewives spent a sizeable part of the war in queues.

Enemy submarine attacks on merchant shipping caused a sharp reduction in the volume of imports. Petrol rationing was introduced at the beginning of the war and private motoring for pleasure eventually became almost impossible. Food rationing began in January 1940. Although few luxuries were henceforth available and the Ministry of Food issued a host of regulations determining, for example, the colour of bread and the proportion of meat in sausage, supplies never ran short. In fact, it is argued that the dieting experts who advised the Ministry in fixing the rations caused an improvement in the nation's health by compelling people to eat more nutritious food. One of the reasons for the success of the food policies was that the Ministry of Agriculture encouraged British farmers to produce as much food as possible and, in particular, to cultivate land which had previously been devoted to pasture.

These policies all involved extending the powers of central government and restricting the rights of the individual citizen. By the Emergency Powers Acts of 1939 and 1940 traditional liberties such as freedom from arbitrary imprisonment and freedom of the press were made liable to suspension. Such authority was used sparingly, but all German nationals and many British Fascists were interned for a while and the Communist newspaper, the *Daily Worker*, was temporarily suppressed. The Ministry of Information operated a form of press censorship by controlling the flow of war news to the papers. From October 1939 everyone was compelled to carry an identity card. Signposts were removed from cross-roads, railway stations lost their name-boards, and stocks of maps were destroyed so that German spies would be mystified.

Air raids emphasized the involvement of the whole population in the Second World War. Now the citizens of London and Birmingham were also in the front line. The events of the Spanish Civil War had led to exaggerated fears of the effectiveness of aerial bombardment. Anticipating the total destruction of the cities and the dropping of poison-gas bombs, the government prepared in 1938 plans for the evacuation of children from London and issued gas-masks to the entire population in September 1939. Strict black-out regulations were also brought into effect: street lights were extinguished, cars might not use headlights, and householders had to black out their windows at night. The principal result was an enormous increase in the number of road accidents.

Immediately on the outbreak of war, the evacuation of primary schoolchildren and mothers with children under five years of age began. Under the official scheme a million and a half people left London and the other major cities (more than half the children and young mothers stayed at home). A further two million were evacuated privately. The movement worked fairly smoothly, but some areas received more evacuees than expected, which led to accommodation and feeding problems. Most of the city children adapted well to the unfamiliar country life, but there were some difficult cases: according to official reports, Evelyn Waugh's hilarious account of a problem family in his novel *Put Out More Flags* is no exaggeration. When no bombs had fallen by January 1940 the majority of evacuees returned home.

Not only the children and their mothers moved out of London. Almost 20,000 civil servants were transferred to safer parts of the country; the B.B.C.'s headquarters went to Evesham; the Bank of England moved to a Hampshire village; and the treasures of the National Gallery were stored in a cave in a disused slate quarry in North Wales.

Heavy German bombing began in September 1940 and continued until the spring of 1941 (see page 198). A total of 30,000 people were killed in the Blitz, and three and a half million houses were damaged or destroyed. In London, the East End and the City suffered the most serious destruction, but every part of the capital was affected. The House of Commons was destroyed, although not during a session, and Buckingham Palace was also damaged. The Blitz led to another round of evacuation, whilst many Londoners sought security at night by sleeping in the tube stations. Incendiary bombs were an even greater menace than high explosives and led Herbert Morrison, the Home Secretary, to institute compulsory

GOVERNMENT EVACUATION SCHEME

The Government have ordered evacuation of registered school children.

If your children are registered, visit their assembly point at once and read the instructions on the notice board.

The name and address of the assembly point is given on the notice to parents.

Posters notifying arrival will be displayed at the schools at which the children assemble for evacuation.

*Faringdon Street Market, London, destroyed by a V2 in 1945. Below Londoners using a tube station as an air-raid shelter*

**The blitz**

fire-watching on all public buildings and to reorganize the Fire Service. Valuable rescue work was done by voluntary air-raid wardens, ambulance corps, and auxiliary firemen. The Blitz grew less intense after the summer of 1941, when Hitler attacked Russia, but in 1944 the bombardment of London was resumed, this time with flying bombs and rockets, the V1s and V2s. These new weapons precipitated another evacuation of the capital, but the danger subsided as the V1s were shot down and the launching sites of the V2s overrun.

Bombing had only a slight effect on communications and industrial production. Nor did it eventually weaken civilian morale, although the first heavy raids seem to have led to murmurs of discontent from the East End of London. After several weeks of nightly attacks the Londoners stopped grumbling, but when the *Luftwaffe* began its assault on the provincial cities the people's first reaction was again horror and sometimes panic. Visiting Southampton on the morning of 2 December 1940, the Bishop of Winchester found

the people broken in spirit after the sleepless and awful nights. Everyone who can do so is leaving the town . . . Everywhere I saw men and women carrying suitcases or bundles, the children clutching some precious doll or toy, struggling to get anywhere out of Southampton. For the time, morale had collapsed. I went from parish to parish and everywhere there was fear.

London showed that people could learn to live with the Blitz. The populations of Russian, German, and Japanese cities proved that civilians could take much more punishment than that. But to underestimate the strain on the people is to fail to recognize the courage and endurance of millions of men, women, and children.

Throughout the war, the B.B.C. made an enormous contribution to morale. Its news bulletins were honest and reliable, it gave Churchill an opportunity regularly to address the people, and it provided a wide range of popular entertainment. The sentimental ballads of Vera Lynn (such as 'We'll meet again' and 'There'll be bluebirds over the white cliffs of Dover') gave heart to the forces, but everyone's favourite was the weekly half-hour comedy programme *I.T.M.A.*, starring Tommy Handley. Surprisingly perhaps, the fairly serious *Brains Trust* was only slightly less popular.

By 1942 it was clear that, although the war might continue for several years, ultimate victory was assured. Some of the government's energies were therefore directed towards planning post-war reconstruction. In December 1942 Sir William Beveridge, who had conducted an investigation of the social services on behalf of the government, issued his *Report on Social Insurance*. Beveridge recommended a comprehensive state scheme of protection for individuals and families 'from the cradle to the grave'. He an-

*Government posters*

**Beveridge Report**

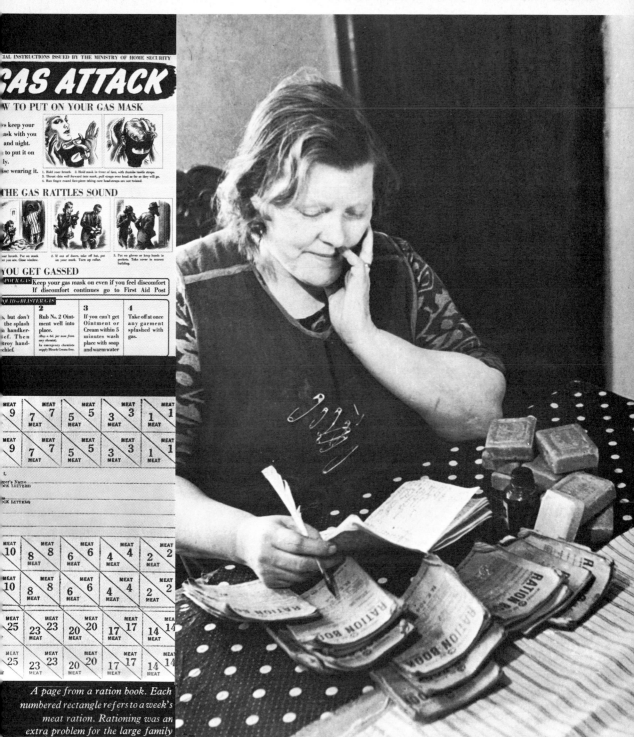

*A page from a ration book. Each numbered rectangle refers to a week's meat ration. Rationing was an extra problem for the large family*

nounced that there were five main enemies which any national social insurance scheme must face: 'Want, Disease, Ignorance, Squalor and Idleness'. He suggested, therefore, that pensions and unemployment and sickness benefit should become part of a service designed to maintain everyone above a basic subsistence level; that there should be a national health service; that the government should act to eliminate mass unemployment; and that vigorous efforts should be made to solve the housing problem and to remove slums. The report became a best-seller but did not win the government's full approval. Many ministers doubted the country's ability to afford such an ambitious scheme after the war.

The other important social measure was Butler's Education Act of 1944. The Act directed that the school-leaving age should be raised from fourteen to fifteen, and ultimately to sixteen. (It was raised to fifteen in 1947 and to sixteen in 1972.) The Act's most important provision was that there should be free secondary education for all children, and it envisaged that this would mean three types of secondary school: grammar, technical, and modern. The old 'all-age' schools would disappear and it would henceforth be impossible to 'buy' a place in a grammar school. The Act caused controversy at the time and since by stipulating that religious instruction should form part of the curriculum of every school.

**Butler's Education Act 1944**

As there had not been a general election since 1935, the party leaders agreed that Parliament should be dissolved as soon as Germany was defeated. Shortly after the German surrender the Labour ministers resigned from the coalition in order to be free to fight the election campaign on party lines. The Conservatives relied on Churchill's prestige and, although the people cheered him wherever he went in his pre-election tour of Britain, they decided in favour of Labour. Churchill himself made the mistake of claiming that his wartime Labour colleagues would, if returned to power, impose their policies ruthlessly and establish something not far removed from a Nazi Gestapo.

The voters, especially the soldiers, sailors, and airmen, rejected the old order. They identified the Conservatives with unemployment, dole queues, the means test, and hunger marches. After six years of war they wanted something better. Labour offered full employment, social security, a house-building programme, and nationalization of the major industries. This was the prospect of an exciting new Britain, and for once the voters became idealists. When the results were announced on 26 July it was found that Labour had won 393 seats, the Conservatives 213 and the Liberals 12. Churchill resigned at once and Attlee became head of the first Labour government to enjoy a majority in the House of Commons.

*Election Result 1945*
| | |
|---|---|
| Labour | 393 |
| Conservative | 213 |
| Others | 22 |
| Liberal | 12 |

Victory in the Second World War had been bought at a high price. Casualties were less than in the First War: 300,000 servicemen, 60,000 civilians, and 30,000 members of the merchant navy were killed. But the financial drain was such that Britain could never again act as a fully independent Great Power. Britain's dollar reserves were exhausted and a huge debt was owed to the United States. In addition, assets in the form of overseas investments had been spent to raise badly needed foreign currency. Bomb damage and the overworking of machinery meant that many industries would have difficulty in readjusting themselves to peacetime conditions. Britain's foreign trading position would thus be difficult, and the loss of overseas markets during the war made the prospects worse. Among the few favourable consequences of the war were the stimuli which had been given to such industries as electricity supply, and the manufacture of motor vehicles, machine tools, synthetic fibres, and chemicals. There was no talk in 1945 of 'a land fit for heroes': few people doubted that the first years of peace would be hard.

# Chapter 11
# The British Economy since 1945

SOME ELEMENTARY ECONOMIC FACTS

Nearly every modern state lives by trading: the cost of its imports from other countries must be met by selling goods and services abroad. Robinson Crusoe, on his desert island, traded with no one and consequently never experienced a balance of payments crisis, but he dressed in goat-skins and did not possess a transistor radio.

**Gold and dollar reserve**
A nation's economic position is similar to that of a family with a weekly income of £50 and with savings of £100 in the bank. It should normally spend no more than £50 a week, although it can occasionally, at Christmas or holiday time, dip into the savings. If it regularly spends more than it earns, however, the bank deposit will disappear and bankruptcy will result. Similarly, a nation like Britain must pay for everything it buys from abroad. If the value of its imports permanently exceeds its foreign earnings, the national bank deposit (the gold and dollar reserve) will be frittered away.

**Wages and prices**
To avoid such a disaster, the government should try to encourage exports and put some restraint on imports. Many different factors affect the success or failure of British exporters, but one of the most obvious is the price of the goods which they are trying to sell. Prices, in turn, are affected by the wages paid to the workers in Britain's factories. A big wage increase for Ford car workers at Dagenham will lead to a rise in the price of Ford cars. Unless the prices of foreign cars are also going up at the same rate, this will mean a decline in overseas sales.

Another effect of wage increases is that the wage-earners are able to buy more, including more imported goods. The net result of a round of wage rises, therefore, may be to reduce exports and increase imports, to bring about, in other words, a worsening of the balance of payments position.

Higher wages do not have to lead to higher prices. If they are matched by an increase in output, the prices can remain stationary. To take a simple example, a shoemaker, working for himself, may make a pair of shoes for £5 and sell them for £6. If he makes forty pairs of shoes a week he earns £40 profit. To increase his weekly earnings to £50, he must either raise the price of his shoes to £6.25 or make ten extra pairs of shoes: an increase in output can make possible an increase in earnings without causing a price rise.

Increased output is best brought about by the modernization of industry, the substitution of new, labour-saving machinery for old, out-dated techniques. If our shoemaker did his stitching by machine instead of by hand, he would increase his output without having to work longer hours. This is known as a rise in productivity. The trouble is that all industrialists, from our humble shoemaker to giants like I.C.I., need money with which to buy the new equipment. Such capital is provided either by firms themselves out of their profits or by private investors. The more firms sell, the greater will be their profits, and the greater the amount of money available for investment.

**Investment**

The quantity of goods sold by a firm is governed, of course, by public demand, which is determined by the price, quality, and desirability of the goods, but also by how much money people have to spend. The amount of money available depends upon the total number of people in work, the size of their wage-packets, and the proportion of their incomes taken from them by the government in taxation. The shoemaker, therefore, striving to save enough money to buy a stitching-machine, may work very hard and produce high quality shoes at a very reasonable price, but still fail to reach his target through no fault of his own. If most of his normal customers are unemployed, or if purchase-tax on new shoes is very high, he may be unable to sell sufficient to pay for the new machine.

**Demand**

The level of taxation, of course, is decided by the government. In the budget, his annual financial statement, the Chancellor of the Exchequer declares how much money he intends to take and in what ways. The obvious and traditional purpose of the budget is to raise sufficient revenue by taxation (income-tax, purchase-tax, customs duties, dog licences, etc.) to pay for expenditure (defence, education, pensions, housing, etc.). The orthodox view was that revenue and expenditure should balance. Between the wars the great economist John Maynard Keynes, looking for a solution to mass unemployment, discovered that a much more subtle use of the budget was possible. When unemployment was high, the government could spend more than it received, thus creating extra spending power and extra jobs, reducing the level of unemployment. A lower rate of income-tax would leave people with more money to spend on, for example, new suits of clothes. This would provide more employment in textile mills and tailors' workshops. Extra government expenditure on road building would mean more jobs for road builders. All these people—mill-workers, tailors, and road builders—would have more money to spend, and so would create employment for others. Keynes's solution meant a budget deficit—expenditure would exceed revenue—but the deficit would

**Keynes**

*Inflation was always a problem, whoever was in office*

228

be temporary and could be covered by borrowing.

The reverse of Keynes's theory is also useful. When too much money is chasing too few goods, prices rise. The government, however, can prevent price rises by depriving people of their extra money through taxation. In such circumstances, the government would be raising more money than it needed, or creating a budget surplus. This policy, commonly called deflation, can also be used to restrict imports—consumers, having less money to spend, will be able to buy fewer luxury goods from abroad.

It is clearly in everyone's interests that wages should rise and prices remain stationary. This would lead to a rising standard of living and a healthy balance of payments surplus. This happy state of affairs can be achieved by encouraging investment with a view to modernizing industry and increasing productivity, securing economic growth.

How can the government contribute? It would seem that low taxation should help achieve full employment and a healthy level of demand. This should lead to full production, high profits, a satisfactory investment rate, and so greater productivity. If taxes are kept low, people will have more money to spend on clothes, cars, spin-driers, etc. and the manufacturers of these goods will make bigger profits. If the firms re-invest these profits in new machinery, output per man will increase with the result that the firms will be able to raise wages without increasing prices.

The snag, however, is that whenever taxes are reduced people do not merely buy more British goods; they also buy more Swiss watches, Japanese cameras, and French wines. Boom conditions, as the economists call them, lead to balance of payments crises. Faced with falling gold and dollar reserves, governments hurriedly deflate the economy: taxes are increased so that people have less money to spend on imports. This solves the balance of payments crisis, but does nothing to help modernize industry.

With relatively full employment, there has not, since 1945, been an army of jobless men eager to work for whatever wages the employers choose to pay. The trade unions have had the whip hand, and have been able to secure wage increases far in excess of the rise in productivity. Governments have sought to stimulate investment and industrial modernization, therefore, not in order to enable employers to pay higher wages, but in the vain hope that increases in output would catch up with wage increases. While growth lags behind wage increases, prices rise—that is, inflation occurs. Inflation can be cured by deflationary measures such as tax increases, but this does not work when unions merely retaliate by demanding, and obtaining, wage increases.

Inflation has been a world-wide phenomenon since 1945. Had it occurred at the same rate in all countries it would have had no

**Deflation**

there's ONE Minister who never loses his job..

229

effect on trade, but Britain's problem has been that her inflation has been more rapid than that of other countries. The result has been a steadily deteriorating balance of payments position. All attempts to achieve the necessary growth to pay for the wage increases have led to soaring import bills and rapid returns to deflationary policies.

What, then, is the answer to Britain's economic problems? Devaluation of the pound, by making exports cheaper and imports dearer, temporarily solves the balance of payments deficit, but it also causes a higher cost of living at home and so leads to further demands for higher wages. Within a year or two of devaluation, rising labour costs can force up the price of exports again, so that the advantage is lost.

The government can, of course, take direct action to influence imports and exports: it can discourage imports by means of heavy customs duties and a quota system, and can grant tax concessions to exporters. Such techniques were extensively used by the post-war Labour government, but they are at variance with a number of international trade agreements, whose general aim is to reduce tariffs and stimulate world trade.

Deflation has been the normal answer to balance of payments deficits and, in the short term, it works. Higher taxes, more severe hire-purchase regulations, and strict rules limiting the amount of money which banks may lend have always reduced consumption and so brought down the import bill. Rising unemployment, how-ever, is an inevitable result of deflation, and no government since the war has dared contemplate a return to the heavy unemployment of the 1920s and 1930s. Industrial modernization and economic growth are also slowed down by deflation, for money is scarce. Nor is there much evidence to show that deflationary policies halt wage demands; even with well over a million unemployed trade unions have not lost their strong bargaining position. Governments which allow unemployment to rise soon become unpopular, however. Short periods of deflation ('Stop') have therefore always to be followed by the lowering of taxes and the relaxation of controls ('Go'). Such 'stop-go' policies, which prevailed in Britain in the 1950s and early 1960s, were generally denounced, but no convincing alternative was put forward.

### THE LABOUR GOVERNMENT 1945–1951

The Labour government which assumed office in July 1945 was in two senses more fortunate than the earlier Labour administra-tions: it had a majority of 146 over all other parties in the Commons and five of its members (Attlee, Greenwood, Bevin, Morrison, and Cripps) had had experience in Churchill's War Cabinet. The voters

**Inflation**

**Devaluation**

**Stop-go**

who expressed their confidence in these men in 1945 probably did not realize the size of the task ahead. The problems of achieving a favourable balance of payments and maintaining the value of sterling were the most critical, but deficiencies of fuel, food, and housing also caused acute anxiety. The new government's task was not only to solve the immediate problems, but also to carry out the social revolution to which the party had committed itself in the general election campaign.

The immediate problem was financial. Britain's gold and dollar reserves had been substantially reduced during the war and an unfavourable balance of payments was anticipated in the first years of peace. Factories could not change immediately from manufacturing war materials to turning out goods for export; after nearly six years of all-out effort, a great deal of machinery was worn out; resources which might have gone into producing exports had to be diverted to the repair of bomb damage. Even worse was the blow to invisible exports. Over £1,000 million of foreign investments had been sold during the war to pay for imports, huge debts had been incurred in India and Egypt to pay for the forces stationed there, and sixteen million tons of shipping had been sunk.

As the Americans ended the 'lend-lease' agreement in August 1945, it was feared that the remaining gold and dollars would quickly vanish and that national bankruptcy would follow. After some hard bargaining, an American and Canadian loan of £1,100 million, to be repaid over fifty years, was secured. The loan prevented immediate disaster, but, as predicted, imports exceeded exports. As in the early 1920s, the volume of world trade did not reach the pre-war level. Britain could not earn enough to pay for her imports from the United States, and by 1947 the loan obtained two years previously was almost spent.

A sudden outflow of gold and dollars in the summer of 1947 led to an acute sterling crisis. There had to be a big increase in industrial production, and most of that increase had to go into the export market. The man charged with this task was Sir Stafford Cripps, who became Chancellor of the Exchequer in November 1947. (Harold Wilson took his place as President of the Board of Trade.) Cripps instituted a policy of austerity. In an attempt to increase production, advisory councils were set up to co-ordinate the efforts of government and managers, productivity drives by national publicity campaigns were launched, and targets were set for individual factories. With the co-operation of the trade unions, Cripps demanded that everyone should work harder, accept the existing wage rates, and refrain from buying the goods which had to be exported. Strict government controls ensured that a substantial proportion of the extra produce was exported. While car exports rapidly increased, new cars were so scarce at home that

*Austerity: Sir Stafford Cripps with the Budget box*

**Cripps's austerity**

one and two-year-old vehicles sold for appreciably more than the new price. Imports were also tightly controlled: some commodities were governed by quotas and licences, while others, such as tobacco, were heavily taxed.

Britain's export drive received considerable encouragement from the renewal of American help for Europe. In 1947 George Marshall, the American Secretary of State, announced that Europe was in need of substantial American aid if famine and economic dislocation were to be avoided. Marshall Aid, which began in 1948, brought American money once more to Europe, including Britain. All European states were invited to participate, but the Communist countries refused America's help. Marshall Aid led quickly to a revival of trade, which permitted Britain to sell her goods in European markets. At the same time, Britain was fortunate in that two of her main competitors in the inter-war years, Germany and Japan, had so far made little progress towards recovery. World trade began to flourish in the late 1940s and early 1950s, whereas it had wilted in the early 1920s (see pages 98–100). Marshall Aid, evidence of the generosity and wisdom of the American government and people, was the main reason why this pitfall was avoided after 1945. The western Allies' failure to impose crushing reparations on

**Marshall Aid**

*Britain's Overseas Trade*

Commonwealth
Western Europe
North & Central America
Rest of the world

Germany and Italy was a further help to reconstruction (compare page 98).

Germany and Italy was a further help to reconstruction (compare page 98).

**Devaluation**

Britain's industrial production and exports increased, but her exports to the United States were still inadequate. Accordingly, in September 1949, Cripps took the critical step of devaluing the pound: henceforth it would be worth 2.80 dollars instead of 4.03. British goods thereby became cheaper abroad and the volume of exports increased. At the same time, imports became dearer, so that the cost of living rose.

By 1950 Britain's exports stood at seventy-five per cent above the 1938 figure and the balance of payments had been restored. But the price had been Cripps's austerity, involving shortages in the shops and little improvement in the standard of living. Wilson, at the Board of Trade, eased some of the controls after 1948. The rationing of bread and potatoes (imposed in 1946 and 1947) ended in 1948, and in 1949 clothes rationing was abolished and the petrol ration doubled.

Shortage of fuel was another of the unpleasant features of the Labour government's period of office. The equipment in many coalmines was out of date and inefficient and the level of production was lower than before the war. The crisis came during the exceptionally severe winter of 1946–7, when the domestic demand for coal and electricity naturally increased, while snow and ice often impeded transport. Factories were forced to close and frequent power cuts added to the general misery. The position improved thereafter, but a bad winter could still lead to chaos.

By 1950 Britain was paying her way. The economic position had been stabilized at the cost of an enormous debt to the United States, with the result that Britain could never again play a fully independent role in the world. To the average citizen (and voter) these matters were not important. As far as he was concerned, the years 1945–50 had been a time when he had been encouraged to work hard and not to demand higher wages despite rising prices, had to put up with food rationing and power cuts, and had the utmost difficulty in obtaining a new house.

The Labour party had pledged itself to a policy of socialism on its next return to office. According to the manifesto presented by Attlee and his colleagues before the 1945 election, this amounted to the nationalization of the country's principal industries and an extensive programme of social reform. Attlee's administration substantially enacted these policies despite the economic and financial problems which the country faced.

The essence of the policy of nationalization, which had been official party policy since 1918, was that the 'commanding heights' of the economy, basic industries like coal, steel, transport, electricity, and gas, should be under public ownership so that the state could

| Percentage of total trade) | | | |
|---|---|---|---|
| Imports | | Exports | |
| 950 | 1967 | 1950 | 1967 |
| 36·0 | 27·4 | 41·5 | 30·4 |
| 24·2 | 36·4 | 26·4 | 38·0 |
| 7·3 | 19·7 | 12·4 | 16·4 |
| 22·5 | 16·5 | 19·7 | 15·2 |

**Nationalization**

control them in the national interest. The question of nationalization always has been, and still is, controversial, although there has been, perhaps, less disagreement between the parties over the public ownership of the coalmines and railways, which were and remain unprofitable. Since these industries provide a necessary public service, it is claimed that their losses should be borne by the state. The Conservative and Liberal parties have always maintained that privately owned industry, which must make a profit, is bound to be more efficient and therefore to serve the nation's interests better.

The nationalization programme was largely carried out in the first three years of the Labour government's life. The Bank of England was taken over by the state in 1946; the coalmines, airlines, and the electricity industry in 1947; in 1948 public transport (docks, railways, London Transport, and road haulage) and gas; and finally, in 1949, the iron and steel industry. There was little political controversy except over iron and steel. In all, the Labour government succeeded in nationalizing twenty per cent of Britain's industry.

The administration of the publicly owned industries was put into the hands of special boards (like the National Coal Board), appointed by the government but enjoying a large amount of independence. They were not controlled directly from Whitehall and miners did not become civil servants. Promises that workers and consumers would share in the direction of the industries, however, were fulfilled only half-heartedly, and the workers often expressed the suspicion that they had merely exchanged one set of bosses for another.

Capital investment to provide new, efficient, and economical machinery was needed in the mines, the railways, and the electricity generating industry in particular. But the government, faced with economic and financial crisis and obliged to pay compensation to the former owners of the nationalized industries, could not afford to spend money on a large scale. The result was continued inefficiency and, in some cases, large annual deficits. The National Coal Board's deficit was made worse by the government's determination to keep the price of coal down, for cheap fuel was vital to the success of the export programme.

Labour won the election of 1950, but its majority was reduced to six. Having struggled to keep the nation's head above water in the first five years of peace, it was threatened by another tidal wave when the Korean War broke out in June 1950 (see page 263). Hugh Gaitskell, who replaced Cripps as Chancellor of the Exchequer in October 1950, had to find the money to pay for an increase in the armed forces. He was also faced in 1951 with a new balance of payments crisis: the Korean War led to a world-wide rise in the price of raw materials, which meant that Britain's import

**Inadequate investment**

*The National Federation of Housewives Association sponsored a petition signed by 100,000 women pressing for the handing back of meat purchasing to free enterprise, March 1951*

**Effect of Korean war**

**Gaitskell and 'stop-go' policy**

bill rose above her export earnings.

Gaitskell's response was to raise income-tax and to impose charges for National Health prescriptions, false teeth, and spectacles. His answer to a payments deficit was, in other words, deflation. This was a much less direct approach to the problem than Cripps's combination of austerity, import controls, and stimulus to exporters, but it set a pattern for the 1950s. Gaitskell may, perhaps, be seen as the originator of 'stop-go'.

## THE CONSERVATIVE GOVERNMENTS 1951–1964

The Conservatives, under Churchill's leadership, won the general election of October 1951, having promised to end food rationing and, by abolishing economic controls, to bring in a period of free enterprise and prosperity. Their policies, however, represented only a slight change from those of Labour's last three years. Only iron and steel and a part of the road transport industry were denationalized. Wilson had already begun to dismantle Cripps's elaborate system of import controls. R.A. Butler, Chancellor of the Exchequer from 1951 to 1955, like Gaitskell used indirect methods, such as alterations in income-tax rates and hire-purchase regulations, to guide the economy along the right lines. There was no abrupt change from socialist planning to Conservative freedom: the term 'Butskellism' was coined to describe what was apparently an agreed approach to economic problems.

Between 1952 and 1954 the new government was entirely successful. Food rationing was ended and building controls were removed, with the result that the Conservatives were able to fulfil their election promise to build far more houses. Butler, by reducing income-tax and easing hire-purchase restrictions, gave the people more money to spend. This heavy demand stimulated greater production and led to a marked increase in prosperity. Expansion at home did not, on this occasion, lead to a balance of payments deficit, partly because the price of imported raw materials had fallen again after the Korean War. Like Cripps, Butler saw that Britain's success depended on the competitiveness of her exporters and his 1953 budget included government grants to firms investing in new machinery.

When he went to the polls in 1955, the new Prime Minister, Sir Anthony Eden, could fairly claim that Conservative freedom had worked. He was duly re-elected with an increased majority. But the favourable circumstances of the early 1950s were already beginning to change. German and Japanese competition had reappeared, to the disadvantage of British exporters. The textile industry of Lancashire had to face the challenge of Japan and India. Furthermore, by 1955 British trade unions had come to expect regular wage increases. Strikes forced employers to grant rises which were not justified by extra production, with the inevitable result that prices rose also. Inflation had set in.

The combined effect of foreign competition and inflation was a balance of payments deficit in 1955. Butler's response was the same as Gaitskell's in 1951: deflation. Income-tax was increased, hire-purchase regulations were made more strict, and the bank-rate was raised, with the result that firms were less inclined to borrow money and the interest rates on house mortgages were increased. The net result was to leave people with less money to spend on imports and so to redress the deficit. On the other hand, the modernization of British industry was necessarily slowed down.

Since 1955 the economic history of Britain has followed a set pattern: recurrent balance of payments crises and runs on the pound have forced successive governments to adopt deflationary policies, which have in turn led to increasing unemployment; concerned over falling popularity resulting from unemployment and anxious about the slow rate of growth, ministers have then relaxed the controls, with the result that imports have once more soared. Economists and politicians have searched hopefully for a final solution, and some think they they have found it in economic co-operation with the rest of Europe.

Six west European countries (France, West Germany, Italy, Belgium, the Netherlands, and Luxembourg) had already in 1950 pooled their coal and steel resources in the European Coal and Steel Community. In March 1957 they signed the Treaty of Rome, creating the European Economic Community, often referred to as the Common Market. The E.E.C.'s aim was complete internal free trade, in food as well as manufactured goods, and a common external tariff. There would, in other words, be no customs duties on trade between France and Italy, and the two countries would levy the same duties on imports from the United States. Britain refused to sign the Treaty of Rome, fearing that economic co-operation would lead to eventual political union, that membership of the E.E.C. would mean dearer food, and that the common external tariff would damage the interests of Commonwealth countries like New Zealand, on whose products Britain charged low customs duties. The main argument in favour of joining was that the E.E.C. would give British manufacturers a much larger market and that more sales would lead to faster growth. It was highly significant that, despite her failure to sign the Treaty of Rome, Britain's trade with Western Europe was increasing rapidly in the 1950s and 1960s. A British attempt to get the best of both worlds by having free trade with Europe in manufactured goods but not food was resisted by the French, and Britain took no part in the European experiment.

The E.E.C.

Another British balance of payments deficit in 1957 was met by the usual deflationary measures, as a result of which unemployment rose to the high level of 620,000 in 1958. Harold Macmillan, who had become Prime Minister early in 1957, insisted that this was intolerable, despite the protests and resignation of his Chancellor of the Exchequer, Peter Thorneycroft. In the second half of 1958 and early 1959 the brake was taken off and the accelerator depressed: bank-rate was cut, hire-purchase restrictions eased, and income-tax reduced. The natural result was an increase in production and consumption and a fall in unemployment. Terrific increases in the sale of consumer goods such as washing-machines, television sets, refrigerators, and cars prompted Macmillan to boast in the 1959 election campaign that the people 'have never had it so good'.

The Conservative government took the credit for the 1959 boom and again increased its majority. Neither it nor the Labour opposition, however, had any clear idea about how to secure steady economic growth. No one liked 'stop-go', but there seemed to be no alternative.

Rapidly increasing wages and a heavy demand for imports brought the usual result of a balance of payments deficit and a sterling crisis in 1961. Macmillan's Chancellor, Selwyn Lloyd, deflated the economy by raising the bank-rate and cutting government spending, but he also introduced some direct measures, more reminiscent of Cripps's approach than any of the Conservative policies of the 1950s. Trying to stem the tide of rising wages, he imposed a pay-pause, refusing to allow any wage increases for government employees, and in 1962 set up a National Incomes Commission, whose purpose was to lay down guide-lines for wage and salary increases in the future. The refusal of the trade unions to co-operate killed this experiment in Conservative planning. Only slightly more successful was his National Economic Development Council, christened 'Neddy' by its critics, which was an attempt to promote co-operation between employers, unions, and the government in balancing economic growth and wage increases.

Such planning could have only long-term effects. The immediate problem in the winter of 1962–3 was rising unemployment, again a direct result of deflation (the maximum figure was 880,000). The government again switched from 'stop' to 'go': Reginald Maudling, who had replaced Selwyn Lloyd, reduced purchase-tax, especially on cars, and lowered the income-tax rate. Maudling's answer to the central problem was novel and bold. He rightly concluded that British industry needed a prolonged period of growth and argued that although growth was always accompanied by a balance of payments deficit, the government should persevere with expansion. Extra production and extra profits would enable manufacturers to modernize their plant and become more competitive in world

**Deflation in 1961**

*'He says he wants to join on his own terms.' Macmillan's Common Market policy 1957*

markets. The increase in output would then catch up with the wage increases and inflation would be halted. Maudling admitted that there would be a year or two of heavy balance of payments deficits, but argued that the gold and dollar reserves would cover them.

Maudling's Conservative supporters applauded his unconventional and imaginative policy. The Labour opposition denounced it as foolhardy. Government spending on roads, bridges, and hospitals was increased and a period of rapid growth began. The Conservatives had been very unpopular in 1962 and 1963, but their prestige rose during 1964 with the result that they very nearly won the election in the autumn of that year. The cost, of course, was a huge balance of payments deficit, and Labour made much of this in the election campaign and after its return to office, but Maudling had expected the deficit and can hardly be charged with irresponsibility. Whether the economy would have reached the plateau of a high growth rate which Maudling claimed to see in the distance is a question which may never be answered.

Concern over the chronic economic sickness led Macmillan's government to decide in 1961 that, despite Britain's obligations to the rest of the Commonwealth and fears about food prices, membership of the European Economic Community might give industry the stimulus which it needed. Edward Heath presented Britain's application skilfully, but it quickly became clear that President de Gaulle of France thought that Britain was still more interested in the American alliance than in collaboration with Europe. He effectively vetoed Britain's application in January 1963.

The Conservative governments did not create Britain's economic difficulties in the 1950s and early 1960s. Nor did they solve them. Towards the end of their thirteen years in office they had recognized, however, that the health of the economy depended very largely on the actions of the government. *Laissez-faire* and unbridled free enterprise were dead and unmourned.

THE LABOUR GOVERNMENT 1964–1967

Harold Wilson's government, which took office in October 1964, enjoyed a House of Commons majority of four and faced a balance of payments deficit of £750 million. There had been much talk in the election campaign of improved social services, to be financed out of rapidly increasing economic growth. Much of this was quickly forgotten as foreign speculators rushed to sell their pounds, fearing that Labour would once again devalue.

During the first hectic months of the new government's life the Bank of England had to borrow 3,000 million dollars to prevent the extinction of the reserves, while James Callaghan, the Chancellor of the Exchequer, raised income-tax, imposed a capital gains

tax, and levied a surcharge duty of fifteen per cent on all imported manufactured goods. This mixture of deflation and direct control of imports was intended both to redress the payments deficit and to show foreign holders of sterling that the government could handle the situation and would not devalue the pound.

The keystone of the Labour government's policy was to be economic planning. George Brown, in the new post of Secretary of State for Economic Affairs, was to develop and extend Selwyn Lloyd's ideas of an incomes policy and planned growth, unaccompanied by inflation or balance of payments crises. He launched the Prices and Incomes Board, an advisory body intended to curb wage and price increases which, unlike the earlier National Incomes Commission, was accepted by both unions and industrial management. His main achievement, however, was to publish a National Plan in 1965. This was a detailed analysis of the state of British industry and a five-year programme of expansion which envisaged twenty-five per cent growth by 1970. Brown was trying to achieve the increase in productivity which Maudling had sought in 1963–4, without risking the payments deficit.

Callaghan's policies were partially successful, and the payments deficit in 1965 was less than in 1964. Public opinion polls suggested that the people were satisfied with the government's performance. Wilson took advantage of the favourable conditions to call a general election in the spring of 1966. Labour increased its majority from four to ninety-eight and now appeared to be strong enough to solve the immediate problem and implement its long-term plans.

Most members of the Cabinet agreed that an effective incomes policy must be a central feature of the government's management of the economy. Trade unions, by calling their members out on strike, could disrupt production to such an extent that employers were glad to grant even excessive wage increases to get the men back to work. Inflated wage settlements, of course, led to price rises and less competitive exports. Also, the strikes themselves harmed the export trade. By 1966 the Prices and Incomes Board had begun to function. Its decisions were well-considered and fair, but its grave defect was that it had no teeth: it could say that a sharp increase in car workers' wages was unjustified or not in the national interest, but it could not prevent it.

The government was reluctant to arm the Prices and Incomes Board, for the unions were strongly against any kind of compulsory wage settlements, and the Labour party itself was financed by the trade union movement. Nevertheless, a small step in the direction of compulsion was taken shortly after the 1966 election, when Parliament passed legislation allowing the government to delay wage increases while they were considered by the Prices and Incomes Board.

Sterner measures were soon necessary. The balance of payments remained stubbornly in deficit and foreign holders of sterling still suspected that a Labour government might devalue the pound. A long seamen's strike in the summer of 1966 lessened Britain's foreign earnings and led to another run on the pound. The alternatives were devaluation and severe deflation. Wilson chose the latter. In July, Callaghan imposed a series of harsh measures, including a total ban on wage increases for the next six months, credit restrictions, and a reduction in government spending. Everything, including the National Plan, was sacrificed on the altar of the balance of payments. To eliminate the trade gap became the government's driving ambition and the Board of Trade monthly figures were scrutinized with as much interest as the newspapers' public opinion polls.

**Sterling crisis 1966**

Under the Conservatives in the late 1950s and early 1960s, economic crisis and boom had alternated. In the mid-1960s, with Labour in power, crisis was permanent. This may be a reflection on the abilities of the two parties, but is more likely to have been a consequence of the fact that British industry was comparatively backward, while its workers were able to demand and secure wage increases which they had not earned.

A further run on the pound in the autumn of 1967, partly caused by a prolonged dock strike, finally forced the government to devalue the pound. Callaghan announced in November of that year that the pound would henceforth be worth 2.40 dollars instead of 2.80. At the same time he resigned from the Exchequer and changed places with the Home Secretary, Roy Jenkins. Devaluation, it was hoped, by making British exports cheaper abroad and by increasing the cost of imported goods to British consumers, would solve the perennial payments problem. But it was also clear that the cost of living in Britain would rise and that this would in turn lead to further wage demands. Unless these were kept in check, rampant inflation would set in and the advantage of devaluation would be lost. In its last three years of office the Labour government sought to achieve a payments surplus. Growth and the National Plan were regretfully abandoned. The optimism of 1964 was lost in the bitter fight for survival.

**Devaluation 1967**

When Macmillan's government submitted Britain's first application for membership of the E.E.C. in 1961, the Labour leaders had been highly critical. By 1966, however, they had realized how difficult it was for Britain to solve her own economic problems. The prospect of a larger market for British exports and therefore a faster rate of growth was so attractive that Wilson's government decided to seek admission in 1966. George Brown, who had sadly watched the collapse of his National Plan, was one of the strongest supporters of the application.

**Second E.E.C. application 1966–7**

As before, the obstacle was President de Gaulle. His motives for opposing British entry appear to have been political—he still thought that Britain was too closely tied to the United States— but he used economic arguments. De Gaulle claimed that the devaluation of 1967 proved that the British economy was too weak to make a useful contribution to the E.E.C. and, as in 1963, he vetoed Britain's application.

The economic problems of the Labour government were more acute than those of its Conservative predecessors, partly because the pressure of rising wages and recurrent balance of payments crises grew worse, and partly because foreign holders of sterling were fairly sure that a Conservative government would not devalue the pound whereas they always suspected that a Labour government might do so. The economic dilemma which has been present since 1945, and which fully emerged in its present form in the mid-1950s, survives into the 1970s.

A SURVEY OF INDUSTRY AND TRADE

*Steel produced*
(million tons)

| | |
|---|---|
| 1945 | 11·8 |
| 1950 | 16·3 |
| 1955 | 19·8 |
| 1960 | 24·3 |
| 1965 | 27·0 |

*Coal produced*
(million tons)

| | |
|---|---|
| 1945 | 183 |
| 1950 | 216 |
| 1955 | 222 |
| 1960 | 194 |
| 1965 | 183 |

*Raw cotton consumed*
(million lb.)

| | |
|---|---|
| 1945 | 717 |
| 1950 | 1017 |
| 1955 | 778 |
| 1960 | 599 |
| 1965 | 492 |

While the economy as a whole expands or contracts, the relative importance of various industries within it is also liable to change. The twentieth century has seen a transformation of British industry. In 1900 its strength lay in cotton, coal, shipbuilding, and heavy engineering; in the mid-1960s motor vehicles, electrical engineering, and the chemical industry were taking over a leading role. Foreign competition and technological progress, stimulated by two world wars, were the main causes of this new industrial revolution.

It is, of course, easy to exaggerate the decline of the older industries. Coal production had slumped between the wars but was rising again in the late 1930s. In 1939, 231 million tons of coal were mined. The figure fell to 183 million tons in 1945, but rose to well over 200 million tons again in the early 1950s, and had settled at about 190 million tons a year in the mid-1960s. In view of the strong competition from oil and, from the late 1950s, from nuclear power stations, the coal industry had kept up a very strong challenge.

Three major changes in the mining industry should be noted. First, coal exports, which had amounted to nearly 50 million tons in 1939, had almost disappeared by the mid-1950s. Secondly, following nationalization, mines were extensively modernized. New machinery and better facilities not only made the miners' lives less unpleasant and dangerous, but led to a reduction in the labour force. Productivity increased by a third between 1949 and 1960. Finally, the National Coal Board began a programme of pit closures. The smaller, less economic mines, such as some of those in the Welsh valleys and west Durham, were closed down and production was concentrated in the large, well-equipped pits, especially those in the east Midlands.

The decline of the textile industry was much more pronounced. Over 4,000 million yards of woven cloth had been produced in 1937, but the average for the 1950s was only a little over 2,000 million yards. The main casualty was the Lancashire cotton industry, which could not resist the competition of cheap Japanese and Indian cloth. A slight textile revival in the 1960s was due mainly to the expansion of firms producing man-made fibres.

The shipbuilding industry, like coalmining, declined only slightly in terms of total production, although its share of the world market fell sharply. Fewer ships were built but, especially in the 1960s, there was a spectacular increase in their size, notably in the enormous new oil tankers. Even if they could secure orders, however, shipbuilders had difficulty in making profits, for prices are agreed when ships are ordered and rapidly increasing wages meant that ships were often built at a loss.

Just as the coalmines were modernized and streamlined after nationalization, so too were the railways. Diesel and electric power had completely replaced steam by the mid-1960s but, despite numerous fare increases, the railways continued to run at a loss. The competition of road freight transport and the enormous increase in the number of private cars were responsible for the decline. Following a survey in the late 1950s and early 1960s, one third of the track was closed down in an attempt to eliminate the least profitable services, but the railways still lost money and people living in remote parts of the country protested against the withdrawal of their rail services.

**Railways**

**The newer industries**

The industries which expanded during and after the Second World War were those which owed most to recent technological and scientific developments: engineering (including machine tools, electrical engineering, and electronics), the chemical industry, motor vehicles, and aircraft. The number of people employed in electronics, for example, doubled between 1950 and 1955. The motor industry made the most striking progress. Britain had produced 400,000 cars in 1939, but the figure reached a million before the end of the 1950s and two million a year in the 1960s. British car firms did very well in the European export market in the late 1940s when there was not much German, French, or Italian competition, but they lost ground later, partly because of unimaginative design and poor after-sales service. By 1963 Germany was producing more cars than Britain, and France and Italy almost as many. Excessive wage increases, too little capital investment, and periodic bouts of government-imposed deflation slowed down expansion in even the most successful industries.

The almost constant government demands for more exports and

**Trade**

regular panics about the balance of payments give the impression
that trade languished after the war. In fact, the total volume of
British exports became two and a half times greater between 1938
and the mid-1960s. The principal increases were made, of course,
by the new, expanding industries. On the other hand, Britain's
earnings from invisible exports declined. British shipowners controlled twenty-five per cent of the world's shipping in 1939, but
their share had fallen to fourteen per cent by 1964. Investment
overseas had been much reduced during the war, but there was a
big increase in the 1950s, mainly in the form of the development
of overseas subsidiaries by British firms, such as oil companies. At
the same time American investment in British industry, particularly
in the car industry, sharply increased.

In the 1930s the Commonwealth countries had been Britain's
most important trading partners, taking over 40 per cent of her
exports and supplying more than 30 per cent of her imports. A
striking feature of the post-war era was the increase in trade with
Western Europe and a comparative decline in exports to and
imports from Commonwealth countries. This led many economists
and politicians to conclude that Britain's best hopes for the future
lay in trying to join the European Economic Community.

Britain's post-war economic problems worried and perplexed
economists and politicians, but most of the population enjoyed a
steadily rising standard of living. The man in the street neither
understood nor cared about the low growth rate or the balance of
payments, but a new car and a television set were realities which
he could comprehend. In some parts of the United Kingdom,
however, the prosperity was not so obvious and the unemployment
of the 1920s and 1930s was more than a half-forgotten nightmare.
Unemployment was always higher in northern England, Scotland,
Wales, and Northern Ireland, because these were the regions which
relied on declining industries such as coalmining, shipbuilding, and
textiles. The average national unemployment rate between 1945
and 1967 was 1·6 per cent, but in northern England it was 2·8 per
cent, in Scotland 3·4 per cent, and in Northern Ireland 7 per cent.
Rising unemployment, as in 1958 and 1963, forced the government
to abandon policies of deflation and try to stimulate more production, but the resulting growth took place in the new, progressive
industries, which were concentrated in the Midlands and the
south-east of England. Governments found that their well-
intentioned policies caused inflation in one part of the country
without curing unemployment elsewhere. The reverse was also
true: the deflationary measures of 1966 caused heavy unemployment
in Scotland and Wales without curbing wage demands in the more
prosperous parts of England.

Special treatment for the areas of high unemployment was

*Unemployment again: Northern
Ireland in the early 1960s*

clearly necessary. The surplus population could not all move to the south and Midlands, for that would make the already serious congestion unbearable. Government subsidies for declining industries, merely in order to provide employment, did not make economic sense. The only possible answer was to induce expanding firms to open branch factories in the distressed areas. Throughout the period successive governments tried to lure firms away from the south-east and Midlands, providing generous grants and loans, tax concessions, and even building factories to be leased or sold cheaply to expanding companies. Some attempt was also made to retrain redundant miners and shipbuilders in skills more appropriate to modern industry.

The regional policies were partially successful. Car factories were opened on Merseyside and in central Scotland and a large number of light industrial concerns were attracted into the development areas, often to trading estates or new towns. But the 'two nations' survived: companies, for sound economic reasons, were reluctant to open factories many miles away from their main markets, while their senior executives and their wives preferred not to move from the civilized south to what they thought of as the barbaric north. In an age when image counted, the out-dated notion survived that the north and Scotland consisted of a mixture of cold, bleak, barren moors and squalid, mean towns, defaced by pit-heaps, factory chimneys, and cobbled streets, populated by uncouth philistines with more than a passing resemblance to 'Andy Capp'.

## SUMMARY

In some senses, Britain has done very well since 1945. Virtual full employment was maintained for almost twenty years and most citizens enjoyed a higher standard of living than ever before. On the other hand, whereas Britain produced twenty per cent of the world's manufactured goods in 1954, her share had fallen to fifteen per cent in the 1960s. Her productivity and rate of growth have been less than those of her main competitors.

Full employment and strong trade unions have led to regular wage demands, often backed by strike action. The resulting inflation has led to balance of payments crises, solved only by deflationary policies which have impeded the growth necessary to provide higher wages. Furthermore, the management of British firms has often responded too slowly to the modern challenge: shortage of investment capital has prevented the modernization of factories, but there is no such excuse for the failures in marketing. British cars, for example, have a high reputation abroad, but many would-be customers have been put off by delivery delays and poor after-sales service.

# Chapter 12
# Political History 1945–1967

DOMESTIC EVENTS—THE LABOUR GOVERNMENT 1945–1951

**Churchill and Attlee**

Never can two consecutive occupants of 10 Downing Street have been so different as Winston Churchill and Clement Attlee. The rotund, ebullient, cigar-smoking Churchill, with his ability to terrorize and stimulate his subordinates, had skilfully and heroically led the nation through its 'darkest hour' and out into the sunlight of victory. Attlee, in comparison, was slight and apparently insignificant. His thin voice and precise, clipped manner of speaking contrasted sharply with Churchill's mastery of the grand phrase. Churchill, and many imitators, liked to pretend that Attlee was a nobody, 'a sheep in sheep's clothing', 'a modest little man with plenty to be modest about'. 'An empty taxi drew up at 10 Downing Street and Mr. Attlee got out', quipped Churchill. But of course these semi-serious jibes were only intended to keep up the morale of his party, which had just suffered its severest electoral defeat since 1906. Churchill, who had worked with Attlee in the War Cabinet for five years, recognized his administrative skill and ability to manage difficult colleagues. What was needed in the first years of peace was not a defiant, obstinate thunderer, but a courageous, meticulous administrator. Churchill might have been able to adapt to the changed conditions; Attlee was certainly well fitted for the role.

In addition to its economic and financial problems, Attlee's government had to tackle the task of post-war reconstruction and to attempt to carry out the programme of social reform to which the Labour party had pledged itself in the 1945 election campaign.

**Food rationing**

Food rationing was retained reluctantly, partly because the government was determined to limit the volume of imports, and partly because there was a world shortage of food. Unable to reach most European markets, the food-producing countries had reduced their output during the war, and were incapable of a sudden increase when peace returned. Also, severe droughts in several parts of the world in 1945 and 1946 curtailed food production. In 1946 a grain shortage forced the British government to introduce bread rationing, which had never been imposed during the war. Potatoes were added to the list in 1947. In 1948 virtually all the wartime food restrictions remained, and most of the rations were

*Attlee's jubilant reaction to the 1945 election results*

below the wartime average. Churchill remarked in 1951 that a week's rations would make one good meal. The only favourable point was that, thanks to the government's subsidy policy, food prices were kept almost stationary. On the other hand it was arguable that this involved high taxes, another cause of discontent.

In 1945, as in 1918, there was a housing shortage, this time made worse by the destruction of homes in air raids. Since building materials were scarce and expensive and skilled labour was at first also scarce, the government drew up a list of priorities and forbade unlicensed building. Schools, factories, the repair of bomb damage, and the construction of new council houses were given priority, and licences for private building were difficult to obtain. The average of 170,000 new houses completed a year between 1947 and 1950 came nowhere near meeting the need; many families spent years on local authority waiting lists.

The social reforms of Attlee's government aroused less controversy than the nationalization programme, although it was thought in some quarters that they were too costly. The Beveridge Report in 1942 had suggested a comprehensive national insurance scheme (see page 222). A Ministry of National Insurance had already been set up in 1944, and between 1946 and 1948 a series of

**Housing**

**National Insurance**

246

Acts made it responsible for family allowances, industrial injuries benefit, sickness and unemployment benefit, retirement and widows' pensions, and National Assistance. The schemes were to be financed, for the most part, by contributions from employers, employees, and the Treasury. These Acts destroyed the last remnants of the old Poor Law, the workhouses, and the household means test; the state became responsible for maintaining all its citizens above the poverty level. But the claim to have eliminated poverty was not entirely justified as, in the following years, prices rose faster than pensions and many old people were too proud to apply for National Assistance.

**National Health Service**

The other major social reform was the institution of a National Health Service in 1946. Its architect was the Minister of Health, Aneurin Bevan, a former miner from South Wales and, with Churchill, one of the last true orators in British politics. Believing passionately in his socialist principles, Bevan had little patience with political opponents and once denounced Conservatives as 'lower than vermin'.

As a result of the National Health Service Act, all medical, dental, and ophthalmic services became free; hospitals were taken over from voluntary organizations and run by the state. The cost was met by the Treasury out of general taxation, although some money came from the National Insurance contributions. There was, at first, strong opposition from the doctors, who were afraid of being reduced to the status of civil servants, but the medical profession was won over by being promised a large share in the administration of the Service. Few people quarrelled with the principle of a National Health Service, but there was again alarm over the cost as the public flocked to obtain free medical treatment, drugs, false teeth, and spectacles. It is probable, of course, that the flood of patients after 1946 included many people who had been in need of treatment for years.

**Education**

No important legislation relating to education was passed; the pattern for the immediate future had been set by Butler's Act of 1944. One of the provisions of the Act was put into effect in 1947 when the school-leaving age was raised to fifteen, but the decision that there should be secondary education for all could not be implemented in all parts of the country as new schools were not yet available. In general, a system of grammar and secondary modern schools emerged, but parts of London and a few other areas experimented with comprehensive schools.

Not only the economy and the social services, but also the lay-out of towns and cities and the siting of future urban development were subject to central planning by the Labour government. It was felt that much of the misery of the nineteenth and early twentieth centuries arose from the failure to plan the growth of towns and

**New Towns Act**
**1946**

247

cities. The New Towns Act of 1946 was an interesting innovation. Entirely new towns, complete with factories, shopping centres and housing estates, were to be built in an attempt to stop the expansion of existing cities, especially London. People were encouraged to move from London and other cities to the new towns, which were to be separate entities and not merely extra suburbs. Eight new towns, including Stevenage, Harlow, and Basildon, were established in the London area and six others, including Bracknell, East Kilbride, and Peterlee, in the rest of the country. Although they flourished, they did not prevent the growth of city suburbs and the enlargement of the class of daily commuters.

Finally, three largely political changes deserve mention. In 1946 the Trades Disputes Act of 1927, limiting the trade unions' rights and weakening their financial link with the Labour party, was repealed. The Representation of the People Act of 1948 finally established the principle of 'one man, one vote' by abolishing the extra business premises vote belonging to owners of shops, factories, and offices of more than a certain value, and by abolishing the university seats in the House of Commons. The Parliament Act of 1949 reduced the power of the House of Lords to delay legislation passed by the Commons: in future Bills could be held up for only one year instead of two.

It would be wrong to claim that the Labour government created the Welfare State. Ever since the Liberal ministry of 1906–14 (and even earlier) the state had been extending its responsibilities for the well-being of its citizens. The legislation of 1945–50 carried that work much further. There were no major changes in education or housing, and the National Insurance schemes were a further penetration of a forest which had been already partly explored. The National Health Service was probably the biggest innovation and the achievement of which the government could be most proud.

The Conservative party had recovered from the disaster of 1945 and was well prepared for the election of 1950. The party's machinery had been reorganized and its policies brought up to date by a research team headed by R.A. Butler and including promising young politicians like Reginald Maudling, Iain Macleod, and Enoch Powell. The notion that Conservatives were against social reform was banished by the Industrial Charter of 1946, which accepted the principle of the Welfare State.

The campaign of 1950 was hard-fought and captured the interest of the public. The Conservatives said that Labour government meant austerity, controls, rationing, and shortages of food and housing; they claimed that the Labour leaders had no fresh ideas and made the most of costly failures like the unsuccessful scheme to grow groundnuts in East Africa. Labour pointed to its record of providing full employment and a Welfare State. No less than

**Political reforms**

*Election Result 1950*
| | |
|---|---|
| Labour | 315 |
| Conservative | 298 |
| Liberal | 9 |
| Others | 3 |

*Hemel Hempstead was one of the post-war New Towns*

eighty-four per cent of the electorate went to the polls and each of the major parties increased its total number of votes, but the Conservative share of the vote was much larger than in 1945. The final result was Labour 315 seats, Conservatives 298, Liberals 9, others 3.

Labour had just managed to retain power, but such a small majority makes life extremely difficult for a government. As a single defeat on a major issue in the House of Commons compels a government to resign, the Labour members had to be constantly on call. The Conservative opposition exploited the situation by inflicting numerous all-night sittings on the Commons. The sheer physical strain on the Labour ministers and back-benchers was enormous.

The men who had led Britain through five years of reconstruction and reform were in any case almost worn out. Ill health claimed first Cripps in late 1950, then Bevin, the Foreign Secretary, early in 1951. They were replaced by Hugh Gaitskell and Herbert Morrison respectively. In his first (and only) budget in 1951 Gaitskell, trying to pay for extra armaments for the Korean War and seeking to prevent inflation, both raised income-tax and imposed charges on National Health Service prescriptions, false teeth, and spectacles. Aneurin Bevan, the Minister of Health and creator of the Health Service, resigned in protest against this retreat from the principle of free medical treatment. His lead was followed by Harold Wilson. Within a few months Attlee had lost four of his ablest colleagues, and he could find no replacements of equal stature.

**General election 1951**

By November 1951 the government was exhausted and Attlee called a general election. Labour again relied on its record of achievement and rather unwisely suggested that the warlike Churchill would be a dangerous Prime Minister at a time of acute international tension. The Conservatives concentrated on domestic matters, again promising to end food rationing and committing themselves to an annual target of 300,000 houses. The 1951 election produced one of the freaks of the British electoral system: Labour won more votes, but the Conservatives gained a majority in the Commons. The Conservatives, with 321 seats against Labour's 295 and the Liberals' 6, were back in office after six years, and Winston Churchill returned happily to 10 Downing Street.

*Election Result 1951*

| | |
|---|---|
| Conservative | 321 |
| Labour | 295 |
| Liberal | 6 |
| Others | 3 |

DOMESTIC EVENTS—THE CONSERVATIVE GOVERNMENTS 1951–1964

**Churchill**

Churchill was in his seventy-seventh year when he became Prime Minister for the second time in 1951. His experience of politics dated back to before the turn of the century; he had first held Cabinet office in Asquith's government before the First World War.

*The Royal Family on the
Buckingham Palace balcony,
Coronation Day, 1953*

His prestige as a war leader, at home and abroad, was enormous. Whether he was the right man to assume the burden of supreme responsibility in the 1950s is more doubtful. His advanced age counted against him and he had never been an economic expert; on the other hand, he was still a splendid orator and for most Conservatives there was no alternative. He did not attempt to exercise the close supervision of government departments which had stimulated his wartime administration and was content to act as a figure-head, showing some interest in foreign affairs.

He was fortunate in having several very able senior colleagues. Anthony Eden, the Foreign Secretary, had been, with Churchill in 1938 and 1939, a severe critic of Chamberlain's pre-war appeasement, had served Churchill loyally during the war, and was universally recognized as the heir apparent. R.A. Butler, now Chancellor of the Exchequer, had to his credit the great 1944 Education Act and the post-war modernization of the Conservative party. In the slightly less exalted office of Minister of Housing was Harold Macmillan, a strange mixture of Edwardian dandy and conscientious social reformer.

*Churchill returns to power, 1951*

Conservative free enterprise, it was hoped, would lift Britain out of post-war gloom and into the bright light of prosperity. A new decade brought new hope and new enthusiasm. There was soon a new monarch also. George VI died in February 1952 at the tragically early age of fifty-six and was succeeded by his daughter, Queen Elizabeth II. The coronation in June 1953, watched by millions on television, was a mixture of pageantry, festivity, and pouring rain. The optimists talked grandly of a 'New Elizabethan Age'.

**Death of George VI
1952**

251

It is a far cry from Drake's triumphs over the Spanish to Macmillan's housing programme, but the fulfilment in 1953 of the Conservatives' promise to build 300,000 houses a year was dramatic news indeed for a population used only to shortages and waiting lists. Some of the new houses were privately built and therefore likely to be out of the reach of the most needy families, but up to 1954 most houses were still built by local authorities. Macmillan's success at the Ministry of Housing was a major reason for his subsequent rise to the highest office.

The Conservatives' economic and financial policies have already been discussed in Chapter 10. They made no attempt to undo all the work of the Labour government, and denationalized only iron and steel and part of the road transport industry. Far more important to the ordinary citizen, the government was able to end all rationing by 1954.

The only really significant piece of legislation in the early 1950s was the Television Act of 1954, which set up the Independent Television Authority. The B.B.C. had resumed its television service in 1946, but there was strong pressure from some parts of the Conservative party in favour of the setting up of an independent, commercial television network. The Act of 1954 created the I.T.A., a public corporation empowered to allocate contracts to companies to provide programmes in various parts of the country. The companies were to make money by selling television advertising time; advertisements were allowed only in 'natural breaks' and no sponsorship of programmes was permitted. The new service was soon successful. The programme companies began making big profits and attracted more than half of the television audience.

The eighty-year-old Churchill finally retired in 1955 and his natural successor, Sir Anthony Eden, took advantage of the government's popularity by calling a general election. The result was never in doubt. The Conservatives' housing record, the abolition of food rationing, rising prosperity, and lower taxation all counted in their favour. Labour, on the other hand, still had no new policies and was continually embarrassed by the conflict between Bevan and the official leadership. Winning 344 seats against Labour's 277 and the Liberals' 6, the Conservatives had a comfortable majority and looked forward to another four or five years of power.

The mid-1950s saw political leadership pass to a new generation of men. Only seven months after Churchill's resignation, Attlee, his former colleague and recent adversary, also retired. He was succeeded by Gaitskell, who fought off the challenge of Bevan and Morrison. Eden alone represented a link with the 1930s.

Aged only fifty-eight when he became Prime Minister in 1955, Eden seemed likely to lead his party for at least ten years. Yet within two years he too had retired. Never a robust man, his health

**Television Act 1954**

**General election 1955**

*Election Result 1955*
Conservative    344
Labour          277
Liberal           6
Others            3

*Election Result 1959*
Conservative    365
Labour          258
Liberal           6
Others            1

*'Supermac', an anti-Macmillan cartoon which probably helped him in the 1959 election*

**General election 1959**

*Macmillan as Housing Minister, 1952, presenting keys to new inhabitants of 'people's houses'*

broke down in the latter part of 1956 when his government was seriously embarrassed by the Suez crisis (see pages 265–266). Butler acted as Prime Minister while Eden was ill and was widely expected to succeed when his leader resigned early in 1957. The Conservative party, however, preferred Macmillan, whose success as a minister was undoubted.

The early years of the Macmillan era were a period of unprecedented prosperity for most British people. Cars, television sets, washing-machines, and refrigerators, previously signs of middle-class affluence, became commonplace possessions. The government took the credit.

Controls such as those applied by the post-war Labour government were unfashionable. The one important measure of these years was the Rent Act of 1957, which eased the restrictions on rent control and meant that eventually landlords would be able to charge whatever rent they could get. Although the Rent Act was exploited by some unscrupulous slum landlords, rents generally rose only slightly.

Despite the Rent Act, the Conservatives remained popular. The government occasionally lost by-elections during periods of deflation, but there were no real signs that the people had regained their enthusiasm for Labour. Gaitskell was skilfully out-manoeuvred by Macmillan in the election campaign of 1959, which gave the Conservatives their third successive victory. Macmillan now had a majority of more than 100: 365 Conservatives against 258 Labour members and 6 Liberals. Gloomy prophets on the Left began to predict the end of the Labour Party.

The recurrent economic crises occupied the Cabinet's attention during much of the last five years of Conservative rule. There were no spectacular new policies.

Nevertheless, some valuable work was done. House building at the rate of 300,000 new houses a year was maintained, while the school-building programme was accelerated and a ten-year plan to build new hospitals was launched in 1962. Universities were expanded and entirely new universities (for example, Keele, Sussex, and Essex) were founded.

The building of houses and schools received less publicity than the Betting and Gaming Act of 1960, which appreciably eased Britain's hitherto strict gambling laws. Betting shops, in which customers could place off-the-course bets on horse races, were now permitted, as were bingo-halls and gambling casinos. The Act had a far greater effect than anticipated: betting shops opened everywhere, bingo became a national pastime, especially among housewives, and night-clubs with gaming rooms opened in most towns. The 'permissive society' was born.

A more important, and more sternly contested, measure was the

Commonwealth Immigrants Act of 1962. Britain's prosperity and a change in the American immigration laws had led to an influx between 1955 and 1961 of 400,000 coloured immigrants, first from the West Indies, then also from India and Pakistan. Immigrants settled in most of the large cities and towns and usually took the less skilled and lower-paid jobs. These extra workers were most useful, particularly in Greater London, the Midlands, west Yorkshire, and south-east Lancashire where there was a shortage of labour. The services of immigrant doctors, nurses, bus-drivers and conductors, station staff, and labourers were valuable and often essential. But their presence was in some places resented by their neighbours. A shortage of housing was the most serious of the difficulties: landlords were often reluctant to take immigrant families as tenants, with the result that they were forced to live in overcrowded conditions in large Victorian terraced houses. In some areas, schools and hospital services were hard pressed to cope with the new demands.

The Act of 1962 drastically reduced the number of immigrants and stipulated that only those with jobs waiting for them or people possessing certain specific skills would be allowed in. It was bitterly opposed by the Labour party and widely denounced as a piece of racial discrimination. Others argued that the housing conditions and employment prospects in some of the areas in which immigrants settled showed that some measure of control was necessary.

During their long tenure of office the Conservatives had suffered from periodic bouts of unpopularity, but had always recovered in time to win the next general election. Lost by-elections and a poor showing in the public opinion polls showed that 1962 was one of their worst years: voters in their thousands were turning to Labour and even the Liberals, more because of rising unemployment than because they disapproved of the government's immigration policy.

Conservative fortunes revived only slightly, however, and in the autumn of 1963 ill health forced Macmillan himself from the centre of the stage. This time there was no heir apparent; several survivors of the 1962 purge felt that they had a chance of becoming Prime Minister. Many people thought that Butler's turn had at last come; Maudling had some supporters; the brilliant, ebullient Lord Hailsham was very popular; the dignified, statesmanlike Foreign Secretary, Lord Home, was widely respected. After several days of secret and mysterious consultations, Lord Home emerged as the new leader. Taking advantage of a recent change in the law, Home gave up his title and, having secured a seat in the Commons, appeared on the Treasury bench as plain Sir Alec Douglas-Home. There was general surprise at the choice; Home was liked and admired, but few people saw him as a Prime Minister. Two

CERVATIVE BRITAIN IS A POWER FOR PEACE

*The making of a Conservative leader: Lord Home (seated, centre) acknowledges the applause of his colleagues at the party conference at Blackpool, 1963, immediately prior to taking over from Macmillan*

members of Macmillan's Cabinet, Iain Macleod and Enoch Powell, refused to serve under him, but the remainder of the party gave him loyal support.

The accession of Douglas-Home to power did not immediately revive the Conservative party's fortunes, and an election had to take place by October 1964. According to the opinion polls, Labour at last seemed to have a chance of winning, despite all its internal quarrels in the 1950s and the sudden death of Gaitskell in 1963. Labour's new leader, Harold Wilson, a more forceful speaker than Douglas-Home and a much more skilful politician, prepared his troops for the coming battle.

**General election 1964**

Douglas-Home waited until the last moment before calling the election, hoping that Maudling's boom policies would recapture the lost votes. Wilson and his colleagues denounced the Conservatives' economic policies, claimed that more money should be spent on the social services, and argued in favour of comprehensive secondary education, while the Conservatives pointed to the return of prosperity and cast doubt upon Labour's ability to pay for its ambitious social policies. The result was far closer than might have been anticipated: the Conservatives won 304 seats to Labour's 317, while the Liberals, having polled over three million votes, gained only 9 seats. Labour was back in office, but only just.

*Election Result 1964*
Labour       317
Conservative   304
Liberal         9

255

In thirteen years the Conservatives had proved that, if they were not radical reformers, they were at least willing to accept the social reforms brought about by the post-war Labour government and to play their part in raising the standard of living of the mass of the people. The Welfare State remained intact, and pensions and allowances were regularly increased; the house-building record of the Conservative governments was excellent and they had made some progress towards providing adequate, modern schools. They presided over the most astonishing improvement in living standards Britain had ever seen and, with a few minor exceptions, maintained full employment. Their failures were economic: 'stop-go' was not good enough, for Britain was beginning to fall behind her competitors.

DOMESTIC EVENTS—THE LABOUR GOVERNMENT 1964–1967

In addition to the economic problems which constantly plagued his government and thwarted its more ambitious projects (see pages 238–241), Wilson faced two serious difficulties in 1964: like Attlee in 1950–1 he had only a tiny Commons majority, and he was supported by a team of inexperienced ministers. Bevan had died in 1960 and, apart from Wilson himself, none of the prominent members of Attlee's government was still on the front bench. The small majority meant that a revolt by even one or two Labour members could endanger the life of the government and that controversial measures, such as the renationalization of steel, had to be postponed.

The new ministers soon learned the ropes, however, and the danger of defeat in the Commons only stimulated the Labour members to extra efforts. The economic perils, on the other hand, were a constant headache. Attlee's government had tackled even worse problems and had carried through a major reform programme at the same time. Wilson and his ministers were preoccupied with economic matters: a continuous balance of payments crisis and frequent runs on the pound caused them to abandon the National Plan, which was to have been the corner-stone of most of their reforms.

No historic Acts of Parliament were passed in these years, although there was a host of technical, administrative reforms. Health Service prescription charges were abolished soon after Labour came to power, only to be restored during a subsequent economic crisis. A rate rebate scheme gave concessions to the less wealthy house-occupiers. An order issued by the Department of Education and Science in 1965 instructed all local authorities to draw up plans for comprehensive secondary education. There was a big increase in house building in 1964–5, particularly in the

**Race Relations Act 1965**

*Election Result 1966*
Labour       363
Conservative   253
Liberal         12
Others          2

number of council houses completed. Such undramatic, but positive, progress indicated that the Labour government had found its feet.

The continuing growth of the immigrant population and its concentration in relatively few areas remained one of the most controversial issues. Labour had voted against the Immigration Bill in 1962 and was thought to be more sympathetic to West Indians and Asians than the Conservatives. It was, indeed, suspected that racial feelings were responsible for at least one Conservative victory in the 1964 election. Once in power, the Labour party realized that vague sympathy for the immigrants was not enough, and reluctantly concluded not only that the control of immigration was essential, but that the number admitted each year had to be reduced. To prove that its motives were not racialist, the government coupled its entry restrictions with a Race Relations Bill, which made illegal many forms of racial discrimination in public places and led to the setting up of special machinery to promote harmony between the different communities. The Act did not, however, cover discrimination in employment or housing.

Having survived, almost unscathed, until early 1966, Wilson felt sufficiently confident of his position to ask for a dissolution of Parliament, in the hope of securing a more healthy majority. He claimed that the Conservatives had left an almost desperate economic legacy, but that Labour was gradually climbing out of the trough. The campaign slogan was: 'You Know Labour Government Works.'

The Conservatives entered the contest with yet another new leader. Sir Alec Douglas-Home seemed ill at ease with the intricacies of modern economics and had withdrawn gracefully in 1965. The new leader was for the first time elected by the Conservative M.P.s, a breach with the old tradition of secret consultation. Edward Heath, like Wilson a representative of the new generation of career-politicians, was elected. But not even a new skipper could save the Conservative ship in 1966. Labour emerged with a handsome majority, 363 seats against the Conservatives' 253 and the Liberals' 12.

One might have expected five years of confident and positive government after the 1966 election. Wilson now had a comfortable majority and had assembled an able and experienced team of colleagues, including George Brown, James Callaghan, Roy Jenkins, and Mrs. Barbara Castle. All such prospects were blighted, however, by the pestilence of the balance of payments deficit. The government survived until 1970, but successive deflationary measures alienated the general public and prevented the remodelling of the Welfare State which was one of Labour's main aims. People who had enjoyed a rapid and fairly constant rise in their standard of living under the Conservatives in the 1950s resented Labour's attempts to resist wage demands, while ministers with their hearts set on ambitious programmes were frustrated by the Treasury's refusal to supply the necessary funds. The left wing of the Labour party was deeply disappointed by Wilson's apparent timidity. Wilson himself was an economic manipulator, not a socialist crusader. The nature of politics had changed.

FOREIGN AND DEFENCE POLICIES 1945–1967

With one outstanding exception, there was little disagreement between the major parties over Britain's foreign policy in these years. Indeed, one of the jibes employed by the more extreme socialists on the Labour back benches against Ernest Bevin, the Foreign Secretary from 1945 to 1951, was that his policies were so popular with the Conservatives. There was also broad agreement on defence, although in the late 1950s and early 1960s Labour did question Britain's ability to retain the status of an independent nuclear power.

If the wartime partnership with the United States was close and cordial, the alliance with the Soviet Union was never more than a 'marriage of convenience'. Churchill had a life-long hatred of Communism, while Stalin always suspected the motives of the western powers. Hitler had tried to take advantage of this hostility among his enemies and hoped, until the very end of the war, that Britain and the United States would change sides and support him in resisting the advance of the Red Army.

As is well known, wartime co-operation with the Soviet Union quickly changed to the dogged hostility of the Cold War. Perhaps there was no chance of post-war friendship and harmony; perhaps fear and ignorance on both sides extinguished the little flame of comradeship which flickered briefly in the spring of 1945.

The leaders of the victorious Powers met at Potsdam in July 1945 and confirmed the Yalta decision that defeated Germany should be divided into four zones of occupation—one each for Britain, the United States, the Soviet Union, and France. Each zone was to be governed by a military commander, and the four commanders were to form a Control Council. Berlin itself, although lying deeply inside the Soviet zone, was to be similarly partitioned.

**Potsdam Conference 1945**

This was the origin of the division of Germany. The Russians never showed any desire to create a united, pacified Germany under a German administration. They treated their zone as conquered territory, ruthlessly removing vast quantities of industrial plant to pay for war damage in Russia, and suppressing all non-Communist political parties. Stalin retained the Polish and Baltic territories which he had seized in 1939 and, without securing the agreement

**The Soviet Union**

258

Territories annexed by U.S.S.R.

Territories annexed by Poland

0    50   100  150 miles

0    100   200 km

Map 16 *Europe in 1945*

of the western powers, compensated Poland with a slice of eastern Germany. The people of eastern Europe 'voted with their feet': by 1947 ten million refugees had fled from the Russian-occupied areas to the western zones of Germany.

As the Red Army had advanced westwards, Stalin had insisted that the countries it liberated from Nazi rule should set up governments favourable to the Soviet Union. Poland, Rumania, Hungary, and Bulgaria thus fell under Communist rule, while Tito's Communist partisans kept control of Yugoslavia. Czechoslovakia was the only democratic outpost in eastern Europe. Western statesmen were naturally afraid that Stalin would not be content with eastern Europe and would try to grab as many countries as possible. Ernest Bevin was not alone in thinking that if the Americans withdrew from Europe as they had done after the First World War, the Soviet Union would take over the whole of Germany and move into Italy and France, where there were already well-established Communist parties.

Were such fears justified? Was Stalin set on the absorption of the whole of Europe, or was he merely trying to surround the Soviet Union with a belt of friendly states? It is impossible to give a definite answer, but most historians now think that Stalin was more concerned with defence than expansion: a cordon of 'satellites' would protect Russia from invasion and provide resources for the massive task of post-war reconstruction. Many western leaders

259

were afraid of Stalin in the late 1940s, but it now appears that he was also afraid of them. Of course, if the opportunity to advance into western Germany had presented itself, Stalin would probably have taken it.

Whatever his motives, Stalin had put most of eastern Europe under Communist rule and had adopted a hostile attitude towards the West. Winston Churchill coined a new phrase when addressing an American audience at Fulton, Missouri, in March 1946:

> From Stettin in the Baltic to Trieste in the Adriatic, an iron curtain has descended across the Continent ... All these famous cities and the populations around them lie in what I must call the Soviet sphere, and all are subject in one form or another, not only to Soviet influence, but to a very high and, in many cases, increasing measure of control from Moscow.

The 'iron curtain' was in position and the unhelpful attitude of Soviet delegates to the United Nations made even the most casual western observer familiar with the Russian word *nyet*.

Bevin watched these developments with alarm, but his more immediate aim was to secure co-operation among the states of western Europe, so that the mistakes of the 1930s might not be repeated. In March 1947 Britain and France signed a fifty-year alliance (the Treaty of Dunkirk) providing for mutual defence in the event of another German attack. One year later, in the Treaty of Brussels, Belgium, the Netherlands, and Luxembourg joined Britain and France in a similar pact. These treaties were, in fact, the foundation on which the subsequent N.A.T.O. alliance was built.

**Treaties of Dunkirk and Brussels 1947–8**

The British government was well aware that, for financial as well as military reasons, the American alliance must be the key of its foreign policy. Attlee and Bevin were therefore relieved to learn from President Truman in 1947 that the United States did not intend to resume its policy of isolation. Addressing Congress in March of that year, he said:

**The United States**

> I believe that it must be the policy of the United States to support free people who are resisting attempted subjugation by armed minorities or by outside pressures.
> I believe that our help should be primarily through economic stability and orderly political processes.
> The free people of the world look to us for support in maintaining their freedom.
> If we falter in our leadership, we may endanger the peace of the world— and we shall surely endanger the welfare of our own Nation.

*Stalin and the western leaders: 'Your play, Joe', says Truman*

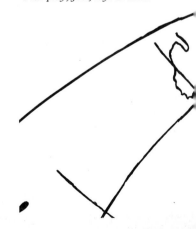

The Truman Doctrine was followed three months later by Secretary of State George Marshall's announcement of the Marshall Plan, a generous offer of economic aid to the whole of Europe. Appreciating immediately the economic significance of the Plan and Truman's promise to stand by the free world, the British government accepted the offer eagerly, as did all European countries outside the Communist bloc.

Without these promises of American support the events of the first half of 1948 would have caused even more concern, for it now appeared that Stalin did intend to embark on a programme of expansion. In February the Communists took over Czechoslovakia and in June the Russians cut all Allied land communications with West Berlin, apparently hoping that the western powers would withdraw from the German capital altogether. But the Allies did not give in. For eleven months the two and a half million West Berliners and the Allied garrisons were supplied by air. The Berlin Air Lift was a monumental effort on the part of the R.A.F. and the United States Air Force: an average of 4000 tons of supplies a day were flown in during August 1948 and a record of 13,000 tons was established on Easter Sunday 1949. Stalin was not prepared to use force and abandoned the blockade in May 1949. The western powers had at last learned the lesson that resolute resistance was better than appeasement.

The Berlin blockade was seen in the west as a clear sign that the Soviet Union had become a potential enemy in a future war, and

**Berlin blockade 1948–9**

**The North Atlantic Treaty
1949**

the success of the Air Lift seemed to prove that determined, collective opposition was necessary to keep Stalin in check and prevent such a war. While the Berlin crisis raged the western powers negotiated a defensive treaty the aim of which was to convince the Russians that any further aggression might involve war with most of the countries of western Europe and North America. The North Atlantic Treaty of April 1949 committed the five signatories of the Brussels Treaty plus the United States, Canada, Iceland, Denmark, Norway, Italy, and Portugal to co-operate in mutual defence. Article Five stated:

> The Parties agree that an armed attack against one or more of them in Europe or North America shall be considered an attack against them all; and consequently they agree that, if such an armed attack occurs, each of them in exercise of the right of individual or collective self-defence recognised by Article 51 of the Charter of the United Nations, will assist the Party or Parties so attacked by taking forthwith, individually and in concert with the other Parties, such action as it deems necessary, including the use of armed force, to restore and maintain the security of the North Atlantic area.

This was the origin of N.A.T.O.—the North Atlantic Treaty Organization. Here, for once, was a treaty which did not consist merely of empty phrases and pious promises. No sooner was it signed than a Supreme Headquarters Allied Powers in Europe (S.H.A.P.E.) was established in Paris. The N.A.T.O. members would not wait to be attacked before co-ordinating their military plans. Bevin played his part in creating the North Atlantic Treaty and could reasonably feel proud that he had served his country better than the pre-war appeasers.

N.A.T.O.'s aim was to preserve the peace by showing that the west was able and willing to defend itself. No one wanted to drive the Russians out of Germany or their east European satellites. Britain and the United States continued to hope that Stalin would agree to the re-unification of Germany and the election of a democratic German government, but by 1949 it was clear that he wanted to keep the Soviet zone under Communist control and realized that free elections would probably mean the return of a non-Communist government. In May 1949, therefore, the western powers agreed to merge the British, American, and French zones into a German Federal Republic, without admitting that the division of the country into East and West was permanent. West Germany at least thus took an important step towards political respectability, and soon, with massive American aid, it was well on the way to economic recovery also.

Her responsibilities as an occupying power in Germany and the tensions of the Cold War, plus her peace-keeping role in many other parts of the world, placed a heavy burden on Britain's military resources. During 1945 and 1946 British forces were serving in

*South Korean marines, 1954*

Germany, Greece, Persia, Egypt, India, Palestine, and the Far East. The pre-war volunteer army was totally inadequate for such a task and in 1947 the Labour government decided to maintain conscription: all young men were to do twelve months' National Service. Apart from the last six months of peace in 1939, this was the first time that conscription had been imposed in peace time in British history. Despite hopes that National Service would soon be abolished, the extra demands of N.A.T.O. forced the government to extend the period of service to eighteen months in 1949.

National Service affected almost every family, but Attlee's government's other main defence policy was a closely guarded secret: it began work on a British atomic bomb. Much of the early research on the atomic bomb had been done in Britain and the secrets of the British physicists had been transmitted to the Americans during the war, on the understanding that the fruits of American nuclear research would be made available to Britain. Truman either did not know of this promise or chose to ignore it, for the post-war British scientists had to begin again, almost from scratch.

It seemed by 1950 that the Western Alliance had thwarted further Soviet attempts to expand in Europe and that the Communists were looking for success in the Far East instead. By the end of 1949 Mao Tse-tung's Communists had taken over in China and had forced the Nationalist Chinese, under General Chiang Kai-shek, to withdraw to the island of Formosa. Then, in June 1950, came news of an attack by Communist North Korea on the non-Communist South.

The western Powers had refused to be drawn into the Chinese civil war, but the events in Korea appeared to be open aggression by one state against another. On the initiative of the Americans, the United Nations Security Council condemned North Korea's action and called upon member states to support South Korea. Many western statesmen believed that the Soviet Union had instigated the North Korean aggression, but this theory could not be proved and, although Russian spokesmen protested strongly against the United Nations' decision, they did nothing to stop it, nor did they give direct help to North Korea.

Sixteen members of the United Nations sent forces to Korea and no less than forty-five states gave assistance of some sort, but the operation was from the beginning overwhelmingly American and its initial commander was the Pacific war hero, General MacArthur. The British government loyally supported the United Nations enterprise, although Attlee urged President Truman to limit the war to Korea. It did, however, cause a big increase in government expenditure on arms and an extension of the period of National Service to two years.

Large numbers of American troops, serving for the first time under

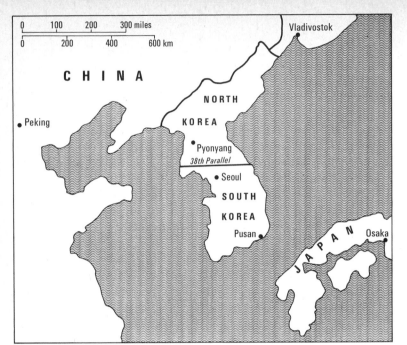

Map 17 *The Korean War*

*Egyptian support for Nasser*

the blue flag of the United Nations, saved the South Koreans from defeat, but they also provoked the Chinese Communists to intervene on the North Korean side. In June 1951 peace talks began, but the war did not formally end until mid-1953.

The change of government in 1951 made little difference to Britain's foreign policy. Churchill and his Foreign Secretary, Anthony Eden, were as determined as Attlee and Bevin to maintain the American alliance and to strengthen N.A.T.O. Effective precautions and resolute action seemed to have succeeded in curbing Communist aggression, for the early 1950s were fairly quiet, apart from the Communist-inspired rebellion against the French in Indo-China. Stalin, in his later years, was either content with his protective screen or convinced that further attempts to expand would fail, and after his death in 1953 the new Russian leaders showed that they did not want to pick new quarrels with the west.

Just as a change of government in Britain did not affect foreign policy, so Eisenhower's Republican government, which took over in the United States in 1953, continued to support N.A.T.O. Eisenhower did, however, ask the other members of the alliance to make a larger contribution to the defence of western Europe. This led to controversy over whether the new German Federal Republic should be allowed to rearm. Understandably, the French had some misgivings about a resurgence of German military power; there was also strong opposition to the proposal from the left (Bevanite) wing of the British Labour party. A compromise was reached in 1954 when Churchill promised to keep four British divisions in Germany (as a contribution to N.A.T.O.'s forces and not as an

army of occupation) and West Germany was admitted to N.A.T.O.

The expense of a large army and the unpopularity of National Service led Churchill's government to look for an alternative way of contributing to western defence. The solution appeared to be an expansion of Britain's nuclear forces. Attlee's government had already begun work on a British atomic bomb; the Conservatives went one step further in 1954 by deciding that Britain would make the hydrogen bomb. This choice enabled the government eventually to end conscription, but it also committed Britain to the increasingly costly research and development involved in sophisticated modern weapon systems.

Post-war British foreign policy was successful because both Labour and Conservative governments accepted that Britain had been eclipsed as a Great Power by the United States and the Soviet Union, and that close co-operation with the Americans was necessary to contain Russia. It is no coincidence that the one major failure was an attempt to pursue an independent policy contrary to the wishes of the American government. The clash between Eden's government's desire to protect Britain's interests in Egypt and the rising tide of Arab nationalism, backed by world opinion, led to a humiliating diplomatic defeat.

According to the Anglo-Egyptian agreement of 1936, British troops occupied the Suez Canal Zone so as to safeguard the Canal, an important international waterway which was deemed vital to Britain's oil supplies. The Egyptian nationalists who ejected the corrupt King Farouk in 1952, replacing him first with General Neguib, then with Colonel Nasser, resented the presence of foreign troops on Egyptian sand. Eden and Nasser accordingly agreed that British forces should leave the Canal Zone.

Eden, however, distrusted Nasser, partly because Communist influence in Egypt appeared to be growing. The opinion was soon reinforced. When Nasser nationalized the Suez Canal in July 1956 Eden, who was now Prime Minister, objected, thinking not only that the Egyptians would be unable to run the Canal effectively, but also that Nasser's high-handed action was a hostile gesture by a trouble-maker who, unless he was dealt with promptly, would disturb the peace of the Middle East and the whole world.

The British and French governments now began to contemplate using force against Nasser. At the same time, the government of Israel, aggravated by attacks by Arab guerrillas based on Egyptian territory, seems to have been planning a reprisal attack on Egypt. Israel's forces attacked Egypt on 29 October and on the following day Britain and France issued an ultimatum to Israel and Egypt, demanding a cease-fire and that each side withdrew ten miles from the Canal. The Suez Canal, of course, lay well within Egyptian territory. When Nasser rejected the ultimatum the British and French first bombed

Egyptian airfields, then began a sea-borne invasion of the Canal Zone. The Anglo-French operation was condemned by most other nations; even the Americans joined in a United Nations cease-fire demand.

After part, but not all, of the Canal Zone had been occupied, Eden did order a cease-fire. The Labour opposition in Parliament criticized the adventure fiercely, although public opinion in the country was largely behind Eden. The almost unanimous disapproval of the United Nations was embarrassing, but the vital factor in the situation was American opposition. Financial speculators began a run on the pound when they noticed the rift between Eden and Eisenhower.

The British and French forces were withdrawn from the Canal Zone, where they were replaced by a United Nations peace-keeping force. The Canal itself, which Nasser had blocked with sunken ships during the crisis, was cleared and reopened to shipping in 1959. But it remained in Egyptian hands. Israel gained very few of her objectives in the 1956 war; Britain and France gained none of theirs. After Suez the 'new nations' of Africa and Asia were much cooler in their relationships with the western democracies.

To many people Suez was final proof that Britain was no longer

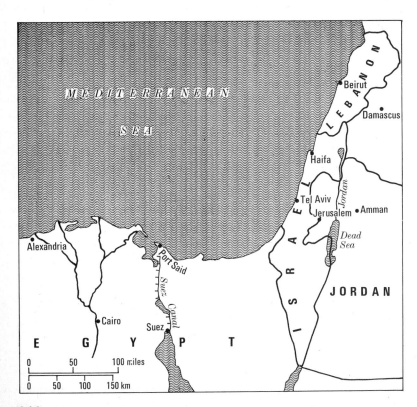

Map 18 *Palestine and Egypt in 1956*

*British troops in the Canal zone, 1956*

**Nuclear weapons**

a Great Power. The government was anxious to prove that, militarily, Britain was still in the first rank, and this meant membership of the 'nuclear club'. Shortly after becoming Prime Minister in 1957, Macmillan announced his decision to proceed with the British hydrogen bomb and to end National Service by 1960.

Having chosen The Bomb, as the press called it, the government next had to solve the problem of delivery: modern defence techniques would soon be too sophisticated for even the V bombers. Research and development work on rockets was almost prohibitively expensive, and Soviet and American technologists were making such rapid progress that even the most costly projects were obsolete almost before they left the drawing-board. Thus, Britain's Blue Streak was scrapped in 1960 after £100 million had been spent on it. Finally, in 1962, Macmillan decided to build a fleet of nuclear-powered submarines and received President Kennedy's agreement to the sale of American Polaris missiles. Britain entered the 1960s with her own nuclear deterrent, although some observers doubted whether it was truly independent.

A by-product of the nuclear policy was the appearance of a protest group, the Campaign for Nuclear Disarmament, which sought to persuade the British government to renounce nuclear weapons altogether. Drawing its support mainly from young, middle-class, left-wing intellectuals, the C.N.D. enjoyed a boom **C.N.D.** in the early 1960s. Its marches and rallies were boisterous, but

267

fairly orderly, and the general public thought of C.N.D. members as well-intentioned but misguided. Such famous men as Bertrand Russell, Canon Collins, and Michael Foot wholeheartedly supported the movement, whose demonstrations were naturally fully covered on television. Briefly, in 1960, the C.N.D. seemed to be on the brink of a major success when the Labour Party Conference voted against nuclear weapons, but Gaitskell and his followers had the decision reversed in 1961.

Britain's main external concern in the late 1950s and early 1960s was the rapid and peaceful transformation of an empire of colonies into a Commonwealth of independent nations (see Chapter 14). She remained a loyal member of N.A.T.O., and so, fortunately, did the United States. Relations between the Soviet Union and the western powers showed occasional signs of improvement, partly because of the more reasonable attitude of the wily and deceptively genial Russian leader, Nikita Khrushchev. A crisis over Berlin in 1959 led to the erection of the Berlin Wall by the Communists in 1960, but to no other change in the European situation. The most serious threat to peace in these years was the Russian attempt to build missile sites in Castro's Cuba in 1962. Prompt action by Kennedy made the Russians withdraw.

Macmillan and his Foreign Secretary, Lord Home, assumed the role of peace-makers. Although the summit conference of 1960 was a failure, they managed to persuade the leaders of the major powers to stop testing nuclear weapons. The United States, the Soviet Union, and Britain signed the Test-Ban Treaty in 1963, pledging themselves not to explode nuclear devices in the atmosphere. But their success was not complete: France and China, both of whom were on the point of perfecting hydrogen bombs, refused to sign.

Just as the change from Labour to Conservative administration brought no alteration in British foreign policy in 1951, so the return to Labour in 1964 meant little more than a continuation along the same lines. Wilson valued America's friendship highly and worked hard to cultivate the friendship of President Johnson. Mainly for reasons of economy, the Labour ministers frequently expressed a desire to restrict Britain's commitments in the Far East. As Johnson found himself drawn more and more deeply into the Vietnam war, Wilson sympathized, but refused to send British troops.

After 1945 the British people and their leaders had to reconcile themselves to the painful fact that Britannia no longer ruled the waves, that militarily and economically Britain relied on American support. In view of the hostile attitude of the Soviet Union, it was therefore fortunate that successive United States governments did not withdraw into the isolation which had been characteristic of

*C.N.D. protest meeting in Whitehall, 1961*

American foreign policy after 1918. Co-operation with the United States was the core of British foreign policy: both Labour and Conservative governments realized its importance, even if patriots regretted its necessity. The Suez adventure finally drove the lesson home. The Anglo-American partnership, most clearly expressed in N.A.T.O., probably stabilized European international relations and may have averted a third world war, for the Soviet leaders recognized that the west was armed and ready to resist aggression.

*In March 1949, the rationing of clothing ceased.*

# Chapter 13
## Social History 1945–1967

Historians and statesmen are apt to see the first sixty years of the present century as a period of British decline: Britain lost her place as one of the world's Great Powers, she ceased to rule a mighty empire, and she was pushed out of her position of economic pre-eminence. The ordinary people, however, might be forgiven for doubting whether any of this mattered. Their standard of living **Prosperity** did not just improve; it was transformed out of all recognition. Of all history's revolutions none has been more materially significant than the sudden blossoming of mass prosperity since the Second World War.

There is no single explanation for this transformation, nor is it a solely British phenomenon—all the advanced industrial nations of the world have experienced the same change. Its main causes have been full employment, rising wages, often boosted by a trade union movement which is more powerful than ever before, technical improvements, which have brought luxury articles within the grasp of wage-earners, and the provision by the government of a range of services cushioning the people against sickness and poverty. It is easy and dangerous to be complacent, of course. The expectation of more and more prosperity creates economic problems which could, if they get out of hand, bring a return to the misery of the dole queues. Nor has poverty been eliminated: the plight of the aged and the homeless is a reproach to what has been called the 'affluent society'. Wealth itself has created problems, ranging from the moral dangers of the gambling boom to the fear that every city centre will soon be choked by traffic. But the central, undeniable fact is that whereas the British working class was underpaid before 1914 and too often unemployed between the wars, it is now better fed, clothed, and housed than ever before.

**Population** The main physical change in the population has been that the number of elderly people has increased. Apart from a sharp rise in the years immediately after the war, the birth-rate has remained low and the population has increased only slowly. The total was just over fifty million in 1951 and had risen only to fifty-three million by 1961—a much slower rate of growth than before 1914. The population figures also testify to medical progress and to the improvement in the standard of living: infant mortality declined from 138 per thousand live births in 1900 to 21 per thousand in

1961; the expectation of life, which was forty-six years for males and fifty-two for females in 1900, had risen to sixty-eight years for males and seventy-four for females by 1960. As old people lived longer and children tended to stay longer in full-time education, so the dependent section of the population grew. In 1969 it was calculated that thirty-three million workers were supporting twenty million dependants.

The distribution of population between town and country hardly changed between 1900 and 1960. Four-fifths of the people lived in towns, half of them in the conurbations of Greater London, the west Midlands, south-east Lancashire, Merseyside, west Yorkshire, Tyneside, and Clydeside, but the continued decline of the old staple industries and the expansion of new, lighter industry caused a more rapid increase in the Midlands and the Home Counties. The inter-war tendency for people to move out of the old city centres to new housing estates in the suburbs, or even to separate dormitory towns, was carried very much further, with the result that the battalions of daily commuters were augmented and a new range of traffic problems created.

This gradually increasing population was more prosperous than ever before, above all because most people had jobs. Between the end of the war and the mid-sixties, an average of less than two per cent of the employable population was out of work, a great change from the five to ten per cent of the thirties.

There was a change in the pattern as well as in the level of employment. Unskilled manual labour ceased to be the normal lot of the working-class breadwinner. As the textile, mining, and ship-building industries declined, men transferred to more skilled and much more highly paid jobs in the engineering, motor, electrical, and chemical industries. To some extent this movement was made possible by the opening of new factories in the older industrial areas, such as Lancashire and central Scotland, but there was some migration of workers to the Midlands and the south-east.

A further change in the employment picture was the extraordinary increase in the number of female clerks and typists. This was due partly to the post-war social convention (and economic necessity) that virtually all single young women should go out to work, and partly to the continuing decline in the number of domestic servants. Before 1914 the unmarried daughters of a working-class family were very likely to go into domestic service; in the 1960s the idea was unthinkable.

Before 1939, a clear-cut distinction between middle class and working class was always possible: differences of occupation, income, housing, dress, leisure activities and even accent separated what were almost two distinct nations. After the Second World War the edges became blurred to such an extent that by the 1960s the

| *Population* (millions) | | |
| --- | --- | --- |
| | 1951 | 1961 |
| U.K. | 48·9 | 51·3 |
| S. Ireland | 4·3 | 4·2 |

| *Population: Age composition* (percent) | | |
| --- | --- | --- |
| | 1901 | 1951 |
| Over 70 | 2·7 | 7·3 |
| 45–69 | 16·8 | 30·4 |
| 20–44 | 39·0 | 31·9 |
| 5–19 | 31·0 | 21·2 |
| 0–4 | 11·5 | 9·2 |
| *Total Population* (millions) | 37·0 | 48·9 |

**Occupations**

**Growth of middle class**

terms had lost most of their meaning and were falling into disuse. The explanation lies partly in the very big wage increases of at least some factory workers, and partly in the enormous expansion of the middle class itself. As firms grew larger and industrial techniques became more complicated, the number of scientists, engineers, managers, salesmen, and advertising executives employed grew also. There was a seventy-six per cent increase in the number of people employed in professional and technical occupations between 1931 and 1951, and a further sixty per cent increase in the next ten years. The 1911 census classified only 5,000 people as scientists; the number had risen to 49,000 by 1951.

The old-fashioned distinction between the workers and the bosses thus broke down. In a highly competitive business world the bosses needed experts, whether they were industrial chemists or sales managers, and these experts came at least in part from the working class. They were the sons, and to an increasing extent the daughters, of factory workers and miners, boys and girls who had taken advantage of better educational facilities and risen to executive and managerial posts.

The throwing open of the doors of the middle class is one of the most outstanding features of the post-war era, but it must not be exaggerated. Nearly seventy per cent of all employed people are still engaged in manual jobs. Manual workers' wages have risen steadily, however, and for this the trade unions are usually given the credit (or blame). But it is important to realize that only a

**Trade unions**

minority of employed workers belong to unions. In 1960 trade union membership stood at the record figure of 9,800,000, but even this represented only forty-one per cent of the total labour force.

**Standard of living**

Higher wages were, of course, accompanied by higher prices. In the 1950s and 1960s the wages of most British people, however, rose much faster than prices. There was, in other words, a rise in real earnings. The following figures show how average wages and salaries increased between the 1930s and 1960:

|  | 1935–7 | 1955–6 | 1960 |
|---|---|---|---|
| Doctors | £1,100 | £2,100 | £2,550 |
| Business managers | £440 | £1,500 | £1,850 |
| Skilled workers | £195 | £630 | £805 |
| Semi-skilled workers | £145 | £505 | £625 |

At first glance the increases are quite startling, but they fall into proportion when one remembers that prices rose by fifty per cent between 1939 and 1945, and doubled in the next twenty years. In fact, doctors' real earnings have never reached their pre-war level between 1945 and 1960. Each of the other groups in the table, however, achieved an increase of about fifty per cent in real wages. Naturally

there are exceptions to such generalizations: coalminers and agricultural labourers doubled their real earnings between 1937 and
1960, while bus drivers, bank clerks, and junior civil servants
enjoyed little or no improvement.

In general, those who gained most were the manual workers and
the 'new middle class'—the managers, advertising executives, and
technologists. The 'traditional middle class' made less dramatic
gains and suffered from much heavier taxation. One important
result of the wage increases has been to draw most manual workers
into the ranks of the income-tax payers. While only four million
people earned enough to be charged income-tax in 1938–9, over
thirteen million had qualified by 1963.

Just as there were many exceptions to the generalizations on
wages, so price increases have been far from uniform. The continuing housing problem, for example, has been accompanied by a
tremendous inflation in house prices. New semi-detached houses
sold for £600 in London and £450 in the provinces in the late
thirties, but prices had increased tenfold by the mid-sixties. Ball-
point pens, on the other hand, have been among the few commodities whose prices have fallen: they cost nearly two pounds when
they first appeared in 1946, but the cheapest varieties could be
bought for less than a shilling (5p) in the 1960s.

The substantial increases in the real earnings of the majority of

*Fourth formers in a London school
are taught all types of office work*

the population have had numerous social effects and, in particular, have led to a change in the pattern of expenditure. While wages were low, most of the weekly pay-packet was spent on essentials such as food, clothing, heating, lighting, and rent. Now, wage-earners can afford not only to supply their families' immediate needs, but have money to spare for what were once undreamt-of luxuries. There has been a sharp fall in the proportion of people's incomes spent on food and clothing and, to take one obvious example, an astonishing increase in expenditure on private motor cars.

The great improvement in the standard of living came only in the 1950s and 1960s, of course; the austerity years, 1945–50, were drab and colourless, mainly because the wide range of desirable articles which later flooded the shops were just not available. By 1959 Harold Macmillan's 'You've never had it so good' was a fair comment: formerly exclusively middle-class possessions such as electric irons and vacuum cleaners were now to be found in most homes, while an increasing proportion of the population could boast ownership of washing-machines and refrigerators. Television provides the best evidence of the social revolution of the 1950s: in the first five years after the resumption of the service in 1946 the audience was confined to a privileged minority, yet ten years later over eighty per cent of homes had sets.

The tendency continued in the 1960s as more and more families became car-owners, installed telephones, and began to buy their own homes. Extra wealth affected people's recreation habits also. Even the most prosperous working-class families could aspire to no more than a week's holiday in a seaside boarding-house in the 1930s, while only a minority of the middle class ventured onto the Continent. Thirty years later travel agents were attracting an ever increasing number of customers with their offers of cheap 'package tours' to the resorts of Spain and Italy.

To some extent, the higher standard of living was due to technical improvements. Manufacturers of washing-machines and television sets, for example, found ways of either producing cheaper articles or at least preventing price rises. Their reward was a boom in sales. At the same time, food prices remained comparatively low, due both to the importation of cheap foodstuffs from Commonwealth countries and to food subsidy policies. Another partial cause of prosperity was the fact that far more married women went out to work. But the main causes of affluence were full employment, and higher wages.

The government also contributed to the rising living standards, both by trying to maintain full employment and by providing a pattern of social services which does much more than guarantee the bare essentials of life to the needy. The National Health Service,

**National Health Service**

by offering free medical treatment to everyone, not only caused an improvement in the nation's health, but relieved people of the fear of hospital and doctors' bills.

Almost everyone has benefited from the National Health Service. Only a small minority of wealthy people have chosen the very expensive luxury of private medical treatment. Although government expenditure on health rose steadily during the 1950s and 1960s the cost of the Health Service as a proportion of the national income has actually declined. The small payments made by most patients since 1951 have not, of course, paid for the Service, which is still financed mainly out of general taxation.

The Health Service's main defects have been inadequate hospitals and a shortage of doctors and nurses. Up to 1960 most hospital buildings were old, many dating back to the nineteenth century, and everywhere there were insufficient beds. The rate of hospital building between 1945 and 1960 was less than in the 1930s. In 1962 the government began a ten-year hospital-building programme which has partially solved the problem. Doctors were in short supply because many newly qualified students joined the 'brain-drain' to the United States, where salaries and conditions of work were supposedly better. To some extent, the deficiency of doctors and nurses has been made up during the 1960s by immigrants from the Commonwealth countries.

**National Insurance**

The National Insurance Act of 1946 was not quite so revolutionary as the National Health Service Act, but its effects have been felt almost as widely. Fortunately, before 1971 remarkably few members of the working population had to take advantage of unemployment benefit, but virtually everyone has at some stage received sickness benefit. Many families have had their incomes augmented by family allowances, while, of the increasing numbers of elderly people, few are nowadays too proud to claim old-age pensions. National Assistance, recently renamed 'supplementary benefit', is the one feature of the scheme which has not entirely lost the old-fashioned charity image.

**Poverty**

The Welfare State was created principally to combat poverty. Although it seems certain that there have been fewer poor people in Britain since the Second World War than ever before, poverty has still not been eliminated; some observers even believe that it increased during the 1960s. Despite all the efforts of what has now become the Ministry of Social Security, two groups of people, the aged and large families on low incomes, are undoubtedly excluded from the affluent society. Seebohm Rowntree, who had discovered a poverty rate of thirty per cent in York in 1900 and thirty-one per cent in 1936, found in his final survey in 1961 that three per cent of the population was still below the poverty line. This looks like an almost miraculous improvement, but the very existence of the

*Aneurin Bevan's National Health Service in action: maternity clinic at Tulse Hill, London, and free school milk at Manchester Grammar School, 1954.*

three per cent is a reproach to the Welfare State.

The least prosperous people in Britain in the 1950s and 1960s were the old-age pensioners. Seven million people were over pension age in 1953, and their numbers have continued to grow. Successive governments have regularly increased pensions, but old people with no other source of income have never had enough money for adequate food, clothing, and heating. Most local authorities have tried to ease the problem by letting special old people's bungalows at modest rents and by providing home-helps and similar services. Despite all such efforts, it was estimated in 1964 that about two million elderly people could not provide themselves with the basic necessities of life out of their pensions. One and a half million were saved from poverty by National Assistance, but the remaining tragic half million, out of either ignorance or pride, failed to apply for the extra money which they needed and to which they were entitled. The plight of the aged, at a time of rapidly rising prices, is the main problem of the social services.

A shortage of housing, which was partly caused by bomb damage, was one of the worst legacies of the Second World War. Such were the economic problems of the post-war Labour government that housing could not come at the top of the list of priorities, and less than a million new homes were built in the first five years of peace. Temporary, prefabricated houses ('pre-fabs') met some of the demand. Intended to last for five years, some of them were still inhabited twenty years later.

The most outstanding domestic achievement of the Conservative governments between 1951 and 1964 was to build four million new houses. At first, most were still council houses, built by local authorities, but private building enjoyed a boom in the late 1950s and the 1960s. Despite the enormous inflation in house prices (see page 274), by 1964 no less than forty-three per cent of families owned, or were buying, their own homes.

By the 1960s new housing estates encroached on the countryside at the edge of every town and, in most parts of the country, blocks of flats had begun to appear in town centres as slums were demolished and redevelopment took place. But not everyone lived in a modern home. A third of the houses inhabited in 1963 had been built before 1900 and a quarter of the total still had no baths. Although most smaller towns had made excellent progress with the work of modernization, the picture in the big cities was far less encouraging. A survey of Scottish housing in 1967, for example, publicized the disgraceful state of Glasgow's slums. Some slum landlords had, in addition, taken unscrupulous advantage of the 1957 Rent Act and, making the most of the housing shortage, were charging excessive rents for houses and flats which were hardly fit

*Tenants in Notting Hill Gate, London, protest against rent increases by landlords taking advantage of the shortage of housing*

**Housing**

*Post-war housing: high-rise flats
replace Newcastle's slums*

for human habitation.

Inflated house prices have prevented lower-paid workers, especially those with large families, from contemplating buying a house of their own. If they live in London or other large cities, these people are still often condemned to overcrowded, sometimes insanitary, accommodation. Local authorities are trying to solve the problem by building council houses and flats, and by offering grants for the modernization of existing property, but the outlook for those families who still face many years on council waiting lists is bleak. One hopeful sign in the later 1960s was that the general public, partly through the efforts of charitable organizations like Shelter and television programmes such as the play *Cathy Come Home*, had at last realized that even the Welfare State had not eliminated the last remnants of the squalor which was typical of slum districts before the war.

The Education Act of 1944 (see page 224) provided the framework for the post-war school system. One of its provisions, that the school-leaving age be raised to fifteen, was carried out in 1947, but its hope that ultimately everyone might stay at school to the age of sixteen was not implemented until 1972. Wilson's Labour government was committed to this policy, but the succession of economic crises forced it to restrict government spending.

The Butler Act envisaged a three-part secondary-education system: grammar, technical, and secondary modern schools. In the early 1950s, however, London, soon to be followed by one or two other adventurous authorities, such as Coventry, began to experiment with comprehensive secondary schools. Permanent selection at the age of eleven, it was argued, was both educationally and socially harmful. Opponents maintained that comprehensive schools were usually very large and therefore impersonal, that the cost of building such schools was prohibitive, and that highly intelligent pupils in comprehensive schools were likely to be held back by their less able fellows.

Unfortunately, perhaps, the comprehensive issue became entangled with party politics: Labour was strongly in favour, while the Conservatives were unconvinced that the change would be worthwhile. Shortly after coming to power in 1964 the Labour government instructed local authorities to submit plans for the eventual conversion of their secondary schools to a comprehensive pattern, and in the next six years most authorities made some move in this direction. Shortage of money, however, made it impossible to provide sufficient new schools, and many comprehensives in the late 1960s were merely amalgamations of existing premises.

The cost of the education system has soared since 1945 and this fact, above all others, is responsible for the imperfections which remain. Governments have had to spend enormous sums on school building, partly because the number of children at school has increased: the school-leaving age has been raised, the 'bulge' in the birth-rate immediately after the war inflated the school population in the 1950s and early 1960s, and many more children have stayed at school beyond the legal leaving age. Furthermore, many existing buildings were old, dark, even insanitary, and had to be replaced,

*Opponents of comprehensive education on the march in Bristol, 1964*

**Education**

while the movement of population to new towns or suburbs has forced local authorities to provide schools there. Between 1945 and 1963, 4,000 new secondary schools and 2,000 primary schools were built, but in the mid-1960s many primary-school children still had to make do with accommodation which was more than seventy years old.

The other major problem was a shortage of teachers. Special training schemes at the end of the war brought a large number of ex-servicemen into the profession, but it was difficult in the 1950s and 1960s to attract sufficient young people into teaching. The shortage of highly qualified mathematics and science teachers was so acute that some schools, especially girls' schools, were forced to abandon advanced courses in these subjects. There was an all-round shortage, however, and many primary schools had classes of forty or more in the late 1960s.

Education has become fashionable since 1945. Employers have ceased to maintain that experience teaches far more than books and are now much more likely to ask an applicant for a job how many O Levels he has, or what is the class of his degree. Examinations have become popular with employers, if not with candidates. Many more secondary-school pupils stay on to take examinations, and the examination system itself has been transformed: the General Certificate of Education replaced the School Certificate in the early 1950s, and the Certificate of Secondary Education emerged in the early 1960s.

Because young people realize the value of education, or at least the advantages of a good educational record, many more of them have gone on to college or university, and the number of further education establishments has increased accordingly. The number of university students increased from 50,000 in 1938–9 to 90,000 in 1956–7 and doubled in the next decade, although it fell far short of the target of 390,000 set by the Robbins Report in 1963. The increase has been made possible partly by the expansion of existing universities and partly by the setting up of completely new universities, such as those at Keele, York, Brighton, and Lancaster.

Cost, again, has prevented the further expansion which both governments and potential students have desired. Governments have, however, realized that they must pay for higher education: universities themselves receive massive financial support from the Treasury, while over three-quarters of students receive maintenance grants.

Nevertheless, in university education Britain lags behind most other advanced countries: far fewer young men and women gain university places than in the United States, for example. In other respects, Britain may claim that her people are better educated than those of other nations. The British buy more books than anyone else, and they also read more newspapers. The boom in the sale of daily newspapers which was a feature of the inter-war years continued during the Second World War and afterwards. The combined circulation of the national dailies, which had reached ten million by 1937, rose to over fifteen million in 1947 and seventeen million in 1957. It was calculated in 1960 that nine out of ten adults were reading at least one daily paper.

**Newspapers**

The wartime shortage of newsprint limited most papers to four small pages, and many of these restrictions continued in the post-war austerity period. As paper became more plentiful, newspapers grew again in size, but this very growth brought problems for their owners. Production costs rose, and prices could be kept down only by attracting more and more advertisers, but firms would buy advertising space only if they were sure that the newspapers would reach a large number of readers. While giants like the *Daily Mirror* and *Daily Express* did very well, less popular dailies struggled to survive. It was for this reason that the *News Chronicle* amalgamated with the *Daily Mail* in 1960.

The chief sufferers in the scramble for advertising revenue were provincial newspapers. Between 1937 and 1959 the number of provincial dailies fell from 28 to 23, while only 900 out of 1,300 weekly papers survived. Those which did continue to appear often passed out of the hands of local proprietors and into the possession of national newspaper chains. In the 1950s and 1960s the Canadian Roy Thomson, later Lord Thomson, bought up large numbers of local papers, and eventually landed some much bigger fish, including *The Scotsman* and *The Times*. Like many other newspaper owners, Lord Thomson also had a strong interest in commercial television.

High-minded critics bemoaned the fact that a newspaper's success was judged by the number of copies it sold and by the amount of money it could extract from advertisers, rather than by the quality of its reporting. They would have been justified if the smaller, more serious papers had been forced to capitulate. In fact, *The Times, The Guardian,* and the *Daily Telegraph* increased their readerships, although their figures were well behind those of their more popular rivals. The same was true of *The Observer* and the *Sunday Times,* while the *Telegraph* even risked bringing out a new Sunday version. The success of the 'quality papers' was due partly to streamlined organization and partly to new attractions, such as magazine sections and colour supplements. 'Success' in this instance, of course, means continued existence; the collapse of *The Guardian* was regularly predicted during the 1960s, but it strode on, complete with misprints, from one financial crisis to the next.

The development of sound broadcasting between the wars had at first alarmed newspaper owners and journalists, but they soon

**Broadcasting**

realized that radio and newspapers complemented each other. By 1939 the B.B.C.'s programmes were reaching most homes in the country, but newspaper circulations were higher than ever before. The peak of sound broadcasting's influence probably came during the Second World War (see Chapter 10), but it remained popular in the first years of peace until it was partially superseded by television in the 1950s. It remained an essential part of the broadcasting service, however, and was beginning, in the 1960s, to assume a new role: in the evening the family settled down in front of the television set, but during the day housewives worked to the accompaniment of soothing background music, while car radios lessened the tedium of many a traffic jam. The small, portable transistor radio opened up the teenage market also. Pirate radio stations proved that there was a huge demand for non-stop 'pop' music, and after the pirates were eliminated the B.B.C. introduced Radio One.

**Television**  Television, however, was the broadcasting revolution of the post-war years. The service, resumed shortly after the war, extended only to the London area at first and made slow progress in the days of austerity. The boom came in the 1950s, when wages began to rise sharply and manufacturers produced reasonably cheap and dependable sets. The Coronation, in 1953, was probably a major stimulus to television sales. By the mid-1950s the number of television licence holders equalled the number of people who had licences for sound radio only, and by the early 1960s over eighty per cent of homes had television sets.

The B.B.C. was, at first, responsible for the only television channel, but the Television Act of 1954 (see page 252) set up an Independent Television Authority. Commercial television was an immediate success. The various I.T.A. companies were attracting between sixty and seventy per cent of the television audience by 1960, and gross advertising revenue amounted to £93 million in 1961. Lord Thomson, the newspaper magnate who had a major share in Scottish Television, remarked that the right to operate a commercial television company was 'a licence to print money'.

The early television programmes were, in accordance with the B.B.C.'s general aims, a tasteful mixture of information, education, and entertainment. News bulletins and documentary films were combined with variety programmes, comedy shows, drama, and often outstandingly good coverage of sporting events. One immensely important discovery by the programme planners was that rather trivial parlour games, such as *What's My Line?*, if skilfully presented, were enormously popular with the television audience. True to its traditions, the B.B.C. maintained a high moral and social tone: during the evening programmes male announcers wore dinner-jackets.

Commercial television brought a change in style and, in many people's opinion, a serious lowering of standards. The independent companies were out to attract a mass audience, so their programmes included few documentaries and very little serious music. Popular series like *Coronation Street* and *Emergency Ward Ten* quickly became national favourites, as did quiz shows, in which lavish prizes were offered to competitors able to answer a few simple questions.

Alarmed at the success of I.T.A., the B.B.C. retaliated by presenting more popular entertainment. Comedy shows such as *Hancock's Half Hour* and *Steptoe and Son*, plus drama series of which *Doctor Finlay's Casebook* is a good example, won back some of the lost audience. The B.B.C. still attempted to cater for the minority who had cultural inclinations, however, and some of its major dramatic productions reached a very high standard. Following the report of the Pilkington Committee on broadcasting in 1962, the B.B.C. was permitted to launch a second channel in 1964, with the result that it could both try to capture a large slice of the mass audience and provide a wide range of documentaries and serious music and drama. A further major step came in 1967 with the first colour television programmes, but the high cost of colour sets deterred many would-be customers.

Television brought men and women into the public eye in a way that films and newspapers had never done. It led the people to believe, wrongly perhaps, that they really knew and understood their public leaders. The converse was even more dangerous: politicians vied with each other in presenting an image—the debonair, unflurried Macmillan, or the earnest, practical Wilson. People's political opinions were formed by their assessment of the party leaders as television performers, not by a sobre examination of their records and policies. Less harmful was the appearance of a new species, the television personality, neither performer nor journalist, usually the genial chairman of a quiz programme or parlour game. Gilbert Harding, Hughie Green, and David Frost would be recognized by more people than the Prime Minister, the Archbishop of Canterbury, or the General Secretary of the T.U.C.

Television was part boon, part disaster. While sound radio had little effect on cinema attendance, television caused hundreds of cinemas to close. The provincial repertory theatre was in a state of continuous financial embarrassment, and survived only when subsidized by local authorities. In many cases, television almost killed the art of conversation. Much of the entertainment provided was tawdry and third-rate, often American in origin. Yet the people whose lives were drab and featureless at best before about 1950 now had a new and comparatively cheap source of pleasure. A flick of a switch could transport them from the back streets of Salford to the art galleries of Florence, or, more often, the plains of Wyoming; they had at their disposal, if they cared to use it, a reliable, intelligent, and up-to-date source of information on every national and international problem. The potential value of television has not been fully exploited, but it has undoubtedly brought warmth, laughter, excitement, and even enlightenment to nearly every home in the country.

The decline in cinema attendance has been a direct result of the development of television, and the numbers going to cinemas have fallen just as the number of television licences has increased. The cinema reached a peak of popularity just after the Second World War: 1,635 million tickets were bought in 1946. Each man, woman, and child, in other words, went to the pictures on average thirty-three times in the year. Many obviously went more often, and it is reckoned that most children went at least once a week. By 1951 the average number of visits a year had fallen to twenty-seven, and ten years later it was down to ten. The number of cinemas had decreased also. Some had become supermarkets, some bowling alleys, some dance-halls, but in the 1960s a very large proportion were converted into bingo-halls.

**Sport**

Television was also partly responsible for the fall in attendances at professional sporting fixtures. Cricket was never as popular as football, but Test Matches against the Australians and the often brilliant West Indians continued to attract large crowds. County matches, on the other hand, drew very few spectators and many county clubs survived only by organizing football pools as fund-raising ventures. Football clubs did very well in the immediate post-war years. A total of more than forty-one million spectators attended Football League matches in the 1948–9 season, but this had fallen to less than twenty-seven million by 1964–5. The most successful First Division clubs, providing a very high level of entertainment and displaying star players valued at tens of thousands of pounds on the transfer market, were never in financial difficulties. Spectators flocked to see Manchester United, Liverpool, Everton, and Tottenham Hotspur, who achieved the Cup and League double in 1961. Rising costs and falling attendances, however, presented the more humble clubs with almost insuperable financial problems. The notable football successes of the period were England's victory in the World Cup in 1966 and Glasgow Celtic's victory in the European Cup in the following year.

**Leisure activities**

While spectator-sports became less popular, there is some evidence that more people were taking part in recreational activities. This was undoubtedly due to the fact that wages were higher, with the result that far more people could afford relatively expensive equipment and club subscriptions. Golf ceased to be the preserve of the wealthy middle class, motor racing in its various forms

*Sitting room in an 'ideal home',
1957*

attracted numerous enthusiasts, sailing became a week-end passion
for many families, while thousands of less energetic people took up
fishing. Others went for drives in their newly acquired cars, or
stayed at home and polished them. Since most of the new council
houses had gardens, digging or rose pruning became for some an
alternative to the delights of Villa Park or Edgbaston, while the
'do it yourself' habit, ranging from wallpapering to house building,
won millions of more or less voluntary converts. Although everyone
mourned the passing of Accrington Stanley (founder-members of
the Football League), there can be little doubt that active participation was preferable to passive attendance. Not only did people
enjoy the thrill of personal achievement, whether it was a 'birdie
at the twelfth' or a well-painted door, but whole families now often
joined in the week-end recreation.

Higher wages influenced holiday habits also. Three and a half
million Britons took holidays abroad in 1961, and their continental
experience undoubtedly influenced their tastes: espresso coffee bars,
delicatessens, and wine shops appeared in places where, thirty
years previously, there had been pawnbrokers and second-hand
clothes shops. The British people's ignorance of food had for long
been a standard joke, but in the 1950s and 1960s Chinese, Indian,

and Italian restaurants appeared in most towns. Eating out became a popular alternative to the cinema.

**Teenagers**

Many of the most striking features of Britain in the 1950s and 1960s—the coffee bars, the vogue for 'pop' music, the sometimes bizarre fashions—reflected the tastes of young people, who now, unlike their predecessors, had money to spend. Wages were high and teenagers' parents expected little in the way of contribution to domestic expenses. Businessmen were quick to spot their opportunity. Young men and women liked to imagine that they were different from their elders, that they had different tastes in music, clothes, and hair-styles. Very often, in fact, they were the victims of manufacturers and salesmen who had discovered a brand new market. The 'cult of the teenager' was an important commercial fact: young people spent £850 million on themselves in 1961.

**Fashion**

It was not until the 1960s that young people's tastes in clothes began profoundly to influence fashion. In the late 1940s the elegant Paris fashion houses continued to lead the world. Dior's 'New Look', with its long, full skirts, and square, padded shoulders, was a reaction against wartime restrictions and a very definite return to femininity. The early 1950s saw little basic change, although the 'A line', with a lower waist, and the straight-skirted 'shift' were variations on the theme. Then, in the 1960s, London took over fashion leadership from Paris and youth began to dictate the main trends. Skirts gradually became shorter until, with the backing of Mary Quant, the 'mini-skirt' arrived. Despite protests from the older generation and counter-attacks from the Paris fashion houses, the rest of the western world followed suit, though in North America and Europe skirts never reached the skimpy extreme of London.

In men's fashion, also, the preferences of the young influenced styles. Wide, padded shoulders, reaching absurd proportions in the suits of the London 'spivs', were typical of the immediate post-war years, but this fashion merged into the 'Edwardian' style, carried to extremes by the 'Teddy boys' in the 1950s. This period saw a return to narrow trousers, a fashion which survived into the 1960s. The 1960s were marked by no distinct styles in men's clothes, except that among the young the traditional lounge suit and collar and tie were often discarded in favour of more casual attire, while long hair and beards became a kind of students' uniform. Such was the popularity of sloppy sweaters and jeans among girls as well as young men, and so long was the men's hair, that the two sexes were often indistinguishable.

**Music and dancing**

Dancing and listening to 'pop' music were by far the most popular leisure activities among the young throughout the period. Ballroom dancing of the type in vogue between the wars survived briefly after 1945, but young people quickly took to the more

energetic jive and jitterbug, violent gyrations accompanied by jazz music. The older generation preferred gentler music, such as the sentimental ballads of Donald Peers, the crooning of Bing Crosby, and the songs from musical shows like *Oklahoma* and *Annie Get Your Gun*. The mid-fifties saw the birth of rock-and-roll, an even wilder dance form which apparently necessitated the ear-splitting efforts of bands such as Bill Haley's. The young delighted in the singing of Elvis Presley, while their elders enjoyed the film versions of a new generation of musicals: *South Pacific*, *The King and I*, and *High Society*.

Just as London displaced Paris as the centre of the fashion world in the 1960s, so Britain took over the leadership in 'pop' music from the United States. First came the individual singers, Tommy Steele, Adam Faith, and Cliff Richard, then the groups, of whom The Beatles were by far the most successful. The Beatles, with their noisy, strident beat music, relying heavily on electronic effects, captivated the world, made themselves millionaires, gave Liverpool an entirely new claim to fame, and were awarded M.B.E.s by Harold Wilson's government. They began a fashion which lasted throughout the 1960s. Although groups like the Rolling Stones and The Animals were also highly successful exponents of the art, The Beatles were unique. The youth of every continent bought their records, performed the twist and similar contortions to the 'Mersey sound' and travelled hundreds of miles to see them in person.

Popular entertainment had become, to a very great extent, the preserve of the young. Anyone over the age of thirty was middle-aged. As they acquired television sets, the older generation went out less frequently and concentrated on either the small screen or a fairly wide range of alternative interests. For the men at least, foremost among these was often the family car.

**Cars**

The enormous increase in the number of private cars was another of the obvious signs of all-round prosperity in the late 1950s and the 1960s. Before the war the car was becoming a symbol of middle-class success, but very few manual workers could afford more than a motor cycle. The enormous extension of car ownership in recent years is a further indication that the old distinction between middle class and working class has ceased to have much meaning.

New cars were scarce in the post-war days of austerity. Most of the vehicles on the road dated from before 1939. Petrol rationing, in any case, made private motoring difficult. The higher wages of the late 1950s and early 1960s, coupled with the streamlining of production techniques, caused the real change. There had been two million private cars on Britain's roads in 1939, but the total had not quite reached two and a half million by 1951. In 1961, however, it has risen to six million, and by 1966 it was not far short of ten million.

*Motor vehicles produced in Britain—cars, motor cycles, buses, lorries* (thousands)

| | |
|------|--------|
| 1945 | 2648 |
| 1950 | 4414 |
| 1955 | 6469 |
| 1960 | 9440 |
| 1965 | 12 940 |

The increase in traffic naturally brought problems, the most serious of which was the risk of accidents. The Ministry of Transport, the local authorities, and the police showed that they were well aware of the danger, but despite their efforts the numbers killed on the roads continued to rise: 5,250 in 1951, 6,900 in 1961, 8,000 in 1966. The death-rate was horrifying, but the relative performance of Britain's drivers over the past forty years has not been discouraging, as the following table shows:

|  | Number of cars | Number killed | Number killed per 1,000 cars |
|---|---|---|---|
| 1930 | 1 million | 7,300 | 7·3 |
| 1939 | 2 million | 6,500 | 3·25 |
| 1951 | 2·4 million | 5,250 | 2·2 |
| 1961 | 6 million | 6,900 | 1·15 |
| 1966 | 9·5 million | 8,000 | 0·85 |

Attempts to make roads safer in recent years have included the introduction of zebra crossings, the employment of special wardens ('lollipop men') to guide schoolchildren across busy roads, the construction of pedestrian subways in city centres, the compulsory testing of all vehicles more than three years old and, in the late 1960s, the breathalyser law, which permits the police to check the level of alcohol in a driver's bloodstream. The figures prove that these measures have been highly successful.

Congestion in town centres is the other disagreeable result of the increase in the volume of traffic. Motorists themselves are delayed by traffic jams, while the exhaust fumes seriously pollute the atmosphere. Local councils have restricted the right to park, have employed traffic wardens to enforce their regulations, and have provided many more car parks. The movement of traffic has, at the same time, been eased by the provision of by-passes and ring-roads and by the marshalling of vehicles into traffic-lanes. Some cities, of which Coventry was one of the first, have gone several stages further by attempting in some areas to separate traffic and pedestrians altogether.

**Motorways**

The most costly assault on the traffic problem has been, of course, the belated construction of a national system of motorways. Work began in the late 1950s on the M1, linking London, the Midlands, and the West Riding of Yorkshire. The initial stages of the M6 in Lancashire and the M5 between Bristol and Birmingham soon followed. By 1962, 190 miles of motorway were open, and by 1967 the total length completed amounted to 458 miles, with a further 129 miles under construction. By allowing cars and lorries to travel quickly and comparatively safely between cities, the motorways have at least in part met the challenge of a quadrupled traffic problem.

*An attempt at the removal of traffic congestion in town centres: the Bull Ring, Birmingham, where the movement of pedestrians and vehicles has been separated*

Traffic regulations and motorways have been the government's response to the extra vehicles. The rising cost of major improvements to existing roads and the construction of new roads illustrates the size of the problem and the extent of official concern: £14 million was spent in 1955, £82 million in 1960, and £182 million in 1965.

There can be no doubt that traffic difficulties will get worse in the future. It is sometimes argued that private cars will soon have to be excluded altogether from city centres. One looks on with alarm as Britain's ancient cities are turned into conglomerations of concrete department stores and office blocks, surrounded by car parks.

The increase in road traffic has come about partly because people have begun travelling more, and partly because they have changed to travelling in their own cars instead of by train. The railways have consequently been in decline since the Second World War. British Rail has come to terms with this change in public habits and has attempted both to restrict its losses by closing down unprofitable lines and, by modernizing its equipment, to offer the best possible service on its remaining routes.

**Railways**

Modernization of the railways began in 1955. Despite the protests of steam enthusiasts and the preference of some engine-drivers, it was decided that steam locomotives had to be replaced by either diesel or electric trains. There had been 19,000 steam engines in 1951, but their numbers had fallen to under 12,000 in 1961, and the only ones left at the end of the sixties were in museums or in private hands. They were replaced for the most

291

part by diesel or diesel-electric locomotives or by multiple-unit diesel cars. Electrification was very expensive: only thirteen per cent of the total track had been electrified in 1966. The route between London and Manchester was electrified in 1966, with the result that fast 'inter-city' expresses considerably shortened the journey, but there was no prospect of an extension of electrification to the whole country.

The closure of unprofitable branch lines and passenger stations was the other main change in the railway system. The total route, which was about 20,000 miles at the time of nationalization, had been reduced to 18,000 miles by 1961, and the Beeching Report of 1963 led to the closure of a further 4,000 miles in the next three years. The number of passenger stations in use was halved between 1951 and 1966, and the staff employed was reduced by forty per cent over the same period.

Largely because of these economies, the railways have become more efficient: there has been only a slight decrease in the number of passengers, and the volume of freight carried has fallen by only a quarter. But in spite of rising fares (they were approximately doubled between 1948 and 1967), the railways have continued to operate at a loss.

The development of air transport illustrates well the idea that war stimulates change. Powered flight of any kind was seen as miraculous before 1914, but the exploits of the air forces in the First War proved that reliable aeroplanes could be made. Nevertheless, aviation was only a sport for most of the inter-war years. The Second World War, however, led to staggering improvements in design, with the result that the great airlines have, since 1945, become major international businesses, while the aircraft industry is now vital to the British economy. Passenger flight statistics are even more impressive than those relating to motor traffic. In 1949, for the first time, a million passengers were carried by air between Britain and foreign countries. By 1966 the total had reached eight million, most of them either holiday makers or businessmen.

The standard of living of the British people in the late 1960s was, without any doubt, higher than ever before. Yet many of them were still unhappy. The economic pessimists, possibly rightly, warned that prosperity might not last. But a new danger—pollution—had been created largely by prosperity itself. Factories, discharging waste material, polluted rivers and the sea; oil tankers were responsible for the appearance of ugly oil slicks on beaches; chemical fertilizers and insecticides upset the balance of nature in the countryside; noise from aircraft, traffic, or even transistor radios, made life hardly bearable at times. These were truly the problems of the affluent society. Man had learned how to create wealth; he had not yet learned how to use it.

*Atomic energy as a source of power became a reality in the sixties with the building of nuclear power stations*

**Air transport**

*Section of the M1 near Sheffield, June 1968. Pollution of the air remained a problem*

# Chapter 14
## From Empire to Commonwealth

Queen Victoria bequeathed to her successor an Empire 'on which the sun never set' and the custody of a quarter of mankind. The Boer War, with which the nineteenth century ended and the twentieth began, brought the last major addition of territory to an Empire which, in the next sixty years or so, was to be transformed from a collection of more-or-less subject dependencies into an association of equal partners. The Edwardians were immensely proud of having built an empire and were deeply conscious of their responsibility for policing and administering it. Their grandchildren were less sure of themselves: some were angry and ashamed that the essence of Britain's power and prestige had been given away; others rejoiced that they had been so enlightened.

The process of change was sometimes smooth and cordial, sometimes violent. There was seldom a direct clash between Britain's attempt to retain her possessions and the colonists' demands for independence. The lesson of the American colonies had been well learned. Rather was there disagreement over the rate of change. The leaders of the Indian and, later, African nationalist movements naturally wanted to be free as soon as possible, whereas British politicians and colonial governors wanted to prepare the subject peoples for independence and feared that a premature British withdrawal might lead to disaster.

### THE DOMINIONS

Until quite recently it was necessary to distinguish between Britain's colonies, territories like Kenya, Nigeria, and Jamaica, which were under direct rule from London, and the Dominions, such as Canada, Australia, and New Zealand, which governed themselves and were virtually independent of Britain. Until 1931 the precise status of the Dominions was difficult to define: they had their own parliaments and governments and made their own decisions on all internal matters, but they accepted the King of England as Head of State, were theoretically subject to his deputy, the Governor-General, and accepted Britain's lead in foreign and defence policies. The first stage in the evolution of the modern Commonwealth was the assertion that the Dominions were Britain's free and equal partners.

*Julius Nyerere and his supporters celebrate Tanganyika's independence*

The distinction between Dominions and colonies was also racial: self-government had been granted to those territories where there was a large European population. Into this category fell Britain's South African possessions, Cape Colony and Natal. But the South African situation was complicated by the existence to the north of two independent Boer republics, Transvaal and the Orange Free State, whose European population was of predominantly Dutch origin and whose people had moved away from the Cape early in the nineteenth century because they disliked British rule.

Relations between Britain and the Boer republics had always been strained, but they deteriorated rapidly in the 1890s when, following the discovery of gold in Transvaal, large numbers of British prospectors moved in. The Boers resented the presence of these foreigners and, although they taxed them heavily, refused to grant them ordinary civil rights. Britain's concern over the ill-treatment of British citizens in Transvaal led to the outbreak of the Boer War in 1899.

Unexpectedly, the British army suffered a series of humiliating defeats in the early months of the war. It was only after massive reinforcements had been sent to South Africa that the tide turned. Besieged British garrisons at Ladysmith, Kimberley, and Mafeking were relieved early in 1900 and the news of these successes was received almost hysterically by crowds in British cities. By August of 1900 organised Boer resistance had collapsed and the war was apparently over. But the Boers did not give in: they organised commando groups and conducted skilful guerrilla warfare for a further two years. The British, now commanded by Lord Kitchener, retaliated by building block-houses and wire fences to divide the country into compartments and moving the civilian population into concentration camps. The policy succeeded, for the Boers sued for peace early in 1902, but it was inhumane: out of 120,000 people in the camps in 1901–2, 20,000 died. Public opinion in France, Germany, and the United States, which was in any case critical of the Boer War, was outraged by the concentration camps. Even within Britain there was some public concern, particularly in the Liberal Party.

The war claimed the lives of 22,000 British soldiers (three-quarters of them from diseases such as enteric fever) and cost the Treasury over £200 million. In view of this, the peace terms, signed at Vereeniging in May 1902, were generous. The Boer republics were annexed by Britain, but were promised eventual self-government; English was to be the official language, but Afrikaans might be taught in the schools and used in the law courts; the British government granted three million pounds to the Boer farmers to help them re-stock their farms.

Towards the Boers, British policy remained magnanimous. The

**South Africa**

**The Boer war 1899–1902**

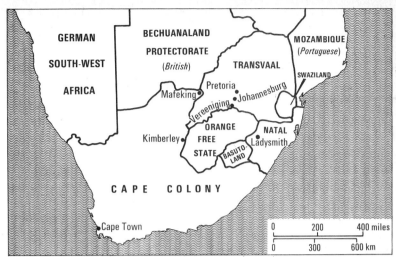

GERMAN

SOUTH-WEST

AFRICA

BECHUANALAND

PROTECTORATE

(*British*)

TRANSVAAL

Pretoria

Mafeking

Vereeniging

Johannesburg

MOZAMBIQUE
(*Portuguese*)

SWAZILAND

ORANGE

FREE

STATE

BASUTO-
LAND

Kimberley

NATAL

Ladysmith

CAPE COLONY

Cape Town

| 0 | 200 | 400 miles |
| 0 | 300 | 600 km |

Map 19 *The Boer War*

promise of the Peace of Vereeniging was fulfilled when self-government was granted to Transvaal in 1906 and to the Orange River Colony (as it was now called) in 1907. Two years later a Union of South Africa, comprising the two British colonies and the former Boer republics, was set up and granted the same rights as the other Dominions. Political power in the new Dominion, of course, lay entirely in the hands of the European minority of the population.

**Union of South Africa 1909**

**Australia and New Zealand**

Australia, unlike South Africa, achieved full Dominion status peacefully. The Commonwealth of Australia Act of 1900 grouped the six existing colonies together in a federal union, thereby following the example of Canada and setting a precedent for South Africa. New Zealand had become self-governing as early as 1854. In 1907 the British government recognised that Canada, Australia, New Zealand, and Newfoundland were self-governing Dominions.

**The Dominions in the First World war**

When the European war broke out in 1914 the Dominions, without instruction from London, all declared war on Germany. The only dissent was in South Africa, where there was a brief anti-war revolt. Dominion forces were used, first, to seize Germany's overseas colonies. Australian troops conquered German New Guinea in September 1914 and the South Africans had control of German South-West Africa by December. The armed forces of the Dominions and colonies played an important part in the major campaigns also: Australians and New Zealanders fought bravely in the disastrous Gallipoli expedition; Indian soldiers took part in the attempted conquest of Mesopotamia; Canadians shared the torments of the Western Front, and their capture of Vimy Ridge in 1917 was one of the few successes of Nivelle's offensive.

The Dominions also made some contribution to the political direction of the war. The Dominion Prime Ministers, meeting in

297

London in 1917, asserted their independence from Britain, but made no important change in the overall strategy. This meeting did, however, bring Lloyd George into contact with Jan Smuts, the South African Minister of Defence, who so impressed Lloyd George that he was appointed to the War Cabinet.

Fighting in the war as Britain's allies, and not merely as auxiliaries of the British army, stimulated the already-growing self-confidence of the Dominions. They had taken part, and had sustained heavy casualties, because they had chosen to do so and not merely because Britain had commanded their obedience. As victorious nations, they consequently sent representatives to the Paris peace conference in 1919, where they were rewarded by being granted, as mandates, former German colonies (see page 112). The Dominion governments also became fully-fledged members of the League of Nations.

Although the decade after the First World War saw no conflict and very little disagreement between Britain and the Dominions, it was clear that the self-governing parts of the Empire were now aware of themselves as independent states and were determined to secure Britain's recognition of this fact. Up to 1914 they had followed Britain's lead in foreign affairs almost without question and did not have their own ambassadors in foreign countries. In 1922, however, Canada negotiated a trade treaty with the United States and four years later appointed a permanent minister in Washington. At the time of the Chanak incident in 1922, when Britain seemed to be on the brink of war with Turkey (see page 115), Canada and South Africa, breaking the precedent of 1914, refused to promise military support.

The most important step forward in the 1920s came with a statement by Lord Balfour, Chairman of the Inter-Imperial Relations Committee, in 1926. He defined the relationship of Britain and the Dominions in the following terms:

> They are autonomous communities within the British Empire, equal in status, in no way subordinate one to another in any aspect of their domestic or external affairs, though united by a common allegiance to the Crown, and freely associated as members of the British Commonwealth of Nations.

Not only were the Dominions independent as regards domestic and foreign affairs, but they were now accepted as Britain's equals, her partners in a 'free association'. Times had certainly changed since 1902, when the 'self-governing colonies' represented at the *Colonial* Conference had 'respectfully urged' the British government to consider the wisdom of adopting policies of imperial preference. The 1926 declaration implied a distinction between

*The Commonwealth Prime Minister's Conference, 1961, when South Africa withdrew from the Commonwealth. Left to right: Nkrumah (Ghana), Diefenbaker (Canada), Verwoerd (South Africa), Nehru (India), Ayub Khan (Pakistan), the Queen, Sir Roy Welensky (Central African Federation), Mrs. Bandaranaike (Ceylon), Macmillan (Great Britain), Menzies (Australia), and Archbishop Makarios (Cyprus). Some premiers are absent from this photograph.*

**Balfour Declaration 1926**

**Statute of Westminster 1931**

Dominions and colonies which had never before been fully recognized, but which was confirmed when in 1930 a separate Secretary of State for the Dominions was appointed to the British Cabinet.

In effect, the Dominions achieved their freedom in the 1920s. Their new status was given concrete legal form by the great Statute of Westminster of 1931, which stated that the British Parliament could no longer pass laws relating to the Dominions unless the Dominion parliaments themselves approved and that the Dominion parliaments were free to legislate for themselves. The Crown was to be a symbol of the Commonwealth members' 'free association'. The Parliament in Westminster, therefore, which could still make laws relating to India and the African, Asian, and West Indian colonies, no longer had the right to interfere in the affairs of Canada, Australia, New Zealand, or South Africa.

While the Dominions drifted constitutionally away from Britain in the 1920s, their relations with the Mother Country were usually cordial. Economic co-operation, for example, was stimulated by such enterprises as the Empire Marketing Board and the limited agreements on imperial preference reached at the Ottawa Conference in 1932. Travel within the Empire became easier: Imperial Airways began a weekly service to India in 1929. Finally, but not least important, harmony was fostered by the overseas tours of Edward, the popular Prince of Wales.

The only Dominion not on friendly terms with Britain during the inter-war years was the Irish Free State, which had achieved Dominion status after the 'Treaty' of 1922 (see page 118). The more extreme Irish nationalists, men like Eamonn de Valera, wanted only the loosest association with Britain, resented having to swear allegiance to the British Crown and were very bitter about the separation of the 'six counties' of Ulster from the Free State.

**Ireland**

When de Valera became Prime Minister in 1932 he took advantage of the Statute of Westminster by having the *Dail* (the Irish Parliament) abolish the office of Governor-General and the M.P.s' oath of allegiance to the Crown. His long term aim, as always, was to set up an Irish Republic, outside the Commonwealth if necessary.

Retaliating partly against these constitutional changes and partly against de Valera's decision to stop paying the land annuities which Ireland was obliged to pay under the Irish Land Purchase Act of 1903 (see page 18), the British government imposed special duties on food imported from Ireland. The Irish government countered with tariffs on imports of British coal and manufactured goods, and the resulting trade war, which lasted from 1932 to 1937, further damaged Anglo-Irish relations.

**Second World war**

When the Second World War began in 1939 Canada, Australia, and New Zealand again demonstrated their goodwill towards Britain by immediately declaring war on Germany. As in 1914, there was a brief crisis in South Africa, where the anti-British Prime Minister, Hertzog, would have preferred to stay neutral, but he was soon replaced by Smuts, who joined the other Dominions on Britain's side. The Irish Free State, however, remained neutral throughout the war and, by denying the Royal Navy the use of southern Irish ports, made the protection of shipping in the Atlantic much more difficult.

Dominion, colonial, and British troops fought side-by-side in the Second World War, as in the First. Australian and New Zealand troops formed an important part of Sir William Slim's Fourteenth Army, which eventually defeated the Japanese in the Burmese campaign; Australians, New Zealanders and South Africans fought in North Africa; the Canadians were prominent in the Normandy invasions and the liberation of Western Europe. Furthermore, Dominion airmen served with the R.A.F. throughout the war, as did 7,000 West Indians. Many thousands of troops from India and the colonies in Africa also served with the British forces, as did many Irish, in spite of Ireland's neutrality.

After the Second World War the notion of the 'British Empire', comprising Dominions and colonies, was gradually replaced by that

**The Commonwealth**

*An advocate of the boycotting of South African goods*

**South Africa leaves the Commonwealth 1961**

of the 'Commonwealth', most of whose members had achieved full sovereignty. India and Pakistan became independent in 1947 and were followed in the 1950s and 1960s by almost all of Britain's former colonies in Asia, Africa and the West Indies (see pages 307 and 310–314). The select 'club' of Dominions was enlarged and lost its predominantly European character; the term 'Dominion' itself was soon dropped.

The constitutional status of the independent Commonwealth countries remained almost the same: it was defined in the Statute of Westminster. A problem arose when some of the states wished to abandon allegiance to the British Crown and to become republics. When the Irish Free State became a republic in 1949 it left the Commonwealth, but India, which took the same step in the same year, was allowed to remain inside. Eventually, most of the newly independent African and Asian states chose a republican form of government, but most of them remained Commonwealth members. Constitutional lawyers produced a splendid British compromise: all Commonwealth countries, including the republics, accepted the British sovereign as 'Head of the Commonwealth', a meaningless term which satisfied everyone.

As the Commonwealth became a multi-racial association, South Africa's continued membership became progressively more embarrassing. South Africa's policy of *apartheid*, or racial separation, which preserved European domination, was universally condemned elsewhere and was especially unpopular among the new Asian and African Commonwealth countries, who felt that racial equality should be one of the Commonwealth's central principles. Harold Macmillan, the British Prime Minister, visiting South Africa in 1960, spoke to the South African parliament of the 'wind of change' blowing through Africa, implying that the South African government should treat black Africans more generously and abandon *apartheid*.

Later in 1960 the South African Prime Minister, Dr. Verwoerd, announced his country's intention of becoming a republic. Several of the newly independent Commonwealth members had already established the precedent that states could be republics and remain in the Commonwealth, but South Africa's decision was taken by the other Commonwealth Prime Ministers as an opportunity to condemn *apartheid*. Such was the criticism at the Prime Ministers' Conference in London in 1961 that Dr. Verwoerd chose to withdraw from the Commonwealth altogether. Many South Africans, especially those of British origin, regretted the decision, but it probably saved the Commonwealth: the black African states would have been most unlikely to remain in the same association as the South African régime.

By 1967 most of the territories controlled by Britain in 1900 had become members of the free association of sovereign states known as the Commonwealth. The purpose and value of this 'club' are often questioned: its members are not united by ideology, legal bonds or military commitments and although there are some economic links the Commonwealth is not a free trade area. Its optimistic supporters argue that, despite its quarrels, it offers the world an example of international co-operation.

## INDIA

Regarded by the Victorians as 'the brightest jewel in the British Crown', India was the heart of the Empire in 1900. Its value was partly economic, for it was Britain's best overseas customer before 1914, and partly emotional: dominion over 300 million Indians added greatly to British prestige. From the late nineteenth century, however, educated Indians were eager to see the end of British rule, but so highly did the British value the sub-continent that they were reluctant to relinquish their control. Most enlightened statesmen saw that Indian independence must come, but the problems of administering India were so complex that they concluded that the transfer of power must be slow and gradual.

Unlike the Dominions, India in 1900 was under direct British rule. The Secretary of State for India was a member of the Cabinet and presided over the India Office in London. The head of the administration in India was the Viceroy, who was assisted by the members of the Indian Civil Service, a carefully selected and highly talented team of British officials who supervised tax-collection, the law courts, medical services, education and attempted to promote agricultural improvement and to relieve the worst ravages of famine. Law and order was maintained by a police force whose senior officers were always British and by a partly British, partly Indian army, which was always under British command. Some parts of India were outside the direct control of the Viceroy and were ruled by Indian princes, who still owed allegiance to the British Crown.

Some attempt had been made by 1900 to give Indians a share in the government of their own country. Central and provincial legislative councils, some of whose members were Indian, were set up in 1892, but they did not have full law-making powers and did not control the Civil Service.

There had always been Indian opponents of British rule, but until the late nineteenth century their efforts had usually been ill-co-ordinated. But the 'raj' provided western-style university education for a minority, some of whom soon became the leaders of a new independence movement. Indian newspapers began to criticise the British and in 1885 a political party, the Indian National

**Indian National Congress**

AFGHANISTAN

KASHMIR

TIBET

•Amristar

WEST PAKISTAN

N E P A L

Delhi•

Karachi•

EAST
PAKISTAN

Calcutta •

BURMA

I N D I A

•Bombay

Madras•

Frontier between India
and Pakistan (1947)

| 0 | 300 | 600 miles |
| 0 | 500 | 1000 km |

CEYLON

Map 20 *India and Pakistan, 1947*

Congress, was established. Congress's aim was a return to Indian self-government, and throughout the last half-century of British rule Congress constantly denounced the authorities for moving too slowly towards its declared goal.

British governments had the permanent dilemma of opposition from Congress and complaints in Britain that India was being 'thrown away'. The Morley-Minto reforms of 1909, the work of John Morley, who was Secretary of State, and the Viceroy, Lord Minto, did not satisfy the Indians, yet were denounced by King Edward VII, among others, for giving Indians too large a share in the conduct of their own affairs. The reforms increased the number of Indians on the legislative councils and provided that some Indians were to be appointed to the national and provincial executive councils, thereby giving them some influence over the actual machinery of government. Ultimate power was left, however, in the hands of the Viceroy.

In 1917 Edwin Montagu, Secretary of State for India in Lloyd George's wartime coalition, announced that Britain's Indian policy was to be

> the increasing association of Indians in every branch of the administration and the gradual development of self-governing institutions with a view to the progressive realisation of responsible government in India as an integral part of the British Empire.

Indians, in other words, were to be given more power. The ultimate aim was 'responsible government', which meant that an elected Indian parliament should be able to control the government, which would in turn be in Indian hands. The process, however, was to be gradual and progressive, that is one step at a time.

The Montagu-Chelmsford reforms, named after Edwin Montagu and Lord Chelmsford, the current Viceroy, were embodied in the Government of India Act of 1919. They produced a highly complicated constitutional settlement and involved the principle of 'dyarchy', or dual control. At both central and provincial levels the government was to be in part subject to control by elected assemblies and in part directly under the Viceroy or provincial governor. The subjects excluded from the influence of the elected assemblies, and therefore reserved for the British administration, included police, justice and most financial matters. The Viceroy was still in command and could over-ride decisions with which he disagreed. The reforms were an important step towards self-government and were consistent with Montagu's declaration, but did not go far enough to satisfy Congress.

The Indians' acknowledged leader throughout the inter-war **Gandhi** years was Mahatma Gandhi, a lawyer who had studied at the Middle Temple in London. Gandhi was an astute and courageous politician who valued the cause of Indian independence much more highly than his personal comfort and success. His conflict with the British began in 1919 following the Amritsar massacre in which troops fired on an Indian demonstration, killing 379 people. Gandhi retaliated by organising a campaign of non-violent disobedience: Indians refused to co-operate with the British authorities. Despite Gandhi's intentions, outbreaks of violence did occur and the Congress leader was gaoled for six years in 1922.

In 1927 Baldwin's government set up a Commission of Inquiry to investigate the prospects of constitutional progress in India. Its chairman was Sir John Simon, a Liberal, and its main fault was that it contained not a single Indian member. Gandhi, when he was released from prison, refused to collaborate with the Commission. Congress, indeed, issued an Indian 'declaration of independence' in 1929, initiating a further programme of civil disobedience.

The Simon Report, when it was published in 1930, naturally did not meet all of Congress's demands, but suggested a further

*Gandhi (in spectacles) on a march protesting against the salt tax, 1930*

**Round Table conferences**

step towards self-government. It recommended responsible government in the provinces, an enlarged electorate and the inclusion of the princes' states in an all-Indian federation. To consider the report in more detail, the British government called a Round Table Conference, attended by representatives of the India Office, the government of India and the Indian princes. Unfortunately, Congress still refused to take part: Gandhi's civil disobedience reached such proportions that 54,000 people were arrested during a period of nine months in 1930.

The first Round Table Conference made good progress. The Simon Report was accepted and the princes agreed to a federation. Then came a major breakthrough: Lord Irwin, the Viceroy, who had already promised India eventual Dominion status, persuaded Gandhi to give up his campaign and to attend a second Round Table Conference in London in 1931. At this, and at a subsequent meeting, Gandhi bluntly demanded immediate Dominion status, but since the Viceroy had given this pledge, the disagreement was only one of timing.

Not everyone in Britain was happy with the progress of the constitutional talks. Winston Churchill resigned from the Conservative shadow Cabinet in 1930 as a protest against the proposal to give India independence. He thought that the problems of governing the whole sub-continent would be too complex, and that a British withdrawal would lead to discord between Hindus and Moslems.

The eventual result of the Simon Report and the Round Table Conferences was the Government of India Act of 1935, which paved the way for Indian independence, but did not yet end the British 'raj'. The Act implemented the recommendation of the Simon Commission that the provincial governments should be responsible to assemblies elected by Indians and partially extended this principle of responsible government to the central administration. But the Viceroy, on behalf of Britain, was still to keep control of some subjects, including defence. The idea of an all-Indian federation, in which the princes should participate, was also included in the Act, but this had not been fully carried out when the Second World War began in 1939.

The Act of 1935 did not, of course, satisfy Congress and Gandhi still refused to co-operate with the British government, even after the beginning of the war with Japan in 1941. Uncertainty about the loyalty of the Indian population seriously hampered the war effort, especially when the Japanese, having conquered Burma, reached the frontiers of India itself. Churchill therefore sent Sir Stafford Cripps, a prominent Labour politician who was known to sympathise with Congress, to India in 1942. Cripps tried to persuade the Congress leaders, Gandhi and Jawarharlal Nehru, to agree to collaborate in the war against Japan in return for a promise of Dominion status after the war. Nehru might have agreed, but Gandhi was adamant. The mission failed, civil disobedience continued and the Congress leaders were sent to prison again.

The Labour government which came to power in 1945 soon decided in favour of Indian independence. Its problem was not one of whether to withdraw from India, but of how to do so without causing catastrophic conflict between the Hindu and Moslem communities. The Hindus, who were more numerous than the Moslems, were represented by Congress, which wanted a united India. The Moslem League, led by Jinnah, on the other hand, favoured partition into Hindu and Moslem states. Lord Mountbatten, who became Viceroy in 1946, did his best to induce the rival leaders to settle their disputes amicably, but it now seemed likely that independence would be postponed by endless wrangles among the Indians themselves.

Attlee and Mountbatten decided to coerce the Moslem League and Congress into agreement by announcing that India would

*Nehru*

**Independence and partition 1947**

become independent by June 1948 and later definitely fixed 15 August 1947 as the date for the British withdrawal. In spite of the continued protests of Congress, partition was accepted as the only way of avoiding strife and bloodshed. The states of India and Pakistan accordingly came into existence, with Mountbatten the first Governor-General of the new Dominion of India and Nehru its Prime Minister.

The transfer of power, however, was not peaceful. Some 200,000 people were killed in riots as millions of Hindus and Moslems migrated so as to live within the borders of India and Pakistan respectively. India's saddest loss was the prophet of independence himself, Gandhi, who was assassinated by a fanatic in 1948. Thus ended the Indian Empire in the bitterness and bloodshed which Churchill and others had long predicted. While Hindus and Moslems perished in religious riots the governments of the new states quarrelled over frontiers, and the province of Kashmir has remained in dispute ever since. The only answer to the argument that by staying the British could have prevented the loss of life is that, had they remained, Hindus and Moslems would have united in opposing them and that violence would have increased year by year.

Ceylon and Burma were both granted independence in 1948, and Burma chose to withdraw from the Commonwealth altogether. The others remained members of the free association, even though India and Pakistan subsequently became republics.

THE COLONIES

As well as the Dominions and India, Britain had acquired, mainly in the nineteenth century, a large number of other overseas possessions. Attempts to find new markets for her products had led her to take over territories in East Africa (Kenya and Uganda), Central Africa (Rhodesia) and West Africa (Nigeria and the Gold Coast). In the seventeenth and eighteenth centuries she had obtained a string of possessions in the Caribbean, while her Asian colonies included Aden, sundry territories in the Persian Gulf, Malaya, Singapore, and parts of Borneo. In the Mediterranean, Gibraltar, Malta, Cyprus, and Egypt provided strategic bases for the Royal Navy. This motley collection was augmented at the end of the First World War when the German and Turkish Empires were dismembered and allocated to the victorious powers as League of Nations mandates (see pages 112 and 114). Britain's most important gains in 1919 were Tanganyika in East Africa and Palestine.

With two exceptions, these colonies caused Britain little trouble until after the Second World War. Colonial administrators maintained law and order, built roads, tried to promote agricultural improvements, fought perennial battles against disease and famine and collaborated with missionaries in providing schools and medical services. Economically the colonies were valuable to Britain, though how valuable is difficult to gauge. They provided cheap basic products—palm oil from Nigeria, cocoa from Ghana, tin from Malaya, sugar from the Caribbean islands—and were a growing market for British manufactured goods. They naturally came to want independence from British rule, also, and this inevitably led to the tensions of disengagement which had marked the latter stages of the Indian Empire.

The two exceptions were Egypt, which was never properly a part of the Empire, and Palestine. Egypt had been a semi-independent province of the Turkish Empire until 1882, when a British debt-collecting mission overthrew the corrupt Egyptian régime and found itself in effective control. Thus Britain acquired an important new colony almost by accident. Its importance was derived, of course, from the Suez Canal, a vital international waterway and a crucial link between Britain and India. British rule in Egypt was far-sighted and enlightened: Lord Cromer, who was in command between 1883 and 1907, had dams and reservoirs built to make better use of the Nile's waters, and eliminated corruption from the law courts and tax system.

**Egypt**

*Illegal immigrants to Palestine, 1946*

The Egyptians, like the Indians, began agitating for independence from Britain immediately after the First World War, however. By a treaty signed in 1922 Britain recognised Egypt's independence, but kept control of the country's defence. Opposition continued, and by a further treaty in 1936 Britain was given the right to maintain forces in Egypt, mainly in the Canal Zone, for a further twenty years. During the Second World War, of course, Egypt was at the heart of Britain's resistance to the Germans and Italians in North Africa: El Alamein saved Egypt as well as Britain. After the war British forces remained in the Canal Zone in accordance with the treaty of 1936, and their withdrawal in the 1950s coincided with Nasser's rise to power (see pages 265–266).

**Palestine**

Britain's presence in Palestine began in confusion and contradiction, led to disorder and almost ended in catastrophe. Its origins lay in promises made to the Arabs during the First World War that they would be freed from the Turks in return for help during the war, and the Balfour Declaration, which pledged Britain to create a 'national homeland' for the Jews in Palestine. The promises were contradictory, for Palestine could not belong to both Arabs and Jews (see page 114).

The League of Nations duly granted Palestine, Transjordan, and Irak to Britain as mandates. The latter two territories soon became Arab kingdoms, but Palestine was kept in British hands. Although there was some immigration of Jews in the 1920s, the flow became rapid in the 1930s when Hitler's persecution in Germany drove many Jews into exile. By 1939 the population of Palestine was 29 per cent Jewish and the Arabs had come to resent their new neighbours. By restricting the number of immigrants the British antagonised the Jews and by admitting any Jews at all they alienated the Arabs.

At the end of the Second World War there were camps full of refugees all over Western Europe. Many of the inmates were Jewish survivors of Hitler's campaign of mass-murder and most of them wanted to go to Palestine as soon as possible. Although sympathetic, the British government was afraid that a large-scale influx of Jews would cause serious trouble. Ernest Bevin, the Foreign Secretary, was also aware that Britain relied for a substantial part of her oil on Arab states, which might restrict or cut supplies if the British government pursued an apparently anti-Arab policy in Palestine. The American government was far from helpful: President Truman, reflecting strong pro-Jewish feeling in the United States, criticised Britain's policy of limiting the number of immigrants.

Illegal Jewish immigration and guerrilla attacks by the Arab and Jewish communities on each other and on the British occupying forces made Britain's position in Palestine almost intolerable. In

1947 Bevin referred the matter to the United Nations, which decided on the partition of Palestine into Arab and Jewish areas; the Arab areas were joined to Jordan and the areas settled by Jews created the new state of Israel. Britain withdrew in 1948 and war between Israel and her Arab neighbours ensued. Despite overwhelming odds and an acute shortage of weapons, the Israelis won, but the Arabs have never accepted the new Jewish state and the Arab-Israeli conflict remains one of the world's most serious international problems.

Britain's performance in Palestine had been far from glorious. She gained nothing from her presence in the area and her attempts to preserve peace lost her the goodwill of all concerned. Her position was from the beginning impossible, due mainly to foolish and contradictory promises made during the First World War.

The history of the remainder of the Empire before 1945 was uneventful. Inspired by the Indian example, talented and ambitious young men prepared themselves for the day when they too could challenge Britain's right to rule, but it was not until after the Second World War that the British government had to contend with independence movements in Africa.

The first major colonial problem to arise after 1945 was the Communist-inspired guerrilla warfare which broke out in Malaya in 1948. This was in part a product of the Communist take-over in China and represented one of the early stages of an eruption of violence which plagued South-East Asia. The British army conducted a skilful campaign against the terrorists in the Malayan jungle and the government promised Malaya independence as soon as the emergency was ended. Violence was stamped out by 1957 and the Federation of Malaya duly became a full member of the Commonwealth. **Malaya**

It was in Africa, however, that the biggest transformation of Britain's role occurred. Apart from South Africa and Southern Rhodesia, which had enjoyed a limited degree of self-government since 1923, all Britain's African possessions were under the direct rule of the Colonial Office in 1945, yet by the early 1960s most of them had become completely independent. **Africa**

There were two basic types of colony in Africa, those with a significant number of European settlers (such as Kenya and Southern Rhodesia) and those whose populations were overwhelmingly African (the Gold Coast and Nigeria, for example). Strangely, perhaps, the transfer of power was more difficult where the Europeans were most numerous, for the settlers resented losing political, economic and social advantages. Within the African colonies the political problems before and after independence were partly caused by the Empire builders. The colonies' boundaries had usually been drawn by European statesmen with little or no

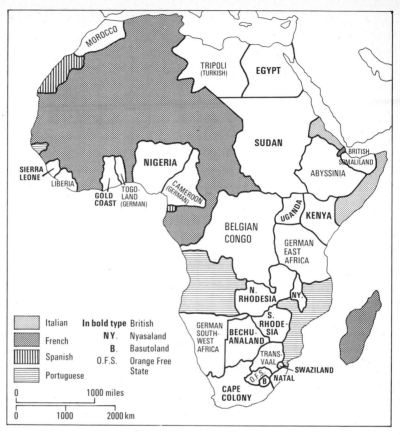

Map 21 *Africa in 1900*

**Legend:**

- Italian
- French
- Spanish
- Portuguese

**In bold type** British
NY. Nyasaland
B. Basutoland
O.F.S. Orange Free State

0          1000 miles
0      1000      2000 km

knowledge of Africa and amounted to compromises between the imperial claims of the powers competing in the 'scramble for Africa'. They were neat straight lines on the map, but took no account of the nationality or tribal loyalties of the Africans themselves. Little wonder therefore that the people of the three major nations and dozens of minor tribes which formed Nigeria found it difficult to live and work together harmoniously after 1960.

The Gold Coast was the first of Britain's black African possessions to achieve independence. Its population was almost entirely African and, being quite small, it was less troubled by tribal jealousies than some of the others. A political leader, Kwame Nkrumah, soon appeared and, following the example of Gandhi and Nehru, he served the regulation terms of apprenticeship in British gaols. When the Gold Coast became partly self-governing in 1951 Nkrumah's party won a decisive victory in the elections and an enlightened administration released him from prison to become Prime Minister. Rapid, if not smooth, constitutional progress followed and Nkrumah had the pleasure of guiding his country, now called Ghana, to full independence in 1957.

**Ghana**

311

The history of Kenya was, in contrast, much more troubled. Substantial numbers of Europeans, who nevertheless formed only one per cent of the colony's population, farmed the best land on the high plateaux. They were alarmed by the prospect of self-government for the Africans, while the latter resented white ownership of the most fertile land. Violence erupted in 1952: African tribesmen, calling themselves the 'Mau Mau', murdered European settlers and destroyed their farms. Within two years British troops had brought the revolt under control and imprisoned Mau Mau leaders, the foremost of whom was Jomo Kenyatta. The rebellion and the problem of the white settlers impeded Kenya's constitutional development, but independence was at last granted in 1963. Kenyatta, like Nkrumah, exchanged his prison cell for the Prime Minister's residence.

Central Africa presented similar problems to Kenya. Southern Rhodesia contained an even larger number of Europeans, and they had been partly self-governing since 1923. Northern Rhodesia and Nyasaland, on the other hand, had few European settlers, but Northern Rhodesia's copper mines gave the colony appreciable wealth. In 1953 the British government merged the three colonies into a Central African Federation, hoping that the political experience and technical skill of the Southern Rhodesians wedded to the economic strength of Northern Rhodesia would provide a satisfactory foundation for a new state which might soon be given independence. The experiment was a failure: the Africans of Northern Rhodesia and Nyasaland, led by nationalists like Kenneth Kaunda and Hastings Banda, would have nothing to do with the white Southern Rhodesians. The Federation was disbanded in 1963 and Nyasaland and Northern Rhodesia, now re-named Malawi and Zambia, became full Commonwealth members shortly afterwards.

Southern Rhodesia was a special, and extremely awkward, case. The Europeans enjoyed far more extensive political rights than the Africans, but British policy throughout the post-war period had been to grant independence on the terms of 'one man, one vote'. Such a formula would have meant the swamping of the white Rhodesians by black Africans and was intolerable to the settlers, at least in the immediate future. However, with every other colony achieving full sovereignty, the Rhodesians felt left out. Lengthy discussions with London led to no agreement: neither the Conservative governments up to 1964 nor their Labour successor would budge from the principle of African majority rule. Finally, in desperation, the Rhodesian government of Ian Smith issued a unilateral declaration of independence in 1965. This was a totally illegal defiance of the British Parliament, which alone had the right to grant independence. The new African Commonwealth states

**Kenya**

*Nigerians attending an adult education class on the use of sprayers in cocoa plantations*

**Malawi and Zambia**

**Southern Rhodesia**

*Hindustan Motors Ltd factory in Calcutta, India*

urged Britain to crush the Smith régime by force, but Wilson felt that British public opinion would not stand for such extreme measures. He applied, instead, economic sanctions: Britain, and most other countries, refused to send goods to Rhodesia or to receive Rhodesian exports. Smith, it was hoped, would be brought quickly to his knees. He was not, partly because his friendly South African neighbour continued to trade with him.

Meanwhile, the British had withdrawn more-or-less graciously from a string of colonies to the north. In Nigeria, Uganda, Tanganyika and elsewhere bands played, soldiers presented arms and the Union Jack was lowered for the last time in ceremonies which at the same time brashly proclaimed the freedom of the new states and revealed the extent of British influence. The process of disengagement in Africa was skilfully and tactfully supervised by a succession of Conservative Colonial Secretaries, Iain Macleod, Reginald Maudling and Duncan Sandys. It was both fitting and ironic that the Conservatives, so long the party of Empire, had presided over its demise.

In Africa the problems of the last stage of the Empire had revolved around potential conflicts between black and white. In Cyprus the issue was between Greeks and Turks. The island's population was mainly Greek, but there was a large Turkish minority. In the mid-1950s the Greeks began to demand *Enosis*, or union, with Greece and, led by the redoubtable Archbishop Makarios, backed up their case with guerrilla warfare. British troops were condemned to yet another thankless peace-keeping role, while Makarios served a period of exile on the Seychelle Islands instead of the conventional imprisonment. By the settlement of 1960 Cyprus became an independent republic with a Greek president (Makarios) and a Turkish vice-president, while the rights of the Turks were strictly safeguarded. The island stayed in the Commonwealth and there was no *Enosis*.

**Cyprus**

In contrast to colonies in Asia and Africa, Britain's Caribbean colonies progressed peacefully to independence. Before 1944 the majority of West Indians had not even had the right to vote for their island assemblies, and government was run by the middle class and by British colonial administrators. Democratically elected governments gradually took control of home affairs in the late 1940s and 50s and economic progress was much faster under these West Indian governments than it had been in the depressed years before the war. The first attempts to federate failed and starting with Jamaica in 1962, the islands gained independence separately.

**West Indies**

Thus, in a very short space of time, Britain's colonial Empire was liberated and merged into the free association of the Commonwealth. All the new states were provided with political institutions which were close copies of the British model—parliament chambers, complete with government and opposition benches, official maces and Speakers' chairs. Party politics, conducted in the British tradition, would, it was hoped, give the people the opportunity to choose their rulers freely. But in Africa, British institutions had no basis in local traditions and in some states governments imprisoned their opponents and banned opposition parties. The reaction, observed in Pakistan, Ghana and Nigeria, was a take-over of power by the army. Communities have not always lived in harmony: rivalry between different ethnic groups precipitated a bloody civil war in Nigeria and the Cyprus compromise soon broke down. Nor have relations between Commonwealth countries always been cordial: India and Pakistan have continued to feud and have twice resorted to war. Commonwealth members all belong to the United Nations, but seldom vote the same way. The Commonwealth is therefore the loosest possible association of sovereign states, with even less formal structure than the United Nations. Its members are bound together by little but sentiment, and it is doubtful whether nostalgia mixed with a little economic advantage will be enough to surmount the trials of the last quarter of the twentieth century.

*Kingston, Jamaica, 1962*

# Index

317

# Acknowledgements

We gratefully acknowledge the permission of the Estate of Harold Owen and Chatto & Windus, Ltd., to reprint a stanza from Wilfred Owen's "Anthem for Doomed Youth" from *Collected Poems* (Copyright Chatto & Windus 1946, © 1963).

We should like to thank the following for permission to reproduce illustrations: Associated Newspapers Group Ltd., 124, 199, 236, 252; Associated Press, 308; Bilderdienst Suddeutscher Verlag, 76; Bulletin (Glasgow) 1926, 124 (bottom); Butlin's Photographic Services, 182; Camera Press, 84 (top), 150, 159 (top), 192, 207, 214, 279, 288, 294; Capa, 209 (see Magnum); Central Press, 84, 151, 156, 189, 257, 291; *Daily Express*, 238; *Daily Mail*, 232; Joan Ellis, 164; Fawcett Library, 35 (centre); Ford Motor Co. Ltd., 181; Fox Photos, 188; *Glasgow Herald*, 142; Hoover Ltd., 145 (top); Imperial War Museum, 40, 69 (top), 72, 74, 75, 76 (top), 86, 90, 91, 194, 195, 196, 212, 218, 219, 220, 222, 223 (top); Keystone Press Agency, 235, 250, 255, 268, 274, 280, 292, 299, 301, 313, 315; James Klugman Collection, 127; Labour Party Library, 18, 20, 21, 22, 28, 96, 99, 141, 142, 144, 226, 229, 270; Location of Offices Bureau, 244; London Express, 264; London Transport, 65; Cartoons by David Low by arrangement with the Trustees and London *Evening Standard*, 135, 137, 261; Magnum, photo by Robert Capa, 209; Mander Mitchenson Theatre Collection, 184; Mansell Collection, 10, 19, 40 (top), 50, 60, 174; Montagu Motor Museum, 12 (bottom); Marconi Photographs, 12, 178; *Morning Star* Co-operative, 125; National Coal Board, 234; National Film Archive, 169, 187; National Library of Ireland, 116; National Museum of Wales, 6 (top), 33 (top); Planet News Ltd., 262; Press Association, 68, 92; Radio Times Hulton Picture Library, 6, 16, 17, 24, 30, 31, 33, 34 (top, bottom right), 35 (bottom), 36, 46, 47, 48, 51–58, 60 (top), 61, 65, 66, 67, 69, 86 (top), 87, 88, 90 (top, bottom), 91, 93, 103–109, 117, 118, 121, 122, 123, 125, 126, 128, 131, 132, 136, 145, 152, 158, 159, 162, 166, 167, 168, 171, 172, 175, 176, 182 (top), 191, 200, 216, 221, 223, 230, 242, 246, 248, 251, 253, 276, 286, 305, 306; Skegness Urban District Council, 65 (top); Sport and General, 35 (top); Syndication International, 34 (bottom left), 126; Ullstein Bilderdienst, 13, 83; United Artists, 186; United Kingdom Atomic Energy Authority, 292 (top); United Press International Ltd., 267, 278; Walt Disney Productions, 187; Worker's Education Association, 62.